Untouchable Fictions

Untouchable Fictions

LITERARY REALISM
AND THE CRISIS OF CASTE

Toral Jatin Gajarawala

FORDHAM UNIVERSITY PRESS   *New York*   2013

THIS BOOK IS MADE POSSIBLE BY A COLLABORATIVE GRANT
FROM THE ANDREW W. MELLON FOUNDATION.

Copyright © 2013 Fordham University Press

Publication of this book has been aided by a grant from the Abraham and Rebecca Stein Faculty Publication Fund of New York University, Department of English.

All rights reserved. No part of this publication may be reproduced, stored in a retrieval system, or transmitted in any form or by any means—electronic, mechanical, photocopy, recording, or any other—except for brief quotations in printed reviews, without the prior permission of the publisher.

Fordham University Press has no responsibility for the persistence or accuracy of URLs for external or third-party Internet websites referred to in this publication and does not guarantee that any content on such websites is, or will remain, accurate or appropriate.

Fordham University Press also publishes its books in a variety of electronic formats. Some content that appears in print may not be available in electronic books.

Library of Congress Cataloging-in-Publication Data

Gajarawala, Toral Jatin.
  Untouchable fictions : literary realism and the crisis of caste / Toral Jatin Gajarawala.
      p. cm.
  Includes bibliographical references and index.
  ISBN 978-0-8232-4524-6 cloth
  ISBN 978-0-8232-4525-3 pbk.
  1. Indic literature—Dalit authors—History and criticism. 2. Indic fiction—History and criticism. 3. Realism in literature. 4. Dalits in literature. 5. Caste in literature. 6. Modernism (Literature)—India. I. Title.
  PK5410.D35G35 2013
  891.4—dc23
                                2012027754

15 14 13   5 4 3 2 1

First edition

For Motamama
A freedom fighter, at home and in the world

CONTENTS

Acknowledgments ix

Three Burnings: An Introduction 1
Dalit Realisms 16

1. The Dalit Limit Point: Realism, Representation, and Crisis in Premchand 32
The Critique of the "Clawless Lion" 63

2. Modernism, Marxism, Metaphor: The Origins of a Literary Politics of Particularism 68
Realist Particularisms 92

3. A Perfect Whole: Knowledge by Transcription and Rural Regionalism 97
Realism and Revelation 123

4. Casteless Modernities: The Contemporary Anglophone Novel and Its Invisible Interlocutors 129
Realism after Modernism? 164

5. Some Time between Revisionist and Revolutionary . . . : Reading History in Dalit Textuality 168
Dalit Realisms Revisited 187
Mimesis: The Representation of Reality in Other Literatures 191

Epilogue: Aesthetics and Their Afterlives 197

Notes 207
Works Cited 233
Index 251

ACKNOWLEDGMENTS

I have dedicated this book to my eldest maternal uncle, Chandrahas Hiralal Shah, professor of agricultural economics, spiritualist, guide, and friend. Motamama, as we affectionately call him, who mingles the *Gita* and Marx, prefers peanuts to almonds—"the food of the common man"—and reminded me that, "Even the Buddha was not always the Buddha." I cannot overestimate what it has meant for me to be close to him in Boston all those years, and what a profound effect he has had on my scholarship, and my life.

This book owes a great deal to two of the most brilliant thinkers of our time, the Dalit scholar and literary critic D. R. Nagaraj and the Brazilian Marxist literary critic Roberto Schwarz, both of whom move seamlessly and artfully between the politics of narrative and the world outside, in the realms of caste and class, the indigenous and the classical, and the delicate dance between freedom and constraint. Their writing on the complexities of the vernacular and the spaces of the poor casts its shadow over the work of this book.

As D. R. Nagaraj says, there are historical beginnings, but there are also metaphorical births. My sincere appreciation goes to two former professors at the University of California, Berkeley—Vasudha Dalmia and Karl Ashoka Britto—with whom I learned to read the literary line and many other kinds of texts. I also wish to thank here Ngugi wa Thiong'o, my first teacher in all things radical, for our earliest conversations on caste and race. Two brilliant readers read every word of this manuscript as well as the tens of thousands that were discarded: Elaine Freedgood and Rajeswari Sunder Rajan. Elaine's comradeship in every intellectual endeavor has moved me, quite literally, towards many possibilities, and Raji's dedication to this project and the course of my career has been unflagging.

Books grow in the small increments of conversation and argument and this one was no different. My thanks goes to those who have been supportive and challenging along the way: Helen Southworth and Jini Kim Watson are colleagues, neighbors, and more importantly, true friends; Simon Gikandi, Martin Harries, Maureen McLane, and Robert Young, all of whom, in one way or another, hastened the emergence of this book. There have been many readers and thinkers who have generously shared their observations, insights, and expertise: Vipul Agrawal, Dora Ahmad, Haytham Bahoora, Rashmi Bhatnagar, Laura Brueck, Joseph Fracchia, Maggie Gray, Sujata Mody, Shalini Perera, Alok Rai, Krishnendu Ray, Naomi Schiller, Gayatri Spivak, and Thuy Linh Tu. I would also like to mention two friends without whom I simply would never have been in a position to move forwards: Sangita Gopal and Mona Chopra, both intellectual confidantes, and sisters.

The completion of this book would not have been possible without the generous support of the Humanities Initiative Fellowship at New York University. My editor Helen Tartar's commitment to the project was unfailing, as were Edward Batchelder and Tom Bishop at Fordham University Press, and Tim Roberts at the Modern Language Initiative, in their effort to see this book through publication. Leigh Raynor's detailed work helped to produce the manuscript. I also thank two wonderful anonymous readers who took the project of reading with utmost seriousness and provided deliberative and incisive comments. I would like to acknowledge my colleagues at NYU for a most supportive and stimulating environment in which to begin, and end, this project.

Finally, and always, family. There are some debts so vast they strain the imagination. We have never been alone. Thank you to my parents for their consistent and unspoken tree-like support, which has seen me through the most challenging times, and the deepest joys. My younger brother Parag is surely the first person to "cite" my work in an attempt to persuade a childhood teacher. My sister has been a mother to my son, and Taimur, a father. And to Tejas, my heart.

An excerpt of chapter 2 appeared in *Modern Language Quarterly* (Fall 2012). An excerpt of the Epilogue appeared in *South Asian Review* (Spring 2012). A portion of chapter 5 appeared in the journal *PMLA* (Spring 2011). I appreciate the permission to reproduce them here.

Three Burnings

An Introduction

The poet is now reflecting not so much on social conditions, as on how to speak of it.
—ANIKET JAAWARE, "Eating, and Eating with, the Dalit"

The traces to be found in the material and the technical procedures, from which every qualitatively new work takes its lead, are scars: They are the loci at which the preceding works misfired.
—THEODOR ADORNO, *Aesthetic Theory*

In Dalit literature, everything is metanarrative. Born from the self-consciousness of any literature of radical protest, Dalit (untouchable caste) literature,[1] engendered by caste oppression and caste consciousness, occasions a self-reflexivity that works at several levels: language and metaphor, political philosophy, and literary production. But its metanarrativity is unusual in that it is firmly cast in an aesthetics of modern realism, both derivative and new, individualized and collective.

Largely a product of the last two decades, Dalit literature has flourished in the Hindi language, across the Hindi belt,[2] in the form of short stories, novels, autobiographies and poetry, generating its own literary apparatus of presses, journals, literary criticism and conferences. This body of work follows the traditions established by Dalit literature in other regional languages—particularly that of Marathi—that date to the mid-nineteenth century and took modern form alongside the political rise of the father of the Dalit movement, Dr. B. R. Ambedkar (1891–1956). Dalit literature is characterized as a literature of protest and historical revisionism, typically with an emphasis on the documentation of the violence, oppression, and structural inequality engendered by casteism. As a result, in Hindi especially, the central question in Dalit literature revolves around issues of realism, the real, and the cult of authenticity. In her analysis of Dalit aesthetics, Laura Brueck studies the critical concept of Dalit *chetna* (Dalit, or caste, consciousness), which has become the marker of that authenticity; writers and critics alike have underlined Dalit *chetna* as expressible in a series of social, political, and literary strategies that necessarily inform a Dalit text. "Dalit chetna is being developed as a strategy for Dalit critical analysis, a kind of 'test' by which Dalit critics can judge the 'dalitness' of any work of literature, whether written by a Dalit or non-Dalit" (Brueck, "Dalit Chetna"). In its broadest conception, Dalit *chetna* implies an anticasteist, antifeudal, and anticapitalist position, a challenge to traditional aesthetics, a critique of "hierarchies of language and privilege."[3] However, the vast complexity of such a model of creative production as well as of criticism, in which political praxis translates into a range of aesthetic strategies, often devolves into a fairly reductive debate on Dalitness: identity, authenticity, and purity. Polemics in journals such as *Dalit Sahitya* and *Apeksha* routinely challenge authors, texts, and criticism as non-Dalit or anti-Dalit on the basis of both birth and ideology.

This is the prerogative as well as the burden of literatures of political protest, which have certain ethnographic imperatives as well as historical ones. If Dalit history is "the narrative of how a new political collectivity was constituted by resignifying the Dalit's negative identity within the caste structure into positive political value," then Dalit literature is its necessary corollary (Rao, *The Caste Question* 2). Dalit literature is inconceivable without a "Dalit movement"; the literary project has long been read as a vehicle for, or transmission of, a larger political project, a form of cultural activism.[4] Eleanor Zelliot, the esteemed historian of the movement, refers to it as both a "school" and "a self-conscious movement" ("New Cultural Context" 79). Scholars read Dalit literature as an addendum to Ambedkarite assertion—the radical program he inaugurated of education and rights-based advocacy for the lower castes—within a framework of accusation (against the oppressors), and revelation (of the conditions of Dalit life) (Zelliot, "Dalit Literature" 451). Centuries of historical elision, as well as the religious exclusion of the Dalit from the cultural sphere, have required that Dalit literature be read as determinedly revisionist. Because of the importance of autobiography, that "artless" genre, to this literary movement, Dalit literature is read as a process of transcription and recovery. Most saliently, Dalit literature is largely understood as the unmediated expression of Dalit identity, now legible in modern narrative and poetic forms.[5] Aesthetic and formal considerations of such texts, therefore, have been subordinated to these political aims, if not evaded entirely. As a result, the ideology of form too, as it has been theorized by much materialist criticism, remains invisible.

Beyond blood, the concept of a Dalit consciousness as a structuring device of literary aesthetics might also be read as one mired in a formal struggle between realism and idealism, between the responsibilities of journalistic disclosure that launch an attack on the system of caste and the demands of inspirational cultural representations that fire a movement. Understood as one political and cultural identarian movement among many others, Dalit prose literature is also, however, clearly intervening in the debates on realism, the de facto style for the literature of social reform, the social novel, peasant literature and so forth. Simultaneously drawing on and denying the canon of mainstream Hindi literature in the twentieth century, while drawing on and debating the "global" pillar of social realism, Dalit literature is poised between a regionalism that revels in local dialect and the nontransferable specificity of caste conditioning, on the one hand, and a broad universalism that invokes a certain global paradigm of protest (both politically and culturally), on the other. Studies of Dalit literature must thus confront the contradiction between Dalit particularity, specificity, and singularity, and Dalit humanism that opens its ranks to many others.

I argue in this book that Dalit literature forms part of a lineage of social realism, speaking, in its formalistic tongue, to Zola, Tolstoy, and Dickens, via Premchand and Mulk Raj Anand in India, but that in doing so it attempts to revise realism's history of representational failures. I turn to Dalit literature, therefore, not only to engage with a crucial literary movement, but also to elaborate a critique of realism, and to explain both its dogged persistence and its new formations. Dalit literature is the space where realism now lives. And yet that realist space is neither blind nor mimetic. As Aniket Jaaware says of the later phase of Marathi Dalit poetry, "The poet is now reflecting not so much on social conditions, as on how to speak of it" (281). Dalit literature in Hindi is a more recent formation, and as such still retains, at least ideologically, its commitment to the elaboration of social conditions, but it also situates itself within a literary tradition and its belatedness and therefore knows "how to speak of it."

A realism that originates as a protest literature will trace a different trajectory than that derived from the standard narrative of Western developmentalism that coincides with the Enlightenment and teleological narratives of progress. And yet, Dalit realisms are clearly indebted to forms of social realism that have characterized Indian fiction in the twentieth century, and derive, in part, from European fictional forms and languages. As a result, Dalit politics and literature, long interpreted as exclusively a problem of identity, also gain from a critique of canon. Dalit writer Surajpal Chauhan, for example, a vocal critic of Brahminism in the literary sphere, claims there is nothing for Dalits in non-Dalit literature, "other than dishonor and deprivation. . . . Non-Dalit writers in Hindi haven't lifted even one brave finger in order to critique the caste hierarchy" (*Hindi* i). Despite its oppositional and exclusionary stance, however, Dalit literature has been irrevocably shaped, and indeed produced, by the critique of the very non-Dalit sphere it excoriates. These uppercaste literary forms function as oppositional parameters, in dialectical fashion; Dalit literature should therefore be read as constructing an *antigenealogy*. This book thus reads Dalit literature against a canon of literary texts in Hindi and English to reveal the range of cultural borrowings and cultural refusals, apparent most saliently in moments of book burning, such as that of the iconic Premchand's *Rangbhumi* in 2004, as well as in more subtle and elusive forms of influence and constraint. The first aim of this book will be to demonstrate the way in which Dalit textuality writes itself in opposition to certain bodies of literature, chief among them: (1) Premchand's social realism and fictions of social reform; (2) Anglophone literary modernism and its construction of the universal; (3) the "rural realism" and village literature of the *anchalik sahitya* movement; and (4) the contemporary Anglophone novel and its conflation of caste and class. What I suggest in this book is a broad genealogy for Dalit writing that complicates an understanding of this fiction as a simple expression of identity, one that moves beyond sociological questions of mimesis or influence. I read Dalit literature here as a history of the negative. It is more than a small public sphere created by Dalits for Dalits or the cultural wing of a militant political organization. Rather, it rereads, and rewrites, a canon of logic on caste questions, arguing, in fact, that a certain relationship to caste was required for fiction to be fiction and realism to be realism. Its real contributions include the provision for a Dalit analytics, a revisionist critique of canon, and a critique of the hegemony of Brahminical culture in the broadest sense. Most importantly, *it demonstrates the work of the negative to be productive of literary form.* It does this via a refashioning of the term "realist," a theoretical elaboration of which is the second aim of this project.

By way of introduction, I will begin here a discussion of the persistence of realism in contemporary Indian literature by tracing an ideological genealogy through three significant moments of book burning: that of the realist novelist Premchand's first collection of short stories *Soz-e-vatan* (*Dirge of the Nation*) by the British Raj in 1908, that of the Hindu sacred text *Manusmriti* (*The Laws of Manu*) by Dr. B. R. Ambedkar, the father of the Dalit movement, in 1927, and most recently of Premchand's 1925 novel *Rangbhumi* (*The Arena*) by activists from the Bharatiya Dalit Sahitya Akademi in 2004. Circling around the epistemological crisis of the "real," these three moments of book burning allow us to construct a debate about the privileges and failures of realism. It is my contention that the story of these three burnings frames the central question of Dalit literature in Hindi today.

2004

In July of 2004, members of the Bharatiya Dalit Sahitya Akademi (Indian Dalit Literary Academy) publicly burned Premchand's famed novel *Rangbhumi* (1925) in Delhi, provoking a maelstrom of praise, condemnation, and controversy. In addition to drawing predictable criticism from the traditional literary establishment, the event fiercely divided Dalit organizations, many of which challenged the position taken by the Akademi.

Premchand (1880–1936) may seem like a strange object of controversy: a progressive writer whose political sympathies lay with the poor and downtrodden. Critic K. P. Singh credits Premchand's writings with "the awareness to recognize the hollowness of the capitalist promises of *swaraj* (self-rule) and see through the ruthlessness and inhumanity of capitalism and warn the people against it" ("Premchand's Ideology" 76). Premchand's novels were undoubtedly groundbreaking for their innovations in terms of modern Indian literature. His politically charged realism capitalized on the narrative features concretized by nineteenth-century French and Russian novelists: the deuniversalization of historical time, the radical shift in subject matter. This displacement of the novelist's worldview from the elite to the peasant, the laborer, or the prostitute was part and parcel of a political program as well as an aesthetic strategy (to challenge traditional formalist notions of beauty and "the beautiful art" and to draw attention to the plight of the masses in the name of Indian nationalism) and crucial to the development of the Urdu/Hindi canon as a progressive enterprise. The democratization of the gaze, in particular, has become synonymous with Premchand's work and established his legacy. "It is the duty of a writer," he propounds in "Sahitya ka uddeshya" ("The Aim of Literature"), his inaugural address at the first meeting of the Progressive Writers Association in Lucknow in 1936, "to support and defend those who are in some way oppressed, suffering or deprived whether they be individuals or groups. He pleads justice on their behalf and considers himself successful when through his efforts the court's sense of justice and beauty is awakened." Premchand's fiction chiseled out avenues of sympathy for women, in particular, but also for the peasant, the "untouchable," even the *zamindar*, the feudal landlord, who had his own particular burden to bear. Like many other writers with political aspirations that lay outside the text, Premchand produced a vast canvas strewn with figures from various castes, classes, and communities—no "imaginary men," as he claims in the essay—that clearly contributed to a national narrative for literary India, while also challenging the inherent elitism of an often uppercaste, upper-class anticolonial movement.[6]

Such a critique of nationalism, and a clear sympathy for the "untouchable castes," would seem to put Premchand on the right side of history. In the 1970s Marathi Dalit writers wrote against the overt casteism of the social sphere, and the failure of literary writing to accommodate caste thus far. But Dalit literature in Hindi has not been solely focused on critiquing partisan casteist fiction, or fiction that overtly promotes "Brahminical" values. Its rise in North India has taken shape in an entirely different *post*-Ambedkarite historical moment, a post-Mandal Commission[7] moment, one that has now been made "conscious" of caste and caste politics. This new world has been educated in the subtle language of reservations and affirmative action, of casteist privilege and caste suppression; it is well-aware of the politics of interdining and intermarriage, and of the persistence of caste-based violence and violation. Dalit literature in Hindi has thus been forced to develop a more subtle critique for more subtle forms of casteism. As a result, one of its primary objects of engagement has been not simply anti-Dalit action but the more sophisticated elocution of the discourse of liberal reform. Unlike the writings of Ambedkar, for example, which routinely cited the overt anti-Dalit prejudice of certain nationalist figures, contemporary Dalit textuality reserves for Premchand a different kind of critique.

The Dalit journal *Apeksha* devoted an issue in early 2005 to a discussion of the burning, in which the president of the Akademi, Sohanpal Sumanakshar, launched a fiery defense. Sumanakshar writes, "We have no opposition to Munshi Premchand or his creative works. We are rather opposed to his *jaativadi-varnvadi* [casteist-*varna*ist] perspective. There are poor Chamars, and poor Brahmins as well. But in Premchand's work the poor Brahmin is worthy of respect and the poor Chamar is treated with scorn" (17). The immediate impetus for the burning was the inclusion of the Premchand novel in the Delhi standard school curriculum; Sumanakshar opposes the introduction of casteist texts—those that use derogatory caste names, as Premchand's do—into schools, as well as young hearts and minds.[8] But it is clear from Sumanakshar's statement that he has entered into a larger debate on literary history. On one side is the *janvadi* (democratic), progressive, often Marxist literary establishment, for whom Premchand connotes certain things; on the other side is the Dalit. For Sumanakshar, as Dalit critic, the celebration of the novel functions alongside a general deification of Premchand, despite what he perceives to be the novel's complicity with a casteist framework. Citing the fact that the Brahmin in the novel is referred to as *garib panditji* (poor priest—the *ji* is indicative of respect) while the protagonist Surdas is only referred to as Surdas Chamar (Surdas the leather worker—a debased "untouchable-caste" occupation), Sumanakshar critiques the *charitraharan* (character destruction) of Dalits (20) in *Rangbhumi*. He accuses Premchand's famed story "Kafan" (1936), of a similar *charitrahanan* (character assassination) and writes that its disgraceful portrait of Chamars is entirely fictional, and could never be verified in real life (18).

I am going to draw from the fascinating charge of "character assassination" to elaborate a casteist critique here. The problem of character is the central vehicle via which the Dalit critique has been launched; this is a critique, in effect, of the poor representation of the poor. The Dalit character, this critique claims, can never be done justice by an inherently casteist lens, even in the case of a novel like *Rangbhumi*, where Surdas Chamar is the object of sympathy and nationalist inspiration. In the novel, it is the plot of land that Surdas the beggar owns that becomes the locus of a struggle among local developers, British administrators, and the peasants of Pandepur. Surdas emerges as a symbol of Gandhian resistance; his literal blindness is indicative of his ability to see. A Dalit critique, however, would argue that for the Premchand text, all this is less important than the "Chamarness" of the Chamar. This critique, therefore, is less about the elision of the Dalit, and pertains rather to the narrative mode of his inclusion—and even his *celebration*: pitiable, downtrodden, insulted. The canonization of Premchand, and the resulting pleasure that uppercaste readers experience in addition to the ideological framework in which they participate, in complete indifference to, or even as a result of, "Dalit dishonor," is part of a larger problem. This is a problem of realism. To call Surdas a Chamar is not only to make concessions to the ethnographic real, but to reify the word "Chamar," which can only function as an insult. In addition to the material critique of misrepresentation, there is the question of the way in which the realist text configures its ethnographic authority on the basis of repetition of caste names, casteized paradigms, and the circumscribed narrative arc of the Dalit figure. If we draw out Sumanakshar's critique, he is suggesting that it is in the name of the nationalist and the humanist that the Dalit character is destroyed.

The burning of the novel *Rangbhumi* in 2004 was an act of intellectual iconoclasm but also, crucially, a critique of canon, one metafictional mode via which a Dalit critique is inaugurated.[9] The act of Dalit critique should be understood as not simply one means of assertion of identity but as a rereading of cultural products via the foregrounding of the problem of caste. New forms of writing, and new forms of realism, are shifting the defined parameters of the Hindi literary canon in order to assert certain claims to literary space. To burn a text of Premchand, heralded as iconic of a certain relationship to the national and the real, would then be to challenge the basic paradigms via which we interpret referentiality.

1927

The act of burning *Rangbhumi* draws its symbolic strength from other burnings: Sumanakshar cites, for example, the burning, and other forms of desecration, of Dalit texts in schools, book fairs, political campaigns.[10] But the burning of Premchand's novel also echoes Ambedkar's burning of the *Manusmriti*, an inaugural moment of

Dalit symbolic critique. By 1927, Ambedkar, had been appointed member of the Legislative Assembly of Bombay province, founded the Depressed Classes Welfare Organization (DCWO), begun the publication of a journal, *Bahishkrit Bharat*, formed two local organizations that fought for social equality, and led a civil disobedience campaign to open access to water tanks and wells for untouchables. Eventually known for the exhortation to "Educate, Organize, Agitate," by the late 1920s Ambedkar had been actively using every means ideologically available to him in order to advance the Dalit cause: *satyagraha* (nonviolent resistance), legal measures, political pressure, public discourse via print media, and localized social movements. Via a large network of political organizing, he created a public platform for the relation of grievance, discussion, and strategizing, and several outlets for the spread of information and knowledge: an incipient Dalit public sphere that produced a vast catalogue of Dalit experience and also provoked a popular movement in support of caste equity that functioned alongside, and in opposition to, Gandhi's nationalist movement.

Already critical of the power of law as accorded by the British government and of potential uppercaste spiritual conversion and benevolence lauded by Gandhi, Ambedkar sought other means to improve the condition of the depressed classes. "If I may say so, the servile classes do not care for social amelioration.... Not bread but honour, is what they want" (*Essential Writings* 144). The burning at Mahad became one symbol of the social movement to restore honor. In December of 1927, addressing a crowd of three thousand, Ambedkar says, "At the outset, let me tell those who oppose us that we did not perish because we could not drink water from this Chowdar Tank. We now want to go to the Tank only to prove that, like others, we are also human beings.... This Conference has been called to inaugurate an era of equality in this land" (Keer 99). On a platform raised in Dasgaon, a few miles from the site of the tank, as conference leaders cited the brutal details of this Hindu text, the infamous *Manusmriti* was burned on a pyre.

At this point, despite his education abroad and his growing admiration for Western liberal forms of governance and state reliance, Ambedkar might still have categorized himself as a Gandhian, a nationalist following a model of *satyagraha*. Indeed, he compared this anticaste burning with anticolonial resistance and the burning of foreign cloth (Rao, *The Caste Question* 80). But the burning of the

Manusmriti was symbolic of the honing of a careful critique of Hinduism as represented both by sacred text and by Gandhi. A series of political failures, including that of the 1932 Communal Award, which would have granted separate electorates to untouchables, would turn Ambedkar resolutely against Gandhi by the end of the 1930s. In his well-known 1946 essay *What Congress and Gandhi Have Done to the Untouchables*, Ambedkar launches a two-fold critique, in effect arguing for a "Dalit" reading of nationalism and Gandhianism. Dissecting the Brahmin-Baniya connection on which the Congress Party was so reliant, Ambedkar argues that postindependence India under the mandate of the ruling classes would serve the untouchables no better than colonial rule had. Beyond the personal prejudices that the political atmosphere of early twentieth-century India legitimized, the entire philosophical premise dictating the relationship between the rulers and the ruled—upon which the right of the former to rule the latter was based—was flawed. "Can anyone who realizes what the outlook, traditions and social philosophy of the governing class in India is, believe that under the Congress regime, a sovereign and independent India will be different from the India we have today?" (Ambedkar, *Essential Writings* 148). The intrinsic paradox was clear: Congress and Gandhi demanded freedom from foreign domination while maintaining the debased status of the lowercastes. Gandhi's praise for the *varna*[11] system, his support for a Hinduism "without untouchability" and for the orthodoxy of text, and his reliance upon support from the propertied classes in whose hands the nationalist movement's direction was determined, allowed Ambedkar to produce a critique of Gandhian nationalism, one that dictates the political parameters of Dalit literature today. In fact, Ambedkar's critique would loudly echo one raised two decades earlier by Swami Acchutanand, an important Dalit figure in North India. Favoring British rule for the missionary education, government jobs, and potential for political representation it offered, Acchutanand saw it "as a source of salvation for the untouchables as opposed to the ill-will of the uppercastes" (Gooptu 170). The lineage drawn by Acchutanand and Ambedkar form the central inspiration for the production of Dalit literature in Hindi today. Delinking the basic association between the novel and the national proposed by Benedict Anderson and others, Dalit literature, from its inception, draws its political critique from the inevitable failures of a liberatory nationalism, turning towards other types of texts, and other types of political community.[12]

When Ambedkar burned the *Manusmriti*, he was making a public statement against the hegemony of the uppercastes. The *Manusmriti* is one of the ancient texts of Hinduism, dated between 100 and 200 AD. Often described as a law book, or a guide, it is a manual for codes of conduct, specifying protocols of marriage, dietary regulations, judicial matters, and, most notoriously, the prescribed relations between, and the specific responsibilities of, the upper- and lowercastes. Infamous for the brutal punishments set out for transgression of caste codes by lowercastes—the pouring of lead in the ears of a Shudra who heard the recitation of the Vedas, for example—the *Manusmriti* became one means to read the religiously sanctioned tyranny of the uppercastes and its codification by text. "No one who knows anything about the *Manusmriti* can say that the caste system is a natural system. What does it show? It shows that the caste system is a legal system maintained at the point of a bayonet" (Ambedkar, *Essential Writings* 164). While the act of burning was concomitant with a broader condemnation of Brahminical privilege and Hinduism, in light of recent temple-entry movements in the south, it was also a critique of a blind reliance on scripture, on text and on textuality as the arbiter of human behavior. In his own way, as an example of the call to education for Dalits that he underscored, Ambedkar was producing a new corpus of writings on caste. In his 1936 speech "The Annihilation of Caste" he expands his critique of Hinduism, now precisely framed as a condemnation of stultified text: rules and regulations that adjudicate without any reference to material reality. Hinduism, he argued, leaves no room for the rationalism necessary to modern man, the reason that allows for the triumph over traditionalism. Composed primarily of rules ("habitual ways of doing things according to prescription") rather than principles ("which are intellectual; they are useful methods of judging things"), Hinduism circumvents moral responsibility. "Under it, there is no loyalty to ideals, there is only conformity to commands" (*Essential Writings* 96). Ambedkar's reading of uppercaste Hinduism was concomitant with a critique of caste politics but it also formed the basis of a positive humanism; his vision exalted the individual and that individual's own unique power of evaluation and contemplation. There was no room within Hinduism, he felt, for the power of rational choice; there was little space for interpretation of, or amendment to, the text and its expression in caste orthodoxy. The new intellectual space being carved out by Dr. Ambedkar was a necessary supplement to, and also material and social incitement for, the creation of new forms of writing that would exalt the individual and the question of rational choice.

Dalit literature is that new text. Dalit literary practitioners often argue their cultural product to be simply an expression of or vehicle for Ambedkarism. But what is Ambedkarism—or what does Ambedkarism mean within the narrative confines of Dalit writing? Although Ambedkar was fairly silent on cultural practice, in a 1948 essay on the origins of untouchability, he cites, interestingly, Maxim Gorky on the linkages between the practice of the artist and the scientist.

> Science and literature have much in common; in both, observation, comparison and study are of fundamental importance; the artist like the scientist, needs both imagination and intuition. Imagination and intuition bridge the gaps in the chain of facts by its as yet undiscovered links and permit the scientist to create hypothesis and theories which more or less correctly and successfully direct the searching of the mind in its study of the forms and phenomenon of nature. They are of literary creation; the art of creating characters and types demands imagination, intuition, the ability to make things up in one's own mind. (*Essential Writings* 117)

Ambedkar shared little with Gorky ideologically, but he was attracted to a methodology that wedded scientific inquiry with its concomitant necessary faculty. When attempting to reconstruct a subaltern history for which existing evidence was not only absent but willfully embedded, "imagination" was central to the proposal of a hypothesis that might then be proven or disproven by other means. Ambedkar therefore prized an evidentiary logic combined with human intuition, precisely because it showcased man's highest mental abilities. There is a faint echo here of the debates on the representation of the real and the ideal in the Dalit text.

Beyond advancing the political program sketched out by Ambedkar, then, Dalit fiction in Hindi has clearly taken up Ambedkar's ideological stance in favor of a rational humanism. "The distinctively human function is reason," Ambedkar would write, in one form or another, throughout his life: in his writings on Gandhi, on caste, on economy, on his eventual turn towards Buddhism (*Essential Writings* 158). The burning of the *Manusmriti* was an act of public protest while also functioning as a celebration of the intellectual faculties of modern man. The Dalit literary text's fixation on the categories of the real should thus be read as an extension of Ambedkar's faith in the rational man; realist narrative would become its highest literary achievement.

Three Burnings

1908

In the story "Duniya ka subse anmol rattan" ("The Most Precious Jewel in the World"), Nawab Dhanpat Rai writes in Urdu that "The land of our fathers and grandfathers has today slipped from our hands and now, we are homeless" (21). The story, part of a collection of five published in 1908 entitled *Soz-e-vatan* (*Dirge of the Nation*), was fabulist, and peopled by a timeless princess and her suitor. But the parable was hardly enigmatic, the characters hardly opaque. "Your stories are full of sedition," the author, a government servant, was told by the district magistrate in Jamirpur. Of the thousand copies of *Soz-e-vatan* printed, the seven hundred unsold were submitted to the district office (Rai, *Premchand* 74). They were burned, and Nawab Dhanpat Rai's career as a writer terminated, forcing the emergence of "Premchand" (1880–1936), the new nom de plume. Rai's career was quite short. Premchand's has been enduring. His vast novels, written from the 1910s to the 1930s, produced the tradition of social realism, inaugurating it in Hindi; his stories, numbering some three hundred, set the stage for the postwar story movement called *nayi kahani*; his essays argued for a literature of engagement for the subcontinent and contributed to a budding literary criticism. Postindependence *anchalik sahitya*, or "regional literature," takes up Premchand's dissection of the village, his interest in rural politics, in the archetypal moneylender, the *zamindar*, and the peasant. Experimentalist writers like Agyeya defined their aesthetic program against Premchand, dissecting the monolith he had become even by the 1940s. Later in the century, when Anglophone writers like Salman Rushdie derided the social realism of vernacular literatures, they evoke a construct established by Premchand.

The burning of *Soz-e-vatan* is often mentioned but rarely "read"; it is seen as a typical instance of colonial domination and political censorship. But the gradual aesthetic shift it signaled allows us to read the nascent link between the novel and the national, and the realist novel in particular. Most accounts of Premchand are dismissive of this first collection of stories for one reason primarily: the stories refuse to cooperate with the notion of Premchand as a social realist. His earliest work, the stories in *Soz-e-vatan*, are largely patriotic and romantic; the characters are Rajput warriors and princesses who demonstrate eternal truths. Critics have ignored this "seditious" writing, demoting it to Premchand's early phase, a phase dominated by Urdu literary paradigms, what Francesca Orsini describes as "the familiar motifs of the Arabo-Perisan romantic-magic quest" (xii). Understood as the strivings of a young, inexperienced writer, raised with the artistic forms produced by Mughal patrons and the practitioners of Urdu poetry, the stories written by Premchand in the first decade of the twentieth century are considered to be of little literary value, and are rarely anthologized or commented upon.

"If we tell the story of two young lovers in a way that makes no impact on our love of beauty and only makes us weep for them because they are apart, what movement have we brought to the mind and taste?" wrote Premchand shortly before his death in 1936 ("Sahitya"). Thirty years after the publication of "Duniya ka subse anmol rattan," ("The Most Precious Jewel in the World"), the previous statement seems like a harsh self-critique. But Premchand himself was the first to castigate his young stylistic predilections. In "Duniya" a prince searches for the "the most precious jewel in the world" with which to woo the princess. He brings back wifely devotion, the ashes from the funeral pyre of a widow who has committed sati, as well as the tears of a repentant criminal on the gallows. But each time, the princess denies him. When the suitor finally returns with the last drop of blood from a Rajput hero dying on a battlefield in service to his nation, the princess is pleased. The transgressive nature of the stories, however, was not masked by the old paradigms of Urdu courtly forms. Blatantly pedagogical, the story functions like a parable. The hero is no ordinary man but, even at the beginning of his quest, compares himself to Sikander (Alexander the Great) and the prince Munir Shami, and dreams of throwing himself off of a mountain to end his misery. And the princess appears archetypal, with wrists of glass, an attendant, a golden curtain, and a throne. The language is lovely and hyperbolic: "the bottomless ocean of sadness," "the most priceless jewel in the world," and epithets like "my lover who is willing to sacrifice his life" litter the story. Premchand constructs a world of extremes: desperate sadness, endless thorny jungles, stunning beauty, fierce devotion. The simplicity of this world is precisely what allows for its smooth pedagogical drive.

But in the next few years, Premchand moved away from the timelessness of the fabulist in order to situate his patriotic vision in the specificities of the "present." Realism offered him the subtleties of historical context and the full range of characterological analysis. While he never insisted on the weighty mode of description, ironic or otherwise, so dear to predecessors like Tolstoy and Dickens, he presented a deep investment in their social scope, and the arena of class society. His writing was to function as a mirror, leading to a Gandhian self-reflection; readers would see themselves, but also their social others, embedded in the network of relations that configured early twentieth-century Indian society. Relying on novelistic form to investigate a social problem while adhering to certain basic literary techniques and philosophical contingencies, his social realism pushed at the boundaries of upper middle class morality; these works drew from discourses of nationalism and women's reform, and aimed to be both pedagogical and practical, expanding the circle of knowledge and sympathy.

Premchand, and the writers associated with the Progressive Writers Association of North India in the 1930s,[13] were instrumental in this regard—in the development of a political literary movement that used the novel, both instrumentally and artistically, to claim a certain relationship to the social real. The rise of the novel in India, the development of the genre, was thus intimately tied to the question of uplift, reform movements, and the psychology of sympathy anchored in the individual. But who was that individual to be? Although it is rarely read as such, that development was produced by a certain type of engagement with caste; realism in the form inherited and practiced by Premchand brought the question of caste into the literary sphere.[14] The new aesthetic forms that Premchand adopts allow for a social and ethical complexity that at some level begets, indeed requires, the representation of caste society. The question of the representational disservice that this subjection of caste affiliation to national belonging might have done is where the critique of Premchand lies.

In "Duniya ka subse anmol rattan," the suitor gains the princess's love. But the story's final line does not focus on their coupling, but rather on the drop of the Rajput warrior's blood encased in a bejeweled box. Written in gold lettering on a tiny placard: "The last drop of blood spilt in defense of the homeland: the most precious thing in the world" (22). A literal engraving appears as the moral of the story, which coincides with the conclusion of a quest and the uniting of lovers.[15] Realism, of the range of all the aesthetic and political formulations available, offered Premchand an ideological complexity, but it also forced him to abandon the transparent and carefully demarcated ethical world of the Urdu fable in favor of the hazy world of readerly interpretation. The form of the realist novel clearly indebted Premchand to certain ideologies, but it also masked and tempered them.[16] Though *Karmabhumi* (1932) would cover budding untouchable caste movements, and *Rangbhumi* (1925) Gandhian civil disobedience against the British, Premchand's writings were never again seized by the British. The realism for which Premchand became famous, developed as a counterpoint to Urdu's rhetorical and political failures, became the cornerstone of the novel of social reform, a genre whose ideological premise Dalit writers will deconstruct late in the twentieth century.

DALIT REALISMS

The production of Dalit literature might therefore be persuasively read as a crystallization of the aforementioned debates: a debate on the politics of form, as in Premchand's abandonment of nineteenth-century Urdu narrative paradigms for the "engaged social realism" of the "Western novel"; a debate on the relationship between realism and rationalism, as in Ambedkar's insistence on the power of cultural production derived from a humanistic individualism; and a debate on the reality of realism, or the fraught relation between its bourgeois liberal impulse, and the radical nature of subjects pushing at its parameters. But in what sense can Dalit literature properly be called "realist"? The intersection of the exposition of social ills with the centrality of human dignity might be the logical point of intervention for a "Dalit realism," the assertion of which is the primary claim of this body of work. Realism, some would argue, maintains a privileged relationship to the human, who can be determined, described and elaborated in his social sphere. For the Marxist critic György Lukács, the realist novel developed by Balzac and Tolstoy had a kind of potential later eclipsed by the early modernist writers, who had no interest in the totality and integrity of the social sphere; it is that radical potential that Dalit writers clearly seek to harness.[17] For Lukács, realism was determined by its historicism, its unique ability to capture the properly historical nature of people and things, to collapse individuals and sociologies, moment and event. The realist novel was therefore not powerful because it was imitative, because of the mimetic power of language, or because of the rigid adoption of a certain aesthetic program, but rather because it was *revelatory*, displaying the totality of the social whole that lay beneath the surface. Unlike expressionism, which according to

Lukács chose subjectivism and formalistic play, realism could never be accused of the obfuscation of history.

But the very realism that Lukács heralds was a product of a radically new relationship to rationalism, positivism and scientific materialism, which in India would be referred to as "the colonial construction of knowledge" (Narayan, *Multiple Marginalities* 15). Generations of criticism have demonstrated that "realism," having traveled abroad literally and metaphorically, revealed itself to be the locus of imperial and orientalist discourses. And yet, it is the serious consideration of the basic tenets of that critically compromised realism that Dalit writing will reevaluate. Dalit literature does aim to reveal the Lukácsian social totality of caste, invisible to the naked eye, just as it espouses the expansion of knowledge. But it does so in the service of a concrete constituency: its own. Thus, contrary to the assumption that India's literary face was consistently turned towards Britain, Dalit literature seems to be equally ideologically indebted to the French and Russian novelists of the nineteenth and twentieth centuries, and bears particular resemblance to the tenets of socialist realism, the official cultural policy propagated by Soviet politician Andrei Zhdanov in the 1930s and '40s, and its later Third Worldist incarnations with which it shares certain ideological imperatives. As a result, though I rely on Lukács's elaborations of the term "realist" and his notion of "critical realism" to characterize Dalit writing, I do so with some qualification. What the term realist comes to mean in Lukács's work was derived from a thorough engagement with Marxism and deduced via a vast reading of very long nineteenth- and early twentieth-century European novels. An aesthetics of realism derived from Balzac, Flaubert, and Tolstoy, made legible through a dialectical materialism, sits uneasily on the writing characterized as Dalit. The primarily short fiction, poetry, and autobiography that form "Dalit realism," produced by Dalit intellectuals and critics often hostile to Marxism and Marxist literary approaches, has, I will argue, other origins. As Frederic Jameson says, "The originality of the concept of realism, however, lies in its claim to cognitive as well as aesthetic status.... The ideal of realism presupposes a form of aesthetic experience which yet lays claim to a binding relationship with the real itself" (quoted in Bloch 198). Irreducible to a series of aesthetic practices, and more compelling as an ideological formation, realist narrative clings to the hope that it is possible to say something, if not everything, about the extraliterary world; it is this assumption that has fueled the reliance by political movements on the realist cultural text. Dalit prose literature, which may vary aesthetically, often relying on forms of first-person narration and chronological play, is clearly the product of a modern subjectivity, if not a modernist one. But it is realist nonetheless, relying on an unwritten compact between reader and writer, asserting a concrete if complex relationship to social reality within the literary text through a certain assumption of referentiality, and committed to the rationalist expansion of knowledge out of which realisms have historically been produced. The literature now characterized as Dalit is clearly invested in the surface materiality of things, and in the relationship between knowledge and mastery, the philosophical underpinning of realist ideology. It also participates to some degree in the ethnographic documentation of culture. There is a dynamic negotiation in the Dalit text between a resistance to realism's failures and an adoption of its privileges—a negotiation that is productive of a certain form. But these texts are realist in that they assume it is possible to make ethical claims about the world, and that such narratives can represent the casteized subject.

The debates regarding the interplay of "real" and "ideal" in a Dalit realist text (effectively, the problem of referentiality) thus require a complex formulation. In an analysis of the Hindi Dalit critique of Premchand, Alok Rai theorizes the concept of poetic justice. Poetic justice, "the underlying idea of imagined, aesthetic worlds being, somehow, compensatory and corrective," he suggests, is one mode via which to read the Dalit response to Premchand, who is never radical enough, whose characters are never angry enough (Rai, "Poetic and Social Justice" 152). Rai cites Dalit writer Kanwal Bharti who says of the character Gangi in the Premchand story "The *Thakur*'s Well," "If only Gangi had fought some battle of liberation, though she may well have lost her life, but it would have become a story of the Dalit fight for recognition" (154). A documentarist vision demands Gangi's subjection; a Dalit realist one requires her revolt. Is there space here beyond what Rai characterizes as a simple demand for "prescriptive militancy," or what Frederic Jameson in the context of socialist realism reduces to "agitational didacticism" (Rai, "Poetic and Social Justice" 154; Bloch 206)?

I would like to suggest a few complements for the real/ideal divide that will help us to do narrative justice to a Dalit realism. Firstly, Jameson's work on realism is illuminating for Dalit writing because it complicates the variable notions of verisimilitude that have haunted the self-proclaimed realist text. In an attempt to characterize the way in which the realist text touches the "real" (and the real here can only mean the historical), Jameson refers to the "trial run," "conditional history," and the "cautionary tale" ("Political Unconscious" 164, 169, 169). The complex problem of realist referentiality here produces a series of narrative times: historical, conditional, possible, inevitable; it moves variably through a series of reals and ideals. The modulating of temporalities and spaces is something that realism, and its later incarnations in the anticolonial and postcolonial realist text, has always done. But in the case of Dalit writing, where historical referentiality is a material problem in that the literary is acting as a supplement for *that which has never been written*, the movement of temporalities is more challenging to characterize. The nature of the utopian vision, the realm of the conditional, of wish-fulfillment, of the possible, is vague in these texts, yet hovering: this is one way to read the critical cliché that the Dalit subject always represents a collectivity. Unlike in a strictly utopian vision or a futurism, however, Dalit realism expresses a commitment to revealing conditions "as they are," precisely in order to justify its otherworldly, othertimely, imaginings. It always necessarily comprises a bifurcated vision.

Secondly, despite the polemical privileging of a "Dalit vision," these texts must be considered in terms of the knotty problem of perspective. In a discussion of the work of Baroda artist Bhupen Khakhar (1934–2003), Ashish Rajyadhaksha derives a democratic realism ("the view from below") and a state realism ("the view from above") (296–317). A state realism mimics an authorial vantage point, a disciplinary gaze; a democratic one is embedded and localized, the insider's view. Often, Khakhar's work contains both in a single work of art, in a single temporal fragment, even. This is an interesting paradigm for the Dalit text, which has one eye turned towards the delineation of subjection, another towards the conditions of liberation. But Khakhar's formulation also elucidates the metanarrative imperatives of the contemporary Dalit text, which participates in a paradigm of atrocity, oppression, and subjectification that is recognizable to an uppercaste readership (state or disciplinary realism) while elucidating its own unique experiential vision. In this way, too, the Dalit text is bifurcated. Dalit texts, like many other texts, contain elements of the traditionally realist and the utopian, the magical, the pedagogical. But they rhetorically insist on the reading of those elements within the framework of a realist epistemology rather than their narrative sequestering as subjectivist, fabulist, "agitational" or "prescriptive." To agree to this would be to grant to the Dalit realist text the privileges the realist text has accrued elsewhere. The Dalit text has to be necessarily concerned with caste status as immutable and fixed, as well as with its transcendence, without which the Dalit text could not *be*. This is less utopian or melodramatic than it is the product of a modern subjectivity. Dalit writing, reorganizing the world according to caste, is using the old categories of realist referentiality to make certain political claims, the elaboration of which require triangulation, circumvention, bifurcation.

This critical realist position is a difficult one to sustain after a century of critique of the positive political attributes of the term realist as either complicit with bourgeois ideology (as Theodor Adorno would attest), or readerly and therefore productive of passivity (as Roland Barthes would argue), or as radically Eurocentric (as would be maintained by Edward Said and Gayatri Spivak). Jameson raises the central question thus:

> Is it conceivable, within the world of immanence, for this or that existent, this or that already existing element, to breathe "the air of other planets," to give off even the slightest hint of a radically different future? . . . An ontological realism, absolutely committed to the density and solidity of what is—whether in the realm of psychology and feelings, institutions, objects, or space—cannot but be threatened in the very nature of the form by any suggestion that these things are changeable and not ontologically immutable: the very choice of the form itself is a professional endorsement of the status quo, a loyalty oath in the very apprenticeship to this aesthetic. ("Experiments" 113)

Even more disturbing is Adorno's critique of the imitative image-making machine of realism, which exploits suffering for the sake of its art: "For these victims are used to create something, works of art, that are thrown to the consumption of a world that destroyed them" (11). The powerful feminist critique of the unitary subject, and that subject as victim, has since the 1980s also demonstrated what has now become a critical assumption: subaltern identities are produced but also deconstructed by the act of writing, not simply reflected in it.

To formulate the charge severely: there has been a Dalit rejection of these later critiques of realism, from the modernist and the Marxist to the postcolonial and subaltern. If the realist novel naturalizes and aestheticizes, elides and obviates, then the realism of a protest literature must necessarily do something else. In a fictional world historically dulled to the penetration of caste and generically and even linguistically ill suited to its narrative accommodation, Dalit realism cannot possibly make the "loyalty oath" that Jameson mentions. The question for us then is not only of what happens when narrative forms travel, but of what happens when there is a dissonance between the purported ideologies encoded and demanded by genre, form, and language and those reenvisioned by a political movement? For Dalit prose narratives to espouse and perform the term "realist," after a century of narrative experimentation, should not be read as belated but strategic. Realism clearly offers certain ideological and aesthetic advantages in the creation of a Dalit subject. Dalit realism favors a realignment of a certain analytics (class, individualism, freedom) in order to privilege the vantage point of caste.[18] What could the narrative "freedom," based on which much novelistic realism typically functions mean in a context of caste hierarchy and uppercaste hegemony? Delinking the relations among the real, the novel, and the national, Dalit realism is immersed in a regional discourse, a regional field, while also creating a literary lineage that reaches towards other histories, narratives, and stylistic modes. Realism here is as much a social movement as it is an aesthetic predilection—in fact, an aesthetics readable in certain features, produced by a social movement. As Priyamvada Gopal writes of the Progressive Writers Association, "Realism, within this framework, is less an aesthetic technique than a philosophy that brings together an affective sense of justice, fairness and harmony with an understanding of all that violates that sense" (27). Dalit writers clearly rely on this sense of realism inherited from the "progressive" writers, while also charging that progressivism in India has implied a certain relation to caste. The modulation of such a notion of realism would require a rethinking of its philosophical underpinnings, and most particularly, the notion of "justice." The putative realism of Hindi Dalit literature, then, clearly derives from sources other than those credited with producing realism in Europe, and its aesthetic origins may be traced through a series of oppositional stances, as this book will outline.

The realist position is also difficult to sustain after much argumentation in favor of the modernness, modernity, and modernism, of, for example, Dalit poetry. Let me first say that Dalit writing is a crucial hallmark of Indian modernity, and produces the kind of subject that has long been heralded as the subject of modernity. And clearly Dalit poetry, in particular, engages with the kind of formal attention, mingling of register, and hybrid diction that might be characterized as modernist, though as Jaaware points out, this is a different type of modernism than the one that has been inspired by the West (285). But this observation presents us with the residual problem of genre and form. In this sense, recent work on non-EuroAmerican realisms is particularly illuminating, for it elaborates the changed nature of the term, as well as the aesthetic, in light of the putative deformation of slavery, colonialism, history. Much like the term, and form, novel, which Franco Moretti has demonstrated to be exemplary only in its continual challenge to, diversion from, and deformation of its supposed European models, realism as an aesthetics is contorted by political circumstance ("Conjectures on World Literature"). To take one recent intervention: Roberto Schwarz argues in *Misplaced Ideas* that European bourgeois realism produced literary "defects" in its transplantation to Brazil. The problem of foreign form, understood as "foreign debt," was not only aesthetic but also ideological, such that the putative liberalism of the modern European novel required contortion, buckled even, when faced with the local conditions of a Brazilian economy dictated by slavery (41). For Schwarz, the pendulum between debt and defect produces the most interesting readings of novelists like Jose de Alencar, who then paved the way for the great Machado de Assis. This is a dance between "detailed realism" and "local color," between the "machinery of plot" and "realist observation," between "European form" and "the local social scene" (Schwarz, *Misplaced Ideas* 66). Despite being grounded largely in the novelistic incarnations of the late nineteenth century, Schwarz's paradigm of "formal borrowings" and their ensuing complications is particularly illuminating for a figure like Premchand, for whom there is a direct economic, linguistic, and generic relevance, but also for a Dalit prose narrative that seeks to embrace certain ideologies and formal tendencies of what has come to be known as realist, while virulently denying others. This is a borrowing less across linguistic and cultural registers, though these are certainly relevant, than across genre, style, and ideology. Dalit writers will often claim that uppercaste literature holds little for them; they are strangers to these fictional worlds. But realist forbearers clearly structure very heavily modern Dalit prose narrative, which has only a tenuous aesthetic relationship to older casteized folk cultural forms. The argument that I am making here thus draws on several paradigms: borrowing, indebtedness, negativity but also, importantly, intertextuality. This is a term rarely linked to the aesthetics of protest, but it is crucial to the construction of an antigenealogy. Dalit literature, like all literature, springs from historical and social contexts, as well as historical and social texts. The decoupling of its modernity from a strictly modernist aesthetics is worthy of consideration.

This book thus collates a rhetorical and political commitment to both an experientially tested, lived reality *and* its utopian vision as they are reformed in the Dalit text, and as they are dictated by a living political movement in various forms, with a broader theoretical deconstruction of realism that suggests that the relationship of the cultural text to the "real" is infinitely triangulated, mediated, and attempted. I wish to insist on realist here as a political and aesthetic gesture, not only in the form of the ethnographic, its shallowest manifestation, but in all the aforementioned ways. An antigenealogy of Dalit realism, however, serves a broader critique, one that it shares with many other times and spaces, and that is a critique of literary progressivism, whether this be the literature of social reform or the contemporary Anglophone novel. From sympathy to nostalgia, from a universalist consciousness to an ethnographic romanticism, Dalit literature is in dialogue with the political, cultural, and *narrative* forms of a majoritarian progressivist thought. Rather than the rightist, religious, and overtly casteist platform, the writing of the Dalit movement launches a frontal attack on the sometimes-modernist, sometimes-Marxist, largely leftist literary establishment. A history of progressivist literary thought would show, despite concerns as divergent as the rural, the urban, English, or the vernacular, an almost fated position on caste. Effectively demonstrating that literary progressivism is indeed produced by a certain relationship to caste—a postcaste consciousness even—the identarian critique does more than essentialize and elevate its own prejudices; it sheds light on its own production. Identarian literary and cultural movements, "identity politics" as they are poorly named, thus reveal the flaws of older cultural projects in the Adornian sense. Radical cultural practices—radical not necessarily conceived politically, i.e., those that emanate from subalternist and nonhegemonic positions—can thus serve to give lie to the foundational premises of majoritarian thought—progressive or otherwise—both in form and content.

CRITICAL CONTEXTS

Dalit literature is now a pan-Indian phenomenon, making use of many cultural forms and present in many Indian languages, most notably Ambedkar's Marathi, where its modern origins lie. Earlier pre-Ambedkarite Dalit cultural production had its roots in traditional folk, often casteized, forms such as the *tamasha* and the *jalsa*, and the explicit activism of the *kalapathak* or Dalit performance troupe (Guru, *Dalit Cultural Movement* 5). But Ambedkar's political movement, his insistence on education, the colleges he founded, his own eloquent expressions, and, as many critics and writers have insisted, his narrative of self-awareness and self-respect, produced a generation of young literary intellectuals. Beginning in the 1940s Dalit writers in Marathi began using the literary to create a narrative of Dalit experience. Published in local newspapers (including *Prabuddha Bharat* of the Republican Party of India) in poetry, in short fiction, in autobiography, these narratives were as yet "fairly gentle accusations of injustice" (Zelliot, "Dalit Literature" 452). In 1972, however, this literary movement took the form of the Dalit Panthers, who drew their political and cultural inspiration from Black America. Under the leadership of Raja Dhale, organizers Arjun Dangle, Namdeo Dhasal, and J. V. Pawar advocated a call to consciousness, complete revolution, the abolition of caste, resistance to uppercaste atrocity, and, importantly, a critique of liberal reform. "We are not looking at persons but at a system. Change of heart, liberal education etc. will not end our state of exploitation. Legalistic appeals, requests, demands for concessions, elections, satyagraha—out of these, society will never change. Our ideas of social revolution and rebellion will not be borne by such paper-made vehicles" (Joshi 146). As an organization, the Panthers honed a critique of the originally Ambedkarite Republican Party of India, the Hindu nationalist Shiv Sena, and state politics more generally.[19] As a literary movement, writers like Dhasal and Daya Pawar, mingling Marxism and Ambekarite Buddhism, expanded the literary canon, introducing a range of casteized social spaces, forms of poetic expression, and political positionalities relying on the deformation of "ordinary" language. Writer and critic Arjun Dangle describes this as an antiestablishment literature, one of "negativism and scientificity" (237). Dhasal's iconic *Golpitha* (1972), a brutal, scathing, and linguistically explosive collection of poems depicting Bombay's seamy underside, was in this way instrumental in the establishment of a paradigm of otherness from mainstream, uppercaste writing. "How deep a chasm there is between the prose of mainstream Marathi literature and that of Dalit literature!" writes Dangle (xiii).

Dalit literature has become so widespread, in languages like Gujarati, Tamil, Kannada, and Telegu, that it has usurped other forms of cultural production, and has become a kind of social dominant. Preeminent Dalit philosopher Gopal Guru argues that Dalit literature has become mainstreamed and co-opted, thereby losing its revolutionary edge, and is no longer able to perform its vital political function (*Dalit Cultural Movement* 2). At the same time, as Aniket Jaaware suggests in a perverse metonymy, Dalit literature allows non-Dalits to "eat the Dalit" without having to "eat with the Dalit" (281). In Hindi Dalit literature, clearly, the same ideological questions are raised, and certain literary stages are necessarily experienced: the initial explosion of autobiography, for example. But this is a post-Marathi Dalit literature, i.e., a body of text self-conscious regarding its "newness," and its "radicalism," which operates within the realm of the regional and yet displays clear kinship with—indeed, derivation from—other Dalit literatures when considered within the context of the national. The questions raised by Ambedkar's burning of the *Manusmriti*, its potential refiguring by Dalit writers, now need to be revised. Dalit literature no longer proceeds solely from the premise of supplementarity, of direct challenge, but from a more subtle form of revisionism.

Circumventing the canonical tradition almost entirely, Hindi Dalit writers often profess to trace their intellectual origins instead to medieval Bhakti poetry, and its democratizing, anticaste ethos. With a focus on social equality, and the individual's particular relationship to God irrespective of status, medieval *nirgun bhakti* traditions were refigured by untouchable caste movements early in the twentieth century; these movements drew on Bhakti poetry in order to privilege the message of caste equality and antihierarchy potentially suggested by the poet-saints, or *sants*. The creation of temples, and accompanying structures of devotional practice throughout the United Provinces, produced a form of Dalit assertion that focused on the recitation of *sant* poetry and the discussion of religious writings. The Raidasis and the Kabirpanthis held festivals and plays, but also *satsangs*, or religious meetings, to read and discuss the teachings of important sect leaders (Gooptu 151). The focus on literacy as a means to participate in these new devotional sects clearly formed part of a program of social assertion more generally. Poetry, some of it formalistically derived from the Bhakti tradition, is today central in terms of Hindi Dalit literary output; many fiction writers publish poetry as well.

But there is a capacious generic ability among contemporary Dalit writers, who move easily and frequently between poetry, short stories, literary criticism, and novels. That prose-writing tradition seems to be intimately tied to the polemic and other forms of political writing that set the ideological stage for many protest movements. In the case of Hindi Dalit literature, prose writing may have its origins in the Adi-Hindu movement, which emerged in North India alongside, or as a result of, Bhakti devotionalism in the early 1920s. The Adi-Hindu movement was predicated on the belief in a pre-Aryan lineage for the Dalits of India.[20] The movement in the North, like the Ad-Dharmi movement in Punjab, arose in several cities (Allahabad, Lucknow, Benares) with large untouchable caste populations, and was led by some of the earliest generation of literate and educated untouchables, people like Ram Charan (1888–1938) and Swami Acchutanand (1879–1933). Swami Acchutanand was central in the creation of the pre-Aryan origin theory, according to which untouchables were the original inhabitants of India, subjugated by Aryan invaders who created caste in order to maintain their authority; he founded his own Adi-Hindu organization and edited a monthly newspaper. While preaching the entitlement owed to untouchables as descendants of the original inhabitants, and the necessary strategies for social advancement, he also asserted self-knowledge, an actively intellectual relationship to worship and God, derived from Bhakti revivalism. The untouchable was therefore once heroic and now deprived, but also reliant only upon his own faculties, not dependent on the perception, treatment, or categorization of others (Gooptu 166). Acchutanand wrote 2 plays—*Ramrajya Nyaya (The Justice of Kingdom of Ram)* and *Shambuka Balidan (The Sacrifice of Shambuka)*—and several other biographical and poetic texts, now recognized as the earliest form of a Hindi Dalit literary tradition, while also inaugurating a fixation on self-knowledge and self-experience that would prove to be determinant in the late twentieth-century outpourings of Dalit writers: *atmavad*. One of the hallmarks of Dalit writing has indeed been the privileging of the experience of the oppressed as a rejection of more systemic epistemological methodologies.[21] Narratively, experientiality has required an embedded narrator, one who has the rhetorical swagger of "omniscience" but the privileged and partial knowledge garnered from intimacy. But it has also required a reframing of a certain literary relationship to history, nationalism, and the event—an often-counterintuitive one. The genre of "popular Dalit history," for example, a kind of revisionist pamphlet sold in stalls and fairs and very widely read, professes a contested relation to uppercaste, nationalist, communalist histories.[22] Swami Acchutanand rhetorically "favored" British rule, as did Ambedkar, both arguing it to be inherently less oppressive and more forgiving towards Dalits than indigenous rule, while also demanding true "independence" for the untouchables, not just the Hindus and Muslims (Gooptu 170–75).[23] Dalit realism, then, while espousing the values of rationalism and tangible experience, suggests a novel relationship to the historical as well as to the national.

The relatively unknown figure of Acchutanand, compared to the well-documented and canonized figure of Ambedkar, presents an interesting intervention into Hindi language politics, which has not been considered in any depth in histories of the period. Modern Hindi—the Khari Boli dialect in the *devnagari* script—was standardized only in the early nineteenth century, ignoring many other "regional forms," as Harish Trivedi calls them, like Avadhi and Brajbhasha. Over the course of several decades, a literary canon for this new language was created, poetry, fiction, religious and pedagogical texts, that could freely break from the complex literary histories and literary forms of Urdu and Braj.[24] By the early twentieth century, this carefully crafted tongue had acquired a powerful constituency as well as national language status (Trivedi 959).

Several critics have demonstrated the way in which the rise of Hindi literature follows various trajectories: a colonialist pedagogical one alongside a more popular one, a reformist one alongside a fabulist and romantic one.[25] Slowly, as Trivedi points out, "a new and perhaps natural demand arose: the language of prose and the language of poetry should be the same in Hindi as in all other developed languages" (959). It was this strain—flexible and accommodating but heavily influenced by a certain conception of the modern European language—that would come to be critically appreciated as modern Hindi; Premchand was constitutive of such a reading. In Hindi in particular, the novel was being created alongside the very invention of Hindi; to write in a Hindi so recently "standardized" rather than other dialects was itself to assert a certain intimate relationship to realism (Dalmia, "Generic Questions" 416).

But alongside Premchand, in Hindi, was the occasional production of a Hindi Dalit literature, sporadic poetry in the prestigious literary journal *Saraswati*,[26] the writings, polemical and otherwise, of social reformers like Acchutanand, and the range of popular materials as yet uncatalogued: folk songs, popular history, pamphlets. These cultural forms were produced in Hindi as well as in those pre- and para-Hindis, and often mingled both. Contemporary Dalit writer Mohandas Naimishraya suggests that because there was no notable Dalit movement in the Hindi-speaking regions, such writing was ignored (Sharma 47). Dalit literature therefore makes a small but crucial intervention into language politics, and the development of Hindi, almost from its inception as a modern language. That is to say, its contemporary intervention, since the 1980s, emerges as a new and powerful iteration of a counterpoint position it has inhabited for some time.

ARCHITECTURE

A word on methodology: in this text the literary work is one that works in symptomatic ways, not only in the manner of those colossi that demonstrate causality and teleology. The loud bastions of readability have rarely served the subaltern. I thus read for those structures that refuse to unmask themselves, yes, but also for the detail, the limit point, the glacier's superficial tip; I read selectively, particularly, partially, and especially metaphorically. This is in part because of a commitment not to read exclusively. The brilliant critic D. R. Nagaraj writes in the preface to the first edition of *The Flaming Feet*, "I have always held that it is better to study the Dalit movement and its different expressions by situating them in the context of other forms of protest: exclusivism can be deadly in these matters" (xxi). Almost all of the texts I consider in this project make, as their readers continue to make, radical claims. One way to test those claims is by the work of a nonexclusivist comparatism.

The logical question that then arises with any comparativist discussion of Dalit literature is, of course, the nature of the politico-aesthetic specificity of caste; the delineation of which is, in fact, one impulse of this project. As an anthropological and sociological phenomenon, caste has been relentlessly studied, analyzed, and archived, as a system of structural hierarchy, a tree-like differentiation of knowledge potential and power, as well as socio-religious demarcation organized around Hindu understandings of purity and pollution. This project is clearly indebted to the entire sphere of knowledge on caste as a social phenomenon, though its sympathies lie particularly with the question of knowledge and power in the realm of casteized cultural practice. But my focus in *Untouchable Fictions* is specifically caste as "a literary object." That is to say, the project argues that there is a literary-aesthetic construction, and repression, of both caste and untouchability that is intrinsically linked to, but clearly triangulated and distinct from, its historical and experiential articulation.

Gopal Guru argues that "untouchability as a dynamic reality is bound to produce experience that is always in excess of its description" ("Archaeology" 49). Caste is thus representable and evades representation. This is an important contribution for any discussion of literary realism, which is often seen as the repository of a naturalistic description. Even if it were, taking Guru's point, it would fail the Dalit movement terribly. If caste as a dynamic phenomenon in this way exceeds the descriptive impulse, then what can the literary offer? I will suggest in this book that caste be read not simply as an abstract difference but in the realm of the aesthetic: language, metaphor, form. Dalit literature in Hindi is a contemporary movement, and, as mentioned, is no longer concerned with simply the overt acknowledgement of caste in the public sphere but rather the excavation of its hidden and much more subtle maneuvers. These may be readable in not only the spectacular violence of atrocity, still a central and terrible preoccupation, but also in the turn of the linguistic, as well as the defamiliarization of narrative.

Guru in fact suggests philosophy, and archaeology, rather than anthropology and sociology, as the disciplines that might better "access" untouchability. He draws on Foucault to argue for the privileging of the form ("those discourses, not as a document, but those discourses themselves, those discourses as practices obeying certain rules") rather than content ("the thoughts, representation, images, themes, preoccupations that are concealed or revealed within"). This is necessary as untouchability now plays out not openly, but secretly, less with feudal authority and architectural demarcation but in the hazy realm of unnamed social relations (54). In his analysis of a conversation between a landlord and potential tenant, for example, Guru tracks the movement from the universal category of the landlord to the specified self of caste-based ownership, "a painful skinning off of layers" (56). Archaeology, he suggests, may be the methodology of the ambiguous. I would argue for the space of the literary then for one compelling reason: it is precisely when the thing itself has become slippery that a critical realism is most powerful. The modern realist text makes claims about the authenticity of experience not through one-to-one correspondence but rather through hyperbole, metaphor, the symptom and the sign. It is in this sense that a critical realism delves below the surface—where caste can no longer properly operate—to access an untouchability submerged.

This project attempts to demonstrate a culturalist antigenealogy, establishing an aesthetic logic for the reading of Dalit literature largely condemned to ethnography, while presenting a critique of literary "progressivism" in its myriad forms. But it must be said that at the most basic level Dalit literature can only be read as a product of a history (and contemporaneity) of caste subjection. The meanings of Dalit literature do not simply circulate through a series of interlaced texts; they derive from the world outside and certain failures of history. Dalit literature is also the outgrowth of caste violence, in all its measurable and immeasurable forms. As a body of work, its development must be tied to the material problems of deprivation, poverty, subjection, and as Gopal Guru adds, humiliation. I quote here at some length from Badri Narayan and A. R. Misra, who write in the specific context of North India and its multifarious production of Dalit culture.

> They were forced to stay away from the historical mainstream, peripheral as they were, deprived of access to education and surrounded by terror. They were not only forced to stay away from history but any kind of leisure, which is such a critical source in the creation of the culture of a community. The very nature of their jobs, and social functions that they were coerced to perform, prohibited them from owning and developing any cultural compartment for themselves or their community. They were not allowed to carry or own any weapon. . . . Thus doomed to serve and comply they were never in a position to be either donors or recipients of the contents of the existing civilization and culture. Orality was their only possession, or medium of communication, of their anxieties, tribulations, deprivations and anguish. They did not even have their religion to console themselves and in such an alienated state, they feared even to entertain the idea of expression of their woes in the world after death; for it were their evil actions in their previous life that had placed them in such a precarious social position and any question pertaining to their existence would be considered to be violative of the divine design. (Misra and Narayan 27)

It has been the unfortunate burden of Dalit literature to supplement an absent historical and cultural archive that is only now being recognized, but its literariness also lies beyond the documentary: in the conjuring of alternate possibilities, in the analysis of subjection as well as its attenuation, in the creative revisions of and commitment to that which never was and may never be. It is precisely in the putatively anachronistic adoption of the realist that a new theory of narrative form emerges.

CHAPTER ONE

The Dalit Limit Point

Realism, Representation, and Crisis in Premchand

We do not believe in imaginary men.
—PREMCHAND, "The Aim of Literature"

Modern Hindi literature, it is said, begins with Premchand. The early nineteenth-century writers of Hindi, producing "literature" in an only recently standardized and consolidated "language," were writing pedagogical treatises, educational texts for students at Fort William College in Calcutta, "fiction" created by the political mandate of the British East India Company. Influenced by the literary world of North India and Urdu, these prescribed texts fit snugly into the generic grids then available to prose narrative: romance, fantasy, social uplift; Lallujilal's 1802 *Premsagar* introduces Krishna, ensconced in the cyclical narratives that characterize Sanskrit but in a simple Hindi prose. There were many other adaptations of Sanskrit tales and epics throughout the nineteenth century, as well as texts like Pandit Gauri Dutt's 1870 *Devrani Jethani ki Kahani* (*The Story of Two Sisters-in-Law*), which fictionally schooled women on appropriate behavior. Later in the century, there would be the pioneering work of Bharatendu Harischandra and the development of the essay, satire, the literary journal, as well as the turn to forms and genres adopted, transposed, and translated whole from English and Bengali.[1] Into this stilted prose fiction world, Premchand's writings appeared as the harbinger of a new era, that which had been the province of Bengali and Marathi for quite some time. The newness of Premchand, I would suggest, is a code capacious enough to signal many things, but it most persuasively refers to his realism. When Premchand switched from writing in Urdu to Hindi, a transition he made throughout his life,[2] realist writing in Hindi was effectively inaugurated, and with it came the subject of the peasant, who remained a constant, the basis of a literary trope that would endure throughout the twentieth-century Hindi literary canon.[3] But if modern Hindi prose literature "begins" with Premchand, Hindi Dalit literature might be said to begin with opposition to Premchand, for precisely the same reasons.

This isn't literally true; the full flowering of Dalit writing in Hindi begins much later, in the late 1980s. But it is the 1920s, during the rise of Swami Acchutanand and the Adi-Hindu movement that argued for a unique and politicized caste identity for untouchable castes, the period during which Premchand most fruitfully wrote, that can be said to have produced the first literary articulations of Dalit identity in the Hindi-speaking belt of North India. In 1914, the unknown "untouchable" poet Hira Dom publishes what may be the first Dalit writing in Hindi in the influential literary journal *Saraswati*, "Acchut ki shikayat" ("The Untouchable's Lament"[4]). Wielding a two-pronged critique against both the uppercastes and their colonial rulers, Hira Dom concludes with a plea for mutual fraternity among castes, drawing on the language of national republicanism. Although that sentiment requires another sixty-five years of caste radicalism and the bureaucratic engines of independence, constitutional protection, and education to produce what we now recognize as Dalit literature, the timing is more than coincidental. An ideological opposition to Premchand and the rhetoric of sympathy he is seen to represent may be where we can locate the first affective stirrings of Dalit literary opposition.

REALISM, THAT CAPACIOUS CODE

When writers from the Bharatiya Dalit Sahitya Akademi chose to burn Premchand's novel *Rangbhumi* in 2004, they burned not only a novel but an icon, a worldview, a genre, an ideology. *Rangbhumi*, written between 1924 and 1925, follows the blind beggar and eventual Gandhian hero Surdas Chamar as he attempts to support the peasant community in the face of industrial land usurpation. Surdas, our protagonist, dies as a saint as the village he attempted to save burns before him. Heralded as one of the most poignant documentations of the crisis of the peasantry in North India, the novel demonstrates a Gandhian vision of sacrifice and *satyagraha* in the face of the brutalities of materialism. Premchand's Surdas Chamar serves as a confirmation of this early phase of Premchand, marked by Gandhian idealism and a rhetoric of sympathy. For Dalit writers, however, Premchand is never simply "Premchand" but a literary figure seeking a role in literary history, attempting "to gain the praises of uppercaste Brahmins who would thereby consider his work 'literature'" (18). This claim, made by the Dalit Sahitya Akademi president, Sohanpal Sumanakshar, reminds us of the vagaries of literary history and the always archaeological work of a historicist literary criticism. Sumanakshar's suggestion is provocative; he claims that Premchand used a certain type of representation instrumentally, and engaged in an extremist form of stereotyping in order to curry favor with those whose sanction established the literary canon. But the hint that the category of literariness and the characteristics of canon have been created at the expense of not only Dalits, but also of Dalitness, is clearly one that resonates with any politics of a democratic literary sphere. Narrative has relied on a certain form of aesthetics, but also on a rigid binarism—not only between upper- and lowercaste themselves, but between their respective languages, politics, and imagery—that has made only certain representational paradigms worthy of literary enterprise. Sumanakshar is thus critiquing the category of literature (thus far almost exclusively the province of the uppercastes and their aesthetics) for foreclosing certain conditions of possibility. In effect, the horizon of literary representation is ontologically constrained for the Dalit character, demonstrated particularly—and most often—by the figure of the Chamar, member of the leather-working untouchable caste of North India, who has come to occupy a certain space in the realist imaginary where the Dalit is concerned. Premchand's characters have become "literary types." *Rangbhumi* may have functioned through repetition of a stereotype, but after a century of circulation, it has archetypal power.[5]

What I will suggest is that the problem is less with Premchand than with the ideological and aesthetic constraints of the realism he employed.[6] "Premchand" as an object of literary interpretation is in a bind, produced in large part by his attempt at "idealistic realism"; his fiction was to be recognizable, in every aesthetic and political sense, despite its "newness," while also being socially conscious, progressive, political. Sumanakshar's critique and the Dalit critique more generally is, in fact, engendered by reading Premchand as a realist, and therefore holding him morally and aesthetically responsible as such. Rather than beginning with the usual question: Who was Premchand? I will begin here with the question: What is Premchand? What does it mean to read the text we refer to as Premchand? How is such a text produced? What are its generic mandates? And what kind of readerly compact does it require?

Even today, Premchand's writings are described by mainstream critics as "the most powerful and authentic accounts of the national movement and people's life . . . and in particular the community life of rural India, peasant commonsense" (Singh, "Premchand's Ideology" 76). They are also described as "in favor of Gandhian ideals, feudal values and the caste system" (Valmiki, *Dalita sahitya* 99). The Dalit critique of Premchand should therefore be read alongside a broader critique of progressive realism, Premchand being its most preeminent practitioner. In particular, it is the model of readerly sympathy engendered by realist writing, on which it in fact relies, that Dalit writing challenges. This chapter traces the chain of sympathy on which Premchand's realism depends in order to illuminate a twofold process: how caste might be revealed as a literary object of analysis, and how the Dalit emerges as a sentimental subject. I argue that the realist novel, despite its insistence that both the woman and the untouchable be "read," was central to a kind of formal erasure of caste as an analytic.

"PREMCHAND"

Unlike in the case of France, for example—where realism's origins had as much to do with an attempt to break new aesthetic ground as they did with a democratic and scientific vision of the world, an engagement with bourgeois individualism and, additionally and gradually, a desire to incorporate the low—realism in India effectively originates with the question of social reform and pedagogical responsibility. Beginning with what Meenakshi Mukherjee refers to as the Christian novel (designed to educate native women on proper postconversion behavior) through the first generation of vernacular novel writing in the mid- to late nineteenth century (in Marathi, Bengali, Hindi, etc.), realist fiction was concomitant with a nascent nationalism and a range of social issues that dominated the public landscape.[7] By the end of the nineteenth century, a large number of novels had been published, in several different languages, most circling around the pressing social questions of the time: widow remarriage, women's education, religious conversion. Produced seamlessly alongside prose narratives that dabbled in fabulism, historical romance, and fantasy, these early social novels set a precedent that Premchand would inherit and refashion, as he navigated the concerns that we now read as central to young nationalism. His realist style, therefore, is inextricably linked to the question of the social problem as narratable, analyzable, and potentially resolvable. The novel *Nirmala* (1928) is situated firmly within a larger discourse on women's roles and responsibilities; *Karmabhumi* (1932) chronicles Gandhianism, *Godaan* (1936) narrates the burdens of the peasantry. Premchand's work, his aesthetic, the generic conventions he produced, can only be understood within the framework of civil society, social critique, and novelistic potentiality.

This has been described as a literature of social reform, a critical realism,[8] a social realism, a naturalism, as well as what Alok Rai calls "the literature of conscience" ("Foreword" 199). Premchand's own term, *aadarshonmukhi yatharthvad*, "idealistic realism" was inspired by the burden of having to produce both social critique and utopian vision.[9] Premchand's work was capacious enough to warrant all the aforementioned categorizations, moving between what we now recognize as classical melodrama and something more caustically interventionist. Priyamvada Gopal reminds us that for Premchand and the writers of the Progressive Writers Association[10] who followed him, this was ideological and not necessarily narratological: "Beauty—our sense of the aesthetic and the affective—has to be recuperated from orthodoxy and redefined" (quoted in Gopal 27). For Premchand in particular, the aesthetic never operated in a realm of isolation; concepts of beauty, poetic form and genre, and narrative ideals were entirely determined by caste and class. In the famous "Sahitya ka uddesya" ("The Aim of Literature"), Premchand's 1936 address to the first meeting of the Progressive Writers Association, the author argues that once literature becomes detached from the patronage of the wealthy ("a particular class"), it has the freedom to be truly revolutionary and challenge the dominant paradigms of the time. In an important essay on capitalism, "Mahajani sabhyata" ("Capitalist Culture"), Premchand bemoans the cultural shift whereby all the arts, literature, music, and fine arts, are determined by wealth (164). "This capitalist culture has established new rules and codes according to which every aspect of today's social arrangement is run" (164). The critique of capitalism, class hierarchy, and the problems of an "engaged" literature occupied Premchand's serious attention throughout his life and effectively created a paradigm for the concerns of an engaged writer.

And yet, the question of caste as such eluded him. Clearly, Premchand was one of the major proponents of lowercaste sympathies and uppercaste critique available at the time. Particularly in his attempts to investigate the potential for a national consciousness, he was concerned about the excesses of the priestly caste, and caste distinction more generally.[11] His prose writing enlarged the circle of fictionality to include not only villainous Brahmins but also untouchable characters, countering centuries of literary evasion.[12] Still, the major critique presented by contemporary Dalit critics is that despite his sympathies, his work betrays lingering faith in *varnavyavastha*, the caste system as a whole. In one of Premchand's later melodramatic novels, the 1931 *Gaban* (*The Stolen Jewels*), when a Khatik family takes care of a Kayastha man in crisis, there is a moment of meditation on caste: "No one raises his status by putting someone up. No matter how much merit a Chamar may benefit from being generous, he'll still be a low-caste Chamar!" "I consider such a Chamar better than a Brahman pundit who always devours the wealth of others," says Jalpa, the young woman, and the ideological winner of this debate in the novel. Reading caste as a problem of birth versus deed is a reflection of Gandhian intervention on the subject; Premchand was clearly indebted to a Gandhian vision that translated narratively into the problematic "change of heart." But the caste problem in this novel is one for the voyeur, a theoretical problem of middle-class acceptance rather than a confrontation with Dalit life. Other novels deal with caste more seriously; *Sevasadan* (1915) and *Karmabhumi* (1934) note its intersection and collusion with patriarchal and colonial power. Caste in these novels emerges as one category of structural consequence amidst others and it is often an intellectual problem; though several short stories paint poignant portraits of untouchable caste life, those stories are excised from the totality of life, such that caste is the essential feature of the very lowest.[13] Sohanpal Sumanakshar argues that Dalits can't be represented honorably by Premchand, constrained as they are to a certain type. Sheoraj Singh Bechain calls Premchand a "Chamar-hating Kayastha" determined solely by Gandhian values: "What one expects to find in the consciousness of a Dalit character with respect to the caste system is rage, anger with respect to inequality—but these are missing in Premchand's characters. Any character who lives in anticipation of kindness, sympathy, generosity and pity, cannot be a Dalit" (11).[14] Critic Dr. Dharamvir goes so far as to say that Premchand's entire outlook was feudal.

There is a danger of placing an anachronistic burden on the social realist text of the 1920s and 1930s, saddling it with a responsibility it could not have culturally borne.[15] The kind of radicalism expected from Premchand by contemporary Dalit writers might seem to charge him with a preternatural gift, one earned only later via generations of struggle and the political successes of Ambedkar. However, it isn't true, as one might assume, that these questions hadn't become discursively available at the time, or that they didn't have popular currency; recent work by Ramnarayan Rawat and Sara Beth indicates otherwise, specifically in the context of the early twentieth century in the United Provinces. Indeed, the range of analytical options proffered on the caste problem in Premchand's realism clearly shrinks a growing body of voices, literary and other, that approached the problems of caste conflict, caste and nationalism, and Dalit identity. I am going to coalesce the range of critiques here thus: caste is what strains the realism of Premchand.[16] The carefree way in which uppercaste Kayasthas in Premchand's novels move in with untouchable-caste Khatiks, as one critic says, may be one example of this. But more importantly, in terms of the "realist," *caste cannot be given causal space*. If for Dalit critics Premchand consistently misreads and misappropriates the referent, the "real Dalit," then this is a characterological critique. But such a suggestion belies the very reliance of the Dalit critique *on character*, which is its only potential narrative avenue for radicalism; once caste as a structural force has been eclipsed, the role of critique is reduced to complaint regarding individual speech and action. The defensive intellectual posture of the Dalit critique, rooted in character, actually locates one of the central problems of realism—reliant upon the demonstration of its mimetic capabilities, but also on the social type, realism is invested *despite itself* in paradigms of bourgeois individualism.[17] Premchand's writing, forged by the intersection of realist aesthetics and a discourse of social reform, has to produce not only an inaugural peasant type, but an object of sympathy, an affective resistance, the only kind of narrative movement available to what one critic calls Premchandian "psychodrama."[18] The problem of "character" is the thematic symptom via which we might read the more pressing problem of the discourse of sympathy.

One of realist narrative's most radical innovations was what critic Linda Nochlin describes as "a democratization of subject matter," the incorporation of the sordid, the marginalized, and the impoverished into its vision (33). Premchand is prototypical in this respect, cited as he is for bringing the village and the peasant into the realm of literary representation and popular consciousness. *Godaan*, for example, occupies near-mythic status for that very reason, as it documents the brutal cycle of peasant debt, the transition to a cash-crop economy, the decay of a feudal notion of social responsibility, and the starkest poverty, filtered through the peasant Hori Ram. Rooted, however, in the logic of character, it is reliant almost entirely on the juxtaposition of the *zamindar* and the peasant to produce the final sense of historical crisis. Thus, painstakingly wrought, one easy condemnation of Premchand is precisely the one that Geeta Patel makes of the Progressive Writers more generally, "The people became an other . . . the life of those others, whose oppression served as literary material, could be easily, transparently rendered" (cited in Gopal 5). The transparent rendering of others has been, in fact, the central concern for the realist novel, largely committed to enlarging the affective circle.[19] For the novel, this required the social "type," and it is here that we may locate the origins of a Dalit critique of realism.

REALISM'S OTHER AND THE QUESTION OF TYPOLOGY

The question of the representation of the other, the question par excellence for the social realists, is the question of the "type." Typology might be seen as the central motif of the realist novel, which travels through a range of exterior spaces. For György Lukács, the defining feature of the type as a literary device is "a peculiar synthesis" between the general and particular, the vehicle via which one demonstrates "the complete human personality."[20] This is less an interest in formalism than a determination to expose the ideological underpinnings of the technique: the type is singularly what gives realism its radical potential. The synthesis on which Lukács relies implies, of course, a dialectical worldview that informs the text. In Balzac, where Lukács sees the most perfect flowering of this technique, the petty-bourgeois gold digger, the archvillain, the social type is socialized—depicted in both his worldliness as well as at his most idiosyncratic. The type thus becomes the pinnacle of the connection between the internal and the external, and therefore the historical, world. Unlike the pure subjectivism of the modernists, or the "pseudo objectivism" of the naturalists, the type remains real in its historicism—it situates the individual amidst the historical forces of his production. This philosophy of history in fiction is central to Lukács's conception of

Marxist aesthetics, of course, but it also masks the concept of proletarian humanism, the object of which is to "reconstruct the complete human personality and free it from the distortion and dismemberment to which it has been subjected in class society" (Lukács, *Studies* 5). Reading Marxism as a proletarian humanism, and perhaps a failed one at that, is precisely what Hindi Dalit critics will claim to be doing fifty years later. Lukácsian realism, therefore, produces a human-centeredness that functions in opposition to the tenets of a contemporary liberal humanism, such that typology is not a problem of individuality but rather the intersection of class consciousness and individuation. Lukács's analysis of the realist type is clearly valuable in a reading of Premchand as well; Premchand's writing institutionalized certain figures—the moneylender, the *zamindar*, and arguably the peasant—all of whom are represented as socially constructed designs.

The complete invention of the type, however, with which early realism in India was charged, requires a different figuration. Alok Rai reads Premchand's short stories as a plea to recognize "the otherness of others," "an effort to represent the poor unglamorized, an act of penitence directed at the arrogant presumptuousness of the insensitive reformers who had wanted to remake the poor in their own petit-bourgeois image" ("A Kind of Crisis" 11). Such a social directive is consonant with the logic of the type, and might be said to allow for very limited conceptual notions and literary configurations for the text. Anchored in a representative logic, the type has to become recognizable *as* a type; this is precisely the opposite of becoming recognizable as real. Literary types are *literary types*. And realist literary types are anchored in the dynamic between the individual and the social—i.e., the individual and his class formation. In Premchand's work, for example, there are broadly two "types" of *zamindar*, the cruel and the compassionate, as there are two "types" of peasant, the pitiable and the angry. Sometimes characters oscillate between the types available to them; *Godaan*'s Rai Sahib makes an ethical discussion of that very trajectory. Literary knowledge in Premchand functions as a closed system—it accretes from text to text, complicates, simmers, and simplifies, adding and subtracting from an array of social types. The nationalist may be pure at heart and he may eventually become heartless; *Karmabhumi*'s Amarkant is both serving and self-serving. But there is only one origin for that distinction and that is class consciousness. Premchand's types spring from the social, and occasionally the radically individual, but the social here can only mean socio-economic. Caste origins are hardly granted formational power. As a result, there is no third way.

Except, of course, in the case of the untouchable. As such, lower-caste characters bear the burden of representativeness but they also must fit the typological paradigms of the peasant, their closest literary kin. One illustration of this might be the change of heart, that "painless device" (Pandey, "Premchand and the Peasantry" 1151) to which Premchand would routinely turn. In several novels, cruel characters are converted via the change of heart, their ways and means having been revealed to them. But untouchable caste characters, even when occupying less peripheral fictional spaces within the arena, cannot bear the arc of the change of heart. The problem isn't only one of two-dimensionality or stereotype, but that their defining feature is caste, not kindness or social class. While the dialectic of the individual and the social leaves room for historical movement, caste fixes and stagnates. The casteized type can thus never be historical.

The typological problem is crucial, as its failure undermines realism's radical potential. But I would like to suggest other modes of reading that aren't so firmly lodged within the problem of character; character, as mentioned, should be read as the problem of content that reveals the tragedy of form. While Dalit critique of Premchand rests firmly on the problem of representation of character, and Dalit literature argues for the humanization of the Dalit subject—Dalit humanism—the figuration of that character moves beyond its literal incarnation. Lukács, again, links realism's designs with the problematic goal of "totality." The world of realist fiction is a world of interdependent parts, of synecdochal links among all the forms that inhabit literary texts, and the final product of the text itself. In a response to the forces of capitalism that seek to fragment, disperse, segment, and parse, the realist novel trades in the organic, if only to demonstrate the real interrelations upon which we all rely.[21] But there are technical demands made to produce that coherence and this is precisely where in ideology of form is most legible. In many novels, chapters oscillate between two locations; in the case of *Godaan*, the move between village and the city creates a rhythmic pull between two dialectically organized spaces. Character is drawn through a perfect distinction between inner and outer lives, between what is meant and what is said, what is felt and what is expressed, what is believed and what course of action occurs. This writing favored a conspiratorial narrational mode that presents a series of dialogues, only to undermine them by capitalizing upon readerly knowledge; the private and public lives of characters are displayed for the reader such that dialogues between characters allow a voyeuristic pleasure in the known and unknown. There is a dualism at work here that is beyond the vast scope of these texts, their representational specificity. Alok Rai writes of how Premchand made certain lives "narratable" and, importantly, "endowed them with an unprecedented coherence" ("Foreword" 2). In "A Kind of Crisis," Rai describes the peasant sections of Godaan, which form roughly half of the text, as "rendered with consummate and unrelenting perfection," as "remorseless and hypnotic" (8). And indeed, as Premchand's final novel, *Godaan* might be read as a case study in such coherence.[22] As a reader, one is left with the sense that nothing falls outside its orbit; everything is included. The narrative disclosures, our access to interiority, the oscillating movement of the text, its very girth—all contribute to a sense of totality created from a sum of various parts. It is the premise of whole-ism, however, that does an extreme disservice to the marginalized, who can only be read as a failure. If the novel as genre privileges a liberal individualism (indeed, this is Franco Moretti's reading[23]), the Dalit character is always a failed individual who rarely has the possibility of transcendence, thereby once again confirming the circular enclosure of the novelistic world. The Dalit critique of realism, then, anchored in a failed type, is also a critique of novelistic holism, which demands an inherent coherence.

Sudhir Chandra interprets the contradictory or vacillating positions on nationalism in Premchand's texts as running from "quixotically radical to humiliatingly timid" (617) via the various opinions represented—those lodged within certain characters are reflections presumably of Premchand's own biography, his individual political transitions. But this is clearly a formal problem as well; novelistic construction requires a range of ideological positions that mimics in some sense the putative intellectual totality of the world to which the realist novel aspires. Within that web, the discourse of sympathy occasionally throws into relief certain pitiable figures, and singles them out for our vision. Sympathy thus emerges as one, perhaps the only, plausible form of narrative justice between the formal demands created by holism and a logic of social type, stymied by caste. I focus here on *Godaan*, the 1936 novel that represents Premchand at his most politically radical. What kind of solutions does a putative literary radicalism offer to the entrenched problem of literary caste?

GODAAN (THE GIFT OF A COW)

Godaan is veritably vast. It moves, using the "meanwhile" structure that Benedict Anderson has identified as crucial to building a sense of national identity, from the village Belari in the former province of Awadh and the city, Lucknow.[24] Balzacian in its scope, it is peopled with peasants of several castes, moneylenders, village headmen, landlords, doctors, philosophers, lawyers, and businessmen. It is nonetheless anchored in the village and has therefore come to be known as a novel of peasant life, culminating a tradition (as Premchand's last complete novel) that began with his short stories and continued through several other works, including the aforementioned *Rangbhumi* and *Karmabhumi*. Critics such as Meenakshi Mukherjee argue that it is the village section that produces a sense of authenticity in *Godaan*, the urban section being largely parabolic (*Realism and Reality* 148). By the time of the publication of *Godaan* in 1936, a few months before his death, Premchand had already become known as a chronicler of rural life, of the peasant folk, though *Godaan* clearly cemented that reputation. The uniqueness of this novel in particular, however, was the vast web of connections created between Belari and Lucknow, between rural tragedy and urban life. Often moving, occasionally contrived, the links between the two produce an epic feel that defies microscopic binocularism. *Godaan* produces a moving portrait rather than an intellectualized diagram of its object. Unlike Premchand's earlier novels and short stories, which provide an easy target for a Dalit critique of the pitiable subject, *Godaan* produces a legitimate sense of structural complexity through its locational politics, and precisely its avoidance of the central casteized character.

Anchored as it often is in the vision of Hori Ram, agricultural laborer, from whom we as readers derive our principle access to the inner life of characters, it is that urban-rural subtext that produces a social critique.[25] Surprisingly little Dalit criticism has been focused on *Godaan*, it being largely reserved for *Rangbhumi* and several salient short stories. But *Godaan* would pose several problems for Dalit critics, such as Sharankumar Limbale or Omprakash Valmiki, who deride Premchand's sententious pity and the moral turpitude of his Dalit characters. The novel's overriding concern is the plight of the peasant in the village and the market, and the attack is less on the culture of caste politics, it seems, than on the culture of capitalism. Critics Alok Rai, Vasudha Dalmia and Meenakshi Mukherjee don't mention caste at all in their readings of the novel and the structure of the novel helps to ensure that the peasant's "other" is less the Brahmin, or the uppercaste moneylender, than the landlord and the moneyed inhabitants of Lucknow.

But Hori Ram's financial worries are intricately bound up with the maintenance of caste practices; social transgression leads to fines, which lead to still more debt. His most impassioned speeches to his fiery wife Dhaniya revolve around caste. "We're all bound to the caste, and we can't break away from it," he says to her. "Life outside the caste was unthinkable," the narrator/character confirms, in a classic moment of free indirect discourse (159). The strictures of caste produce the tragedy of Jhuniya, whose widowhood makes her unmarrigeable, as well as that of Siliya the Chamarin, the Brahmin boy's lover, both of whom additionally burden Hori's family. Various village subplots are anchored by the question of caste as well, demonstrating it to be central to the functioning of the narrative and crucial in maintaining Hori Ram's penury. The symbolic weight of the *godaan*—the gift of the cow—can only be understood in a context of caste religiosity. Particularly because of the initial juxtaposition with the Rai Saheb, the feudal landlord, however, Hori identifies and is identified as a peasant, whose victimhood is ensured through sharecropping, levies, usury, weather, and greed, delinked from caste subjection.[26] This is a very subtle elocution; there is a rhetoric of caste propriety and caste burden in the text, and an attention to its financial consequences. But somehow, despite this, caste emerges as a *social* phenomenon in that the conditions of Hori's peasantness a priori are never linked to caste. Hori is not an "untouchable"; there are Chamars in the novel for whom he feels pity. Hori can then be constructed as a somewhat casteless victim, and it is from the initial envisioning of the peasant victim, and the deconstruction of the "peasant mentality" that the entire novel proceeds.

The ideological framework of the novel is therefore set from the beginning: the *zamindar* versus the peasant. Although Hori's son Gobar gives expression to an impotent class rage, a workers manifesto, and a critique of the hollowness of religion, the prototypical materialist critique, that his decision to abandon the village is also a casteized one, is hardly considered. Hori appears as an apologist, a peasant whose world has been irrevocably shaped by the feudal order, as well as Hindu notions of karma and dharma. He knows better, at some level, and his belief is hardly unchecked, but he is certain that the new system would fail him as well. "Where could we get jobs?" he muses (34). From this debate, in which Hori represents the traditional problematic of feudal servitude, bound by religion, social ties and the conditions of slavery, and Gobar the materialist, egalitarian challenge, a world of just such polarities ensues: the city and the village, wealth and poverty, leisure and labor, encapsulated in an argument between young and old, son and father. This neat grid of certainties doesn't go unchallenged throughout the novel but nevertheless remains, somehow, firmly rooted in place.

Such a structure is concomitant with the demands of realism in its most orthodox version, but particularly for the "critical realism" with which Premchand is charged. It is also, I would add, central for a new realism—and by this I mean the introduction of a literary genre to the reading public. In the case of *Godaan*, the self-sacrificing logic that Hori Ram espouses, a choice that is determined to be hardly a choice, is confirmed by the figure of Malti, the uppercaste doctor who willingly abandons her life of luxury for Gandhian ideals of service. In a damning confirmation of inequity, the daily nonvoluntary sacrifice of the peasant is trumped by an act of volunteerism, a charitable enterprise by a social reformer. It is in this way that the world of the realist novel comes full circle. The only logic that shakes it is the logic of sympathy. In the form of the early realist—and progressive—novel, sympathy, not social justice, is the narrative channel by which the Other is accorded space.

THE CIRCLE OF SYMPATHY

Sympathy has a long history of engagement with the novel; constructively, sympathy is an essential project of realist fiction and its democratization of the gaze. The work of the realist novel, as many have suggested, has been to expand the circle of readerly sympathy. Such a project required a figure eminently readable—identifiable and possible to identify with—who was produced by a kind of melodramatic realism. The sympathetic subject may not be specific to realist writing but it clearly is one of realism's most enduring aesthetic legacies. But the significant amount of criticism on the production of sympathy in the eighteenth- and nineteenth-century novel, in women's writing, in colonial discourse, and in the debates on slavery, have all demonstrated one broad generalization: the discourse of sympathy (and this may be particularly true in the novel) is at least as much concerned with the sympathizer as the putative object of sympathy.[27] Sympathy concerns sharing and potential identification, but the writer is in fact entrusted with not only the production of an object of sympathy, but the staging of the affective process of the sympathizer. The language of this discussion is rooted in questions of intimacy (how well can one know the other?), time (when does one know the other?) and, importantly, distance (how far away is that other?).[28] If realism in India effectively originated with the question of social reform, such that the late nineteenth- and early twentieth-century realist novel is often a social reform novel, and such that Premchand's realism, in particular, was designed in part to accommodate "the social question," it should be said that the realist novel in India also performed the crucial function of consolidating uppercaste identity. The presence of sympathy in the novel in fact assumes a victimized object who may be a woman, or a peasant, but at the same time necessarily assumes an uppercaste sympathizer. Modern subjectivity is thus produced by the ability to sympathize, to see beyond oneself. Alok Rai refers to the "guilty reader" who is willing to countenance injustice but may also be pushed too far, after which his loyalties and sympathies may wander; it is a delicate dance, this readerly compact.[29] But on what basis might the literal and metanarrative reader, within and outside the text, flee? The terms of this compact were intimately colored by social categories that remained largely submerged in the space of the novel. Traced in various European and American contexts as a hidden affective politics of race, in Premchand's novels the architecture of sympathy rests on caste and gender.

That history of sympathy as a discursive project in India has yet to be written, and I'm unfortunately unable to trace it here. But I will rely on Dipesh Chakrabarty's important scholarship on the widow, suffering, and the modern subject, which lodges that history within two intertwined discourses: the first derived from the "natural theory of sentiment" suggested by Adam Smith, David Hume, and other Enlightenment thinkers, whereby sympathy is a product of reason, and the second derived from the *rasa shastra* or Sanskrit theories of aesthetics and taste, whereby sympathy was a product of an intrinsic "heart" (127). The latter was a limited capability, but the former was premised on a potentially learnable trait, a self-recognition as a potential sufferer. If we accept Amit Rai's suggestion that it is the residue of an eighteenth-century mode—a "formal borrowing," as Roberto Schwarz would put it, one that Chakrabarty's research qualifies, we are still presented with certain problems chief among them, that the borrowed object of sympathy, potentially *you*, was invariably the gendered subject.

Pity, sympathy, guilt: these are the emotions that move plots in the world of early Premchand. The literary goal, however, was less structural transformation than, as Alok Rai so aptly puts it, "the writhings of conscience" ("Foreword"). This was in part an acknowledgement of the limitations of the form of the novel; essentially part of a Gandhian movement, Premchand's novels were to effect changes of hearts and minds in uppercaste readers through a complex interplay of sympathy, guilt, and outrage.[30] Sudhir Chandra and Alok Rai both suggest the novel as means to manage collective social guilt, a means of expiation by which moments of outrage and potential radicalism were encased in an essentially conservative generic form. "Insofar as [concern for the poor] offered only a personal release from collective guilt and was not employed to acquire an understanding of the self in relation to society, it could not become a social force capable of sustaining an organized movement for the transformation of society" (Chandra 620). Chandra reads this within a model of self-critique; Premchand too was wrought of the petty-bourgeois educated background, as were the rapacious nationalists he sought to hold accountable to the poor. It was in this context of affective management that the vehicle for those convulsions of consciousness became the female subject. The protagonist's plight in *Nirmala* (1924–25), that of a young bride married off to an older man with whom she is physically, intellectually, and socially mismatched, thereby producing a series of complicated interactions with her similarly aged stepsons, or that of Jalpa in *Gaban* (1930), responsible in part for the misdeeds of her husband because of her seeming desire for wealth and jewels and her subsequent penance, center that sympathy, guilt, and outrage on certain, and often on a series of, female characters. The fervent debates on the "women's question" demanded this; Premchand's writings were in that sense a central part of the collective zeitgeist: widow remarriage, female education, dowry, prostitution. Within Premchand's novels, almost all of the collective problems of patriarchy are pondered, anchored by an object of female sympathy.

This didn't necessarily have to be so; just a decade or so later, the question of sympathy seems to have been deconstructed in the writings of progressives like Sadat Hasan Manto. "Sympathy," writes Priyamvada Gopal, "reveals itself to be a pointless emotion" (116). Within a few short decades, narrative would choose other channels of radicalism in order to move beyond the "writhings of conscience." Gopal's is a post-Partition analysis, however; it is clear that in Premchand's writing sympathy had a certain instrumental value, inherited from the rhetoric of the social reformers that Chakrabarty analyzes. This is why Alok Rai refers to this body of work as the "literature of conscience" ("Foreword"); sympathy was one aesthetic and political strategy to awaken a readership, and potentially to "arouse a critical spirit" (Premchand, "Sahitya" 157). The significant factor in the case of Premchand, is that sympathy was seen as intimately tied to the real; only a literary realism could produce the desired effect. "It becomes [the writer's] duty to help all those who are downtrodden, oppressed and exploited—individuals or groups—and to advocate their cause. . . . He knows that the more realistic his story is, the more full of expression and movement his picture, the more intimate his observation of human nature and human psychology, the greater the effect he will produce" (Premchand, "Sahitya" 157). Sympathy must then be read as one means of advocacy, measurable in readerly convulsion; it is one gift that can be accorded, in an affective contest, one means by which to adjust a tally of wrongs. In the realist system of weights and measures, small adjustments to a static system are made in the interest of readerly fluctuation. I argue here that this model, one that relies essentially on some form of kinship between the reader and the victim, a kinship on which pivots the cycle of sympathy, guilt, and outrage, is curiously the one that is superimposed onto the caste question—insofar as the phrase "the caste question" is not a complete anachronism. A form of sympathy and pity carefully honed and patterned to deal with the women's question rests uncomfortably on the grid of caste.

PROGRESSIVE LITERATURE AND THE PROBLEM OF CASTEIST SYMPATHIES

In *Godaan*, the oscillating movement between the world of the *zamindar* and the peasant, or the city and the village, isn't replicated in the case of caste. The periodic shift between the home of the landlord and the peasant's hut is designed to eventually reveal the structural web that binds them; when the Rai Saheb speaks of exacting taxes, the next chapter reveals the peasant's desperate attempts to procure the money. Bound by labor and a shared economy, the rhythmic movement of the novel formalizes interdependence. But Hori's world is just as intricately tied to that of the uppercaste moneylender and the priest, who might as persuasively be read as his normative "other." The very structure of the novel, however, preempts the extension of the same oscillating logic to the caste question, which must therefore be read as exclusively a problem of the village, one to be brokered *within* rather than beyond the rural sections. Outside the village, the casteized subject is most easily read as generic peasant, i.e., *the peasant as a type*. In the face of a series of characterological others, all of whom identify occupationally, economically, but castelessly, Hori too becomes indicative of an abstract class positionality. For caste *as such*, for caste prior to its metaphorization, the novel chooses instead to take the questionable route of love.[31]

Let's take the example of one prominent subplot: the lecherous Matadin the Brahmin, son of Datadin the elderly *pandit* (priest), moneylender, marriage maker, and veterinarian, is having a relationship with Siliya, a young Chamar girl. Matadin and his father survive according to Brahmin patronage, their small landholdings, and the *pandit*'s money-lending ventures. Siliya, passionately in love, lives on the edge of their compound; as a Chamarin she is not permitted inside. She is an abject figure who works for the household, according to her station and caste propriety, with the joy of a new bride. "I'm staying with him though, whether he cares or not. I won't leave him even if he starves me and kills me. How could I desert him after bringing all this trouble on him? I'd rather die than act like a common prostitute. I gave him my hand once; now I'm his forever," she declares (308). But Siliya is not a bride. The work that Siliya does as a lover, in the service of a domestic ideal, is read by Matadin as labor; he callously dismisses it as "not *begaar* [forced labor]." When her own family comes to redress the impropriety of this relationship, by "making" Matadin a Chamar (and feeding him beef), she refuses to go with them and is cast off by both her lover and her family.[32] The drama of this subplot lies in Matadin's "conversion"; Siliya's father Harkhu brings fellow Chamars to defile Matadin by placing a bone in his mouth. Siliya emerges as an object of sympathy through her mistreatment by Matadin, the cruel treatment meted out to her by her mother, and her abandonment by her family. The sympathetic reader would also take his/her cue from Dhaniya, who offers her a space in her home, a benevolent gesture born from pity. She is, after all, a woman scorned.

A Dalit critique of the story of Matadin and Siliya might begin with the "dishonorable" portrayal of Siliya and the Chamars; Siliya is a slave, and her family appears brutish and violent despite the fact that the novel puts them clearly in the ideological right. But a different kind of analysis altogether might ask what role the untouchables play in this novel more generally: what kind of formal purpose do they serve? To say that their role is negligible is true; the novel does not need them. But they do serve to indicate a kind of vigilante justice—direct, brutal, vindictive—they defile Matadin, they beat Siliya. The Chamars occupy a peripheral space, both ideologically and structurally, in that they espouse a different kind of logic from our protagonist, the dutiful, though doubting, casteless peasant. They use their limited and collective physical might to right social wrongs though they work in the realm of the symbolic: they defile Matadin precisely because they do not intend for him to become a husband. It is a swift and partial justice. But ultimately they are failures. Matadin abandons Siliya at that very moment, and undergoes ritual purification to regain his caste status. And when he does take up with Siliya again towards the end of the novel, this time renouncing his caste to live with her, he does so not via coercion but via the time-honored plot device: change of heart. Casteist assertion is featured, concomitant with a liberal sentiment, as one means of social change, but is trumped, in a sense, by the individualized social conscience. In contrast, the legitimate ferocity of untouchable assertion manifests as a caste rage, a form of vengeance. The sentiment that provokes it, which the sympathetic reader may be inclined to swallow insofar as the object of its anguish is a woman upon whom social legitimacy through marriage can never be conferred but only imagined, is somehow hollowed out by Matadin's defilement and Siliya's miserable acceptance of her rejection. What purpose does this push and pull serve?

Colonial modernity played an important role in the creation of a new discourse of rights and wrongs; the notion of underserved suffering, and its resultant discourse of sympathy, became possible through new conceptions of time and space. The wrongs of the past could no longer justifiably be satisfied in the confines of the bodily present and suffering was required to follow certain logical paradigms.[33] In the context of "the women's question," the unmarried, the widowed, the child bride, the fallen woman—in short, the woman wronged by social custom—could now legitimately become an object of sympathy. Insofar as Siliya is read as a woman first and a Chamar woman second, her ritual abandonment by Matadin the Brahmin allows the pendulum of sympathy to swing towards her. But the sympathy for Siliya works alongside the pure disdain Matadin provokes in the novel, as is seen in this scene of his undoing. "All the men in the vicinity had gathered around . . . but no one, surprisingly, came forward to prevent this sacrilege. . . . They were inwardly pleased at his predicament. Outwardly, of course, they had to assert their superiority over the Chamars" (306). Hori, the Shudra, despite seeing the injustice of Siliya's situation, has distaste for the action taken by the Chamars—it is only his wife Dhaniya who, out of a sisterly compassion, takes Siliya home. The untouchable-caste woman, however, was never the subject of the discourse on "the women's question," confined as it was to a bourgeois movement for upper-class women and male reformers. As a result, once Siliya's Dalitness is "revealed," or narratively thrown in relief, the women's question becomes the caste question and falls into corresponding neglect. When Siliya's Chamar family enters the scene and insists on the "conversion" of the Brahmin, their Dalitness becomes required reading. The carnivalesque conversion—a revision of the failed Arya Samaj project of *shuddhi*[34]—is stripped of its political critique, the Chamars go home, and the social space of the narrative is restored as Matadin goes through the rituals of purification. The problems of Siliya, who critics argue is the representative of Dalits in the narrative, are eventually resolved through a specifically non-marital yet domesticated relation whereby she becomes ineligible for sympathy. Caste exploitation is clearly economic and sexual, but it is also easily displaced as such: in a novel dominated by the construction of a peasant type, Siliya's problem, a love story, may be collapsed into "the women's question" and putatively reconciled through a quasi-normalized social relation. On the one hand, only certain characters—particularly feminized subjects, not casteized ones—are accorded sympathy; on the other hand, sympathy is all they are accorded![35]

The subplot of Matadin and Siliya is its own short story, in a sense, and functions according to the logic of Premchand's short stories on caste, which Geetanjali Pandey also suggests operate differently from his novels; they are by and large freed from the drive towards resolution that dominates the novel (Pandey, "Peasantry," 1152). The realist novel doesn't typically allow for the same open-endedness: Siliya and Matadin must be reconciled, but, importantly, they are featured alone, an act of daring iconoclasm, excised from family, caste, village, and all sympathetic narrative voices. This might very well be read as an example of the clash between formal constraint and local conditions beautifully theorized by Roberto Schwarz in the context of the Brazilian novel: resolution of all subplots is a technical necessity in order to draw attention to the crisis of the central protagonist, but that resolution is challenged by the demands of local verisimilitude (46). While marriage was the narrative pillar of a conventional bourgeois realism, it is also a central feature of caste radicalism. There is an echo here of the Satyashodhak and Self-Respect marriages advocated by reformers like Phule and Periyar in the late nineteenth and early twentieth century, marriages based on self-choice, equality, conducted without a Brahmin priest, from which Ambedkar derived his position (Rao, *The Caste Question* 53–56). But Siliya and Matadin's reconciliation, occurring long after the birth of a child, and after the social devaluation of Matadin's Brahminness by fellow villagers as a result of his "conversion," sits uneasily here. This is one reason why what might be read as a radical Ambedkarite solution—i.e., intercaste marriage—doesn't present itself exactly as such: it is transformative only for the Brahmin boy; it requires his excision not only from family but also community, without which caste and anticaste as concepts lose their meaning; and finally, it is a "marriage" only metaphorically.

This may be confirmed by returning to our point of departure. Chakrabarty asks what kind of subject, in the late nineteenth century, is interested in the suffering of others, in those others as humans, and their documentation: one, he says, who experiences "a certain moment of self-recognition on the part of an abstract, general human being" (119). And how, asks Chakrabarty, "would society train itself to make this compassion a part of the comportment of every person?" I would suggest that when the casteized subject might potentially strain the process of "self-recognition," that training would occur via the sympathetic figure of the woman in the realist novel.

We are thus presented with the cruel irony of Dalit critique, which is required to dispute the unequal distribution of sympathies (in and of itself a failed project of liberal reform) and is required to do so in a kind of narrative competition with the gendered subject, its closest kin. The turn to sympathy, in this case via the time-honored trope of a love story, emerges as a narrative option precisely because caste assertion at this point in the history of the novel cannot emerge as anything else. Narrative sympathy is a last resort, and caste as a social problem is undercut through its firm lodging in individualized character, whose potential arc maintains the illusion of narrative freedom. And of course, these arcs aren't universally available; while Matadin is free to abandon his Brahminness, and he does so in the end, Siliya remains a Chamarin. Realism's reliance on the logic of sympathy in the context of the social reform novel, as a narrative act, might be read as a keen methodology for the cordoning off the question of caste, intertwined as it is with other forms of exploitation. While caste exploitation reveals itself to be economic and sexual, in the metonymic food chain of novelistic sympathies, caste must often take second place.

SYMPATHETIC REVISIONS

A canon like Premchand's anchors a discourse of sympathy in very particular ways, as I have demonstrated; one way is by modulating a narrative of sympathy for the female victim and transposing it to the untouchable-caste victim. Beyond victimhood, the Dalit problem is relegated to the margins of a text that has other primary concerns. In this section, I will focus on other possible architectures of affect for Dalit characters, and for Dalit texts. Dalit texts may be labeled as such not only on the basis of identity but through a different narrative structure, one that aspires to a solidarity rather than a sympathy.

The radical shift in worldview is the preeminent mode by which this occurs. It isn't enough to say that Dalit literature seems to be about Dalit peoples, in Dalit spaces, doing "Dalit things." Replacing a hegemonic space and time with a Dalit one, or Dalit ones, reanchors ideologically every narrative moment, plot turn, dialogue, action. Following a tradition set by realist writers in many places and times, Dalit writing creates new literary spaces (a Valmiki home, for example) and new literary actions (the prototypical animal skinning), as narrative forms of compensation, and demands that they be read. Dalit characters do not simply happen upon a predetermined hegemonic stage but rather are legitimate actors in spaces no longer contrived elsewhere; the ideological debates that ensue are in fact born from that space rather than prefabricated. It is now the adversary—the moneylender, the *thakur*, or the uppercaste teacher—who enters the narrative space as an interloper, and Dalit characters who have legitimate narrative arcs. In Dalit writing, the Lukácsian problem of type is inherent; Dalit characters always collapse the social and the individual. This is a political practice by which one can be representative of many, but which also accords a dignity to the individual. The central problem of Lukácsian realism, by which the massive web of societal transactions and transmissions is represented and revealed, the problem of "holism," is dismissed; the narrative world is weighted towards the Dalit and the structure of revelation is weighted towards caste.

One mode by which this occurs is through a form of triangulation that I would suggest revises the old narrative channel of sympathy. I will focus in this section on the writings of Omprakash Valmiki, probably the leading Hindi Dalit writer, who has written autobiography, short stories, poetry, and literary criticism throughout the last fifteen years. He is now anthologized routinely, and his work of literary criticism, *Dalita sahitya ka saundaryashastra* (*The Aesthetics of Dalit Literature*), has become the seminal text of the field. Located in the villages and provincial towns of Uttar Pradesh, Valmiki's writing largely traverses the problems of education, assimilation, and integration, set in an atmosphere of ubiquitous casteized social relations. The following text is one of several that entertain a particular form of dualism, the relationship between student and teacher. As a leitmotif of Dalit literature and, in part, its generative force, education appears as the civilizing mission par excellence, the road to upward mobility, a metaphor for brutality and occupation, a type of migration, and many other things. The school, in particular, is replete with longing as well as misery, and many Dalit texts in Hindi problematize the putative evolutionary narrative of education. I am going to suggest that Dalit realism attempts to move away from a logic of failed typology, holism, and sympathy, to textual solidarity. The deconstruction of the ideology of liberal reformism is a narrative problem; a revision of the standard functioning of realism is required.

I want to stress that my methodology here is less a comparison than the tracking of a revision. The juxtaposition of Premchand's writings, particularly the large novel *Godaan*, with Valmiki's short story may indeed seem problematic. But if generic forms impart their own logical constraints, as I believe they do, then a willful disinterest in the novel must be read as not only a material choice but an aesthetic and ideological one. Dalit writers who determine to use the short story may do so precisely because the failures of realism are particularly palpable in the novel, which in Hindi has become synonymous with Premchand. I don't mean to suggest that Dalit writing en masse consciously chooses its vocation via the genre of the short story— there are now several Dalit novels in Hindi—rather, that the forms that the short story engenders are particularly suited for different explorations of the realist paradigm.

By the time of the emergence of Dalit writing in Hindi, the theoretical problem of pity and sympathy had largely been deconstructed philosophically. Alok Rai argues that late Premchand, and even *Godaan*, demonstrates an acknowledgement of the failed power of pity ("A Kind of Crisis," 6). More recently, Amit Rai, working within the Gothic novel as well as on colonial, missionary and abolitionist discourse from Britain, traces sympathy as a crucial eighteenth-century European ideological formation, one that implies a distantiation and othering from the pitiable and largely inert object as well as a gendered project of mastery and violence. The complicated sentiment of sympathy implies identification but only across a vast power differential. More importantly for this reading is that Amit Rai theorizes sympathy as a perverse gift, one that requires the incurring of a certain debt. Unlike the current form of solidarity to which many movements aspire, sympathy is seen by him as an outmoded form, invested in scenes of suffering by which the subject *earns*. Rai's analysis is rooted in a British imperial history and therefore relies upon a form of racial binarism that is implicit in every instantiation of sympathy that he reads. But beyond the assumption that lowercaste bodies are racialized, or feminized, in the context of a Dalit reading of Premchand, new questions of sympathy arise. The *zamindar* "feels" for the poor in a very different way than the abolitionist felt for the enslaved; the kind of distantiation necessarily assumed in Rai's work is necessarily diffused by a caste logic. Untouchability is "otherizing," to put it mildly, while also being wholly domesticated. If Dalit writing preemptively shifts narrative space and microscopes the Dalit figure, the earning of that affective debt simply cannot occur in the same way. Still, one way we might read the emergence of Dalit solidarity is via an undoing of the literal, metaphorical, and metanarrative debt assumed by older forms of realist writing.[36]

NARRATIVE INDEBTEDNESS

In Dalit literature that treats the school and the teacher, the figure of Shambuka haunts the text. One of the few lowercaste characters featured in both the *Mahabharata* and *Ramayana*, Shambuka is punished for hearing the Vedas; lead is poured into his ears. Less a symbol of resistance than a reminder of impending injustice, Shambuka's story in the epic ends there, with the act of listening. In a form of symbolic haunting, however, Shambuka's story, alongside that of Ekalavya, hovers over fiction that treats the educational process, the relationship to the teacher, the problem of upward mobility, and the structural failures of casteized institutions. The narrator of Mohandas Naimishraya's *Apne-apne pinjare (Cages of Our Own)*[37] mentions the awe with which his illiterate father carefully pores over his Hindi and English primers, and more so over his own son's writing, now a textual rival to the schoolbooks. In the Sushila Taakhbhore story "Siliya" (1997), a narrative of education concludes with the educated daughter's revision of her father's gender politics. The fraught environment of the school is produced by both the powerful dynamic of caste relations and the potential for transformation or rewriting of both narrative and metanarrative, largely depicted as a threat to the authority of the school.

In Valmiki's story "Paccis chauka dedh sau" ("25 x 4 = 150"),[38] education is the process by which the Dalit subject undoes a history of caste oppression, both literally and metaphorically. While the protagonist Sudip is reciting his times tables, his father, listening with satisfaction as his son, a laborer's son, does his school work, and overhears him saying "25 x 4 = 100." When his father corrects Sudip, saying, "25 x 4 = 150," the son protests, presenting in his defense his teacher's words, as well as those of the math textbook. Both are discredited. "No, father, 25 x 4 = 100 . . . see, it's written in my math book." "Son, why show me the book? I don't even know how to read. For me these black letters are like black buffalo. Still, even I know for sure that 25 x 4 = 150. . . . Your book could be wrong, otherwise, what, do you think the *chaudhari* [village headman] would lie? The *chaudhari* is a much bigger man than your book" (5).[39]

In Dalit writing, the binary opposition between the school and beyond is also one between the home and the world, but this is not an entirely unidirectional system of pressure. The written word is a fickle thing, unreliable as well as incomprehensible; experience and family history are trustworthy. Sudip's father has no desire to examine the contents of the text, not only because of his illiteracy but because his "reading" of the statement "25 x 4 = 150" is derived from the experience of borrowing money from the village headman. Besides, the book belongs to a new world, the world of school, his son's world (as he points out with "teri kitab" [*your* book]). The representation of the father's speech as such (plus the metaphor of the black buffalo), as explicitly different from the narrator's standardized, urban Hindi, attests to this fact. But when the father's knowledge is offered in the classroom, despite being based on the trusty experience with the *chaudhari*, it collapses.

> "25 x 4 = 150."
> Master Shivnarayan interrupted him. "25 x 4 = 100."
> Startled by Master's interruption, Sudip shut up and looked at his teacher's face in silence.
> Master Shivnarayan Mishra was squatting with his feet on the chair. Taking a long puff from his cigarette he said, "Hey, son of a Chuhra, why did you stop? What, did you forget?" Sudip started his tables again. "25 x 4 = 150." Master Shivnarayan Mishra now scolded him angrily. "Hey! Blackie, not 150, 100!"
> "Master! Pitaji says 25 x 4 = 150!" stammered Sudip fearfully.
> Master Shivnarayan became furious. Grabbing him, he struck a blow on the boy's cheek. He glared at him and screamed, "Abe, if your father is such a wise man then why is your mother here . . . (a word that cultured people forbid in literature) . . . bastard, you people, no matter how much we teach you, you stay in the same place . . . your brains are just full of garbage. You will never be part of the world of learning and education" (7).

Represented as a verbal battle between teacher and student in which the rest of the classroom fades into the background, the argument proceeds from the dialogic premise of equality but the master's words are met with fearful stammering and silence, propelled by the injection of the respected *pitaji* into the classroom. The teacher's reaction is not only a response to the challenge to his authority presented by the student's mention of his father, which evokes a life that is to remain outside the school boundaries, but a response to a societal problem, the essence of which has crystallized in the classroom. Engaging a pervasive metaphor of dirt and pollution, the teacher's response is a product of a post-Mandal Commission antireservation sentiment echoed in many arenas.[40] The teacher's reaction, however, is importantly divergent, a different type of casteism overlaid with the discourse of liberal meritocracy; somewhat tolerant of postindependence integration, the teacher is skeptical of its outcomes, waiting to be triumphantly proven correct on the basis of biological determinism. That paternalism is clearly reflected in an earlier scene showing Sudip's father's experience of enrolling his son in school, in words, gesture, and posture: his pleading and respectful voice, hands together, bending submissively. This, of course, is the only type of distinction that the teacher is ideologically capable of maintaining, cornered by a system of democratic education that insists on clean slate-ness, and on formal equality.

The irony, of course, as is made plain by narratorial intervention, is that it is the cultured and revered teacher who is using foul language, speech that is considered inappropriate not only for the classroom but for literature as it has been thus far defined. In fact, this comment evokes a long-standing debate on the very nature of Dalit writing and its place in Hindi literature. Dalit literature has often insisted on the use of a grammatically nonstandardized Hindi (itself a fairly recent invention), on a vocabulary informed by various regional dialects and casteized speech, and on frequent epithets in order to question, precisely, the "standard" conception of both Hindi as a language and Hindi as a literature.[41] The teacher's insult undermines itself at one level, while asserting his authority at another (only certain figures have the privilege of certain speech), reminding us that assimilation to the culture of the classroom is not merely a question of language. The editorial decision on the part of the narrator to omit the profanity and leave it to be guessed by the reader, in turn, critiques the teacher as the standard that students are to follow, while questioning the terms of Hindi literature by putting the controversial language in the mouth of an uppercaste figure rather than the Dalit.

But narrative intervention at this moment serves other purposes as well. Metanarrative commentary breaks the haze of dramatic realism and reminds the reader not to excise this episode from its Dalit context, while also asserting the eminently partial sympathies underlying the narrative process. If the authorial voice is sympathetic to Sudip's plight here, that sympathy functions on a very different basis than in the classic paradigm. In effect, Sudip is plagued by the same crisis as his father: if his father is right, the book and his teacher must be wrong and if Sudip's teacher and the book are right, then the *chaudhari* must be wrong. Both he and his father are students. Although what is at stake here is more than arithmetic, there is no room within the narrative for the shaky world of interpretation. Later in the story it is revealed that Sudip's father, many years ago in time of need, borrowed money from the village headman to buy medicine for his ill wife. She recovers as a result. When Sudip's father goes to the *chaudhari* to settle his debts four months later, he is told that he will be charged 25 percent interest per month. His fee is therefore 150 rupees, as 25 x 4 = 150. The gracious headman, seemingly taking pity on the poor man, decreases the debt to 130 rupees. Sudip's father, understanding this as an act of benevolence rather than one of trickery, praises the *chaudhari* and recounts his moment of generosity to many. The story, through repetition, has become one of legend in the village, cementing the *chaudhari*'s reputation, particularly for the father, whose analysis of the situation is revealed with pride: it is an analysis of character rather than caste. Unlike others of his caste, the village headman has proven himself to Sudip's father. It is in this way that the man's putative act of generosity and the weight of his caste are compounded, thereby confirming mathematical fact. For Sudip's father, if his son's textbook is correct, then the *chaudhari*, and more importantly his own judgment and faith in this particular uppercaste man, is wrong.[42]

STUDENTS AND TEACHERS

Why doesn't the story produce Sudip as an object of sympathy? Firstly, Sudip has a narrative arc, which makes it impossible to read him as a static figure. The story climaxes in the revelation of deception, the goal towards which the plot inevitably moves. Now Sudip, educated and adult, is on his way back home to the village, his first-ever wages in hand. But in addition to paying his respects to his father at this special time, Sudip has gone home to play teacher, becoming the schoolmaster himself, to his father, the student. Using real currency rather than a book, bills neither he nor his father have ever before held in their lives, Sudip forces his father to unlearn the lesson taught to him by the *chaudhari*, which he in turn had passed on to his son. Making piles of the bills he is holding in his hands, Sudip helps his father to count out the four stacks of twenty-five rupees, note by note.

The father's re-education, and Sudip's emergence as an adult, clearly don't allow for a discourse of pity. Sudip's embrace of the social capital that education allows ensures that, despite the casteized experience of pedagogy, positivism, empiricism, and indeed rationalism (all realist and metarealist values) produce him as an actor. But I would argue that a narrative of solidarity emerges much earlier in the story. Even in the moments of the duel between teacher and student, the father appears as a third space, asserting his own forms of knowledge. The presence of the father (and the father here might be a wife, a friend, anyone else, really) tilts the conflict between teacher and student in Sudip's favor, at least at an affective register. It is impossible to read the previously cited scene without the hovering presence of the father, who is not literally, but metatextually, watching the scene unfold. Unlike the classic "meanwhile" of the realist novel described by Benedict Anderson, in which events unfold coterminously, a structure that characterizes Premchand's *Godaan* perfectly, in "Paccis," a unitary narrative (within one framed by memory), the movement from the space of the home *into* the space of the school masks the familial relationality that is contiguous throughout. Sudip brings his father with him to the classroom, so to speak, and as a result he never appears excised from a framework of sociality, caste relation, and fraternity. In this body of Dalit writing, every subject is a casteized one, and naming names is a crucial process. The presence of the father gives Sudip a name, a history, a genealogy, and a caste identity. Although Dalit writing that features the school is often about an evolutionary progression through the stages of education, it isn't bildungsromanesque. The bildungsroman, after all, requires the complete excision from old sociality into new forms.[43] In Valmiki's story, those forms of sociality are not supplanted, but relied upon to shift the narrative weight of the story. This is how solidarities might be constructed in the text.

What kind of narrative compensations are required to transform a model of sympathy to one of solidarity? Historically, the notion of underserved suffering was to arise with modernity and more secular conceptions of the outlines of human life. To suffer unjustly was concomitantly to produce a discourse of sympathy and pity for those who could no longer be said to be bearing the sins of the past. But the context of uplift and social reform grafted on to this discourse produce a figure of sympathy who functioned within a limited narrative register. Oblivious to the social construction of his or her making (the politics of patriarchy, for example), the object of pity moves through softer channels of affective power: misfortune, insult, grievance, indifference, disaster. The ideals of Lukácsian realism, by which social conditions are revealed via a flurry of transaction, negotiation, coercion, and compliance, by the holism and constant collisions of the social sphere, are challenged by the novel of social reform that is required to carve out a special space for victimhood. That space is rarely entered by anyone other than the reader. When Premchand's Nirmala suffers, for example, she suffers inside, and narrative interiority alone reveals her pitiable state, otherwise inaccessible to others. That suffering is then endowed with moral capital.

A narrative of solidarity firstly requires a space of transgressive boundaries. Dalit literature is about Dalits, yes, but it magnifies the segregated space of the pitiable and the marginal into a spatial whole. This is now the substitute for the fictively organic and it is from here that any holism must spring; it is into this space that others now tread. In the case of "Paccis chauka dedh sau," it is tread upon by the father of the protagonist Sudip. Sudip is locked into a losing battle with his teacher, who berates him, ostensibly for his multiplication tables but more so for his Dalitness. In his derision of the knowledge produced by the father, the master—expressing the brutality of casteism—might have left us with a pitiable subject. But the scene of dialogue doesn't allow for it, giving Sudip no space to speak, and, told in retrospect, the scene quickly returns us to the *present* of a grown Sudip, riding on a bus. Why, when Sudip is so clearly victimized, does the affective logic of the text refuse to produce a "sympathetic subject"? Having enlarged the narrative timeline of Dalit literary life, Sudip becomes an actor, an individual, revising the logic of caste oppression. Dalit literature is often characterized as a resistance literature. It so clearly is that this appellation unfortunately blinds us to its other contributions. I would suggest that it is the narrative hovering of Sudip's father in the scene that produces a counter to a discourse of sympathy. Despite his mistake, the presence of the father creates room for a counterdiscourse rarely available to the pitied subject and prepares us for an eventual undoing.

Secondly—and this is crucial—Sudip cannot be an object of sympathy when he is himself a sympathizer; the story opens with Sudip on a crowded bus, a witness to a mean-spirited harangue against a villager by the bus conductor, who is described as a wild boar, fangs reddened by *paan*. "Feeling frightened, Sudip looked at his fellow traveler, who wore an indifferent air, lost in his thoughts. He then glanced at the villager, who still couldn't extract himself from his pitiable state" (79). Sudip's expression of pity for the villager, in and of itself noteworthy, is preceded by an act of looking and his characterization of the conductor as a wild animal. As the bus conductor is flattened into metaphor, and the villager into an object worthy of pity, Sudip gains a kind of narrative authority. But that authority is predicated on a very different type of relationality; in an atmosphere of alienation, where fellow travelers are indifferent to the harassment of a compatriot, Sudip singles out the villager for attention. His pity is also a fledgling connection—he too is disturbed by the conductor's behavior. The only other character who receives the adjective *dayaniya* (pitiable) is Sudip's father.[44] In a social space of indifference, pity is one form of relation, but its negative connotations are undercut by Sudip's own experience as potentially pitiable. Solidarities emerge when the distance between the sympathetic and the sympathizer collapse but also when narrative weight is shifted to a present of vindication.

In Valmiki's autobiography *Joothan*, the 1993 publication of which perhaps signifies an inaugural moment of modern Hindi Dalit literature, there is another student-teacher scene. Autobiography has its own generic compulsion, of course, though I would disagree with overreading generic distinction in this particular case. In the Dalit case, the autobiography clearly plays a central role in the distribution of as well as challenge to, a discourse of sympathy as it has been constructed in fiction.[45] Many critics have discussed the testimonial nature of Dalit autobiographies, their insistence on a certain truth-value, their attempt to engage the reader, but also to exhort the downtrodden subject. Still others have pointed out the "constructed" nature of the Dalit autobiography, which is required to follow a certain prototype.[46] As such, and as a most important genre in Dalit literary production, autobiography finds its own particular ways to interrogate the problem of sympathy. In the following example, the power of the written word is made manifest as it underlines the question of historical representation. When the narrator reflects on eating *maand* (rice water), he recalls the occasion in school when his teacher and classmates became tearful at the thought of a character from *Mahabharata* being forced to feed his son flour mixed with water out of poverty. Although this meal, and worse, was a daily occurrence in the narrator's home, he notes that no great poet had deigned to write about his life. Gathering his courage, he asks the teacher about this historical elision.

> The whole class stared at me, as if I had raised some ridiculous question. The teacher let out a shriek. "The dreadful Kaliyuga has come upon us . . . that an untouchable is daring to talk back!"
> The teacher made me sit crouched in the *murga* [rooster] position. This meant squatting on my haunches, then drawing my arms through my inner thighs, and pulling down my head to grasp my

ears, a painful, constricted position. He stopped teaching and went on and on about the fact that I was an untouchable. He ordered one of the other boys to fetch a long shisham cane.

"Son of a Chuhra, you dare compare yourself to Dronacharya.... Take this, I'll write an epic poem on you...." He brought the cane down on my back with a crack-crack and composed his own epic with the swishes of his stick. That epic poem is inscribed on my back even today. In the wretched moments of a hungry and helpless life, this epic poem of feudal sentiment didn't just leave a mark on my back but every fiber of my being.... In literature, one can only imagine hell. For us the rainy season was nothing short of hell. We have been subjected to this hell while still living. The epic poets were not even able to touch upon the cruelty of village life. And this is the horrible truth.[47]

In addition to a depiction of corporal punishment and bodily marking, the narrative stages an attempt to challenge a canonical literary representation, and notes the violence with which that revision is encountered. What the student is attempting to do, in effect, is rewrite the character of Dronacharya in a way that democratizes this figure of reverence. Dronacharya is actually most well known for the Ekalavya episode, the story of a lowercaste archer who comes to him for his guidance, wishing to study archery under him. In that episode of the *Mahabharata*, the guru, who only takes well-born students, asks Ekalavya to prove his devotion by cutting off his thumb, thereby disabling him. This story of the teacher's crafty violence, however, is not discussed here, in favor of his penury and goodness. By comparing his own situation to that of this character from the epic, the narrator is attempting to historicize a condition rather than allowing for continued uncritical compassion; he attempts to alter a long-established narrative. This attempt is perceived as so threatening that the teacher must repeat and assert the narrator's untouchable status, and involve other students in his punishment. In addition, this punishment is framed as a writing, a correction of the narrator's attempted revision, and that writing must be inscribed on his body. The unwritten narratives of Shambuka and Ekalavya hover over the text as their bodily mutilation here becomes the protagonist's bodily inscription.

THE CRITIQUE OF THE "CLAWLESS LION"

Though the previous passage is one of many in this autobiographical text that reevaluates the tormented relationship between Dalits and uppercastes through narrative performance, it sheds a particular light on the problem of sympathy. Beyond the slippage between the body and the book, which has a certain resonance for theories of Dalit culture and the Dalit condition as one of casteized labor, the narrator's revision reveals the historical failure of a logic of sympathy, which misreads its object! While the class turns a compassionate eye towards Dronacharya, precisely because he is a literary and religious figure, an archetype, it is unable to read the narrator's plight in the same way. Hierarchies of sympathy, literary ones in particular, derive, in fact, from the excision of the material realm. The narrator's critique of the epic as a casteist document functions alongside the antirealist realism of the literary. This is not a claim based on the generic constraints imposed by epic or other forms, but rather, a critique of the problem of the literary, which has become one crucial avenue by which we learn to exercise our sympathies. Dislodging those intuitions, literary and extraliterary, is a violent process. In this example, it is the autobiography—a narrative form that claims a privileged relationship to the real, particularly in the case of Dalit writing—that is being used to challenge a literary logic of sympathy derived from the epic and to problematize such a concept outside the text.

In a commentary on his work, Valmiki challenges the narrative presentation of uppercaste texts. "In their writings, struggle and revolt are like a clawless lion trapped in a cage." The sympathetic sensibilities of Hindi writers, he suggests, function as a mask for their lack of political commitment, making uppercaste literature seem artificial and contrived (quoted in Gupta 1). For the reading of Dalit literature, Marathi writer and critic Sharankumar Limbale suggests empathy. Empathy is the philosophical challenge because it obliterates the distance on which realist sympathies rely. Limbale is working with a different literary paradigm, however, in which Dalit writing is a testimonio, an articulation of suffering, which always already has its own implicit truth-value. The basic premises of fictionality require a different formulation. In Premchand, sympathy has to be constructed precisely because the generally acknowledged truth-value of caste oppression wasn't widely available. Sympathy is one slow step in a larger narrative evolution, a process by which one creates sentimental subjects. But even sympathy is only partially available to the Dalit figure, since caste distinction doesn't properly obtain. Dispersed neatly between figures of the peasant and of the woman, the sympathetic subject, constructed largely by gender, is challenged by caste, which adds one degree too many of separation between the sympathizer and his object.

Valmiki's writing demonstrates that sympathy, even properly allocated, is in and of itself deeply problematic. "Paccis chauka dedh sau," for example, is also an analysis of structural crisis. When the *chaudhari*'s fiction is revealed, caste hierarchy is also revealed; it can no longer be read as a structure of benevolent protectionism. The putative pity of the *chaudhari*, who "reduces" the debt of the Dalit because of his impoverished state, is an act of supreme guile. In *Joothan*, sympathy can only extend sameness, but can accommodate neither the real, nor the different. Sympathy produces a debt economy, as Rai has mentioned, whereby the object of pity is in a kind of affective deficit, but it rests on a shaky basis. Valmiki's writing would suggest that if you extend that sympathy towards others—as Sudip does towards his father and the anonymous fellow traveler—others who are like you, the debt is erased.

This doesn't mean, however, that self-pity isn't a powerful tool in Dalit narrative. Dalit literature, like other protest literatures before it, relies on certain conventions of melodramatic realism and self-pity in order to make certain ethical claims. To return to the aforementioned moment, Valmiki writes, "We have been subjected to this hell while still living. The epic poets were not even able to touch upon the cruelty of village life. And this is the horrible truth" (27). Self-pity is a structural requisite, simply because the very premise of autobiography and life-writing is a privatized, nontransferable, secret suffering. Functioning as a revelatory genre, autobiography *reveals* a suffering not necessarily unknown, but unknowable by the other.[48] Based on an ontological separation between casteized knowledges, *self*-pity becomes the only legitimate possibility. And self-pity, counterintuitively, once again puts the affective power of sympathy in Dalit hands.

Social realism and melodramatic realism of the sort exhibited by Premchand ensured the presence of not only his object of investigation and creation—the peasant, the woman—but also the bourgeois nationalist, the intellectual, the *zamindar*, the Brahmin. While this served to express the totality of society and the most basic level of interdependence, it also provided the reader with an imitative model. We learn the discourse of sympathy from within the novel; when the *zamindar* suffers the emotional burden of his tenants, *we suffer too*. This wasn't an expression of the inherent "goodness" of the North Indian educated uppercaste readership. Rather, expressions of sympathy were something the educated readership had specifically learned *not* to offer; the novel was central in undoing that emotional practice.

In a discussion on the nature and definition of Dalit literature, Valmiki's *Dalit sahitya ka saundaryashastra* (*The Aesthetics of Dalit Literature*) offers a now oft-repeated anecdote: In response to the Hindi writer Kashinath Singh's quip, "Can only a horse write about horses?" Valmiki responds that, "Only a horse, tied to his stall after the day's work, knows how it feels, and not its owner" (*Dalit sahitya* x). If there are different epistemological means showcased here, then sympathy can only be a failed project of knowing, a valiant attempt perhaps, but too underscored by hierarchical relations to offer much affectively. Valmiki's story, therefore, and Dalit writing more generally, clearly demonstrates new forms of relationality within a realist paradigm. Dalit literature should be read as modulating a particular convention of progressive fiction and making it transitive, reorienting it; sympathy now emerges as a new form of relationship, something you might pass on. A Dalit critique reveals that the sympathy on which old forms of realism rely is a kind of affective performance, a unidirectional affective movement, available in close confines, to categorically confined objects. Within Dalit literary texts, it would be called something else.

It is in this sense that the development of a social and melodramatic realism were formally crucial to a kind of erasure of caste in the earliest moments of the formation of Hindi literature, while simultaneously being exalted for showing a laudatory concern for the peasant. The representation of varied forms of nationalism, from a moderate Anglophilia to anarchic extremism, still served to confirm a national consensus; digging too deeply into caste division could only do the opposite. The problem of caste politics for the nation is a thread that runs throughout this project, and becomes a central ideological conflict for almost all the bodies of text mentioned; most anti-caste agitators were questioned regarding their patriotism. Literary texts, however, have encountered and sidestepped a similar confrontation whereby they are read as progressive despite their active devaluation of caste analysis. Social realism, devoted as it was to a range of social places, an intersection of class societies and the multifarious facets of modernity, couldn't possibly tackle the basic segregation of the casteless, or the structural conditions of their impoverishment. In *Godaan* in particular, creating the casteized subject as a gendered one extended the life of a narrative problem; "marrying" her, at the end of the novel, solved it. This isn't to say that questions of gender subsumed those of caste, but that they allowed a deferral of caste questions, which could not receive proper narrative space—sympathy could too easily be exhausted.

This is why, I think, a debate about the mimetic abilities of the realist severely challenges the potential for reading Dalit texts. When Alok Rai interprets the demands made by Dalit writers that fictional texts demonstrate caste assertion and caste radicalism as "poetic justice" or "prescribed militancy" in the vein of socialist realism, this seems like a debate about historical potentiality. Why, says the Dalit critic, weren't Dalits represented by Premchand not only *as they are* but also *as they might be*? But prescribed militancy is no less ideal, no less utopian, no less ideological than the "prescribed sympathy" that Rai himself describes as a form of imprisonment "in hegemonic systems of representation, in the narratives of other people" ("Poetic and Social Justice" 165). Alok Mukherjee writes, "Unable to imagine the untouchable Other out of existence, Brahminical literature now sought to confine it within a discourse marked by 'sympathy' and 'compassion'" (5). This is less a debate about historical referentiality than a question of the invention of a literary mode by which the introduction and creation of caste others occurs, and the concomitant containment it engenders. Sympathy, as a narrative channel, helped to produce a literary Dalit, but more importantly, a literary type with a limited potentiality. Types have socio-cultural longevity as well as political implications that are clearly more real than realism. The radical gesture of the Dalit literary movement is its refusal of a sympathetic discourse that has been central to a progressive realism—and, in fact, to unearth sympathy as the faulty affective architecture via which the old mode of realism was deemed progressive at all. The assertion of the narrative "I," a singular, nonexchangeable, often autobiographical "I," is the negation of the frequent "she" and occasional "he" that have been constructed by literary sympathies for caste others.

CHAPTER TWO

Modernism, Marxism, Metaphor

The Origins of a Literary Politics of Particularism

It seemed to suit him, to give a homogeneity, a wonderful wholeness to his body, so that you could turn round and say: "Here is a man."

—MULK RAJ ANAND, *Untouchable*

As the principal hero of our books we should choose labor, i.e., a person, organized by the processes of labor, who in our country is armed with the full might of modern technique, a person who, in his turn, so organizes labor that it becomes easier and more productive, raising it to the level of an art.

—MAXIM GORKY, "The Craftsmen of Culture"

The question of Dalit *chetna* (consciousness) is the central question of contemporary Dalit literature, a revision of a very old problematic that has haunted the literature of progressivism, social realism, socialist realism, anticolonialism and protest: How does the literary text articulate and propel an explicit political awakening? The consciousness of rights and resistance—often *the* singular factor in the determination of the protagonist as *protagonist*—is the most prescribed aspect of the Dalit literary text, which may vary thematically, politically and aesthetically, contingent upon its evocation of such sentiment. As such it becomes one of the most defining features of the genre, particularly by the guardians of literary countercanonicity.

For example, Tej Singh's *Aaj ka dalita sahitya* (*Contemporary Dalit Literature*), a recent work of Dalit literary criticism, seeks to delineate the unique position of the socio-literary text. In this largely thematic study, Singh mentions some of the major preoccupations of recent Dalit short-story writing: the demonstration of the "irony of caste division and the obsession with touching" in light of putatively democratic sentiment and principles; the relation between caste and sexual politics; the elaboration of an explicitly Ambedkarite platform; and most significantly, the problem of labor and the stigma of casteized occupation (15). But the central factor that unites these thematic concerns is the evocation of a radical consciousness. In the work of several fiction writers, Singh reads *as a trope* the emergence of a figure of Dalit resistance who challenges, retaliates against, and rectifies injustice: in effect, a literary paradigm. What Singh does not explicitly mention, what is taken for granted, is that such fiction is realist in its basic elaboration and structure. For these fictions to be read experientially and pedagogically, they must be realist, and it is in the problem of the evocation of consciousness that the most vexed question of referentiality lies.

In some ways, then, the realist is a kind of departure. Modernist writing, no easily definable entity, has long created itself as the aesthetic metalanguage of revolt, particularly after the failures of the realist to radicalize society had been revealed. Simon Gikandi writes, "It is my contention that it was primarily—I am tempted to say solely—in the language and structure of modernism that a postcolonial experience came to be articulated and imagined in literary form. The archive of early postcolonial writing in Africa, the Caribbean, and India is dominated and defined by writers whose political or cultural projects were enabled by modernism even when the ideologies of the latter were at odds with the project of decolonization" (Gikandi, "*Modernism*" 420).

In other words, literary revolt and the evocation of consciousness in the colonies had long been the province of a modernist ethic and, often, aesthetic. This is a broad claim, one that parses variably at the regional, local, and linguistic level. However, it is true that even caste became a preoccupation of modernism, most famously in the example of Mulk Raj Anand's 1935 novel *Untouchable*. What kind of literary potential was evoked by the epistemological and aesthetic debates inaugurated by modernism and what did this do for "the caste question"? I want to suggest in this chapter that a reading of the stark realism of the contemporary Dalit text is incomplete without its modernist genealogical roots. One of the central questions for a proper reading of the Dalit literary text is of why a certain modernist aesthetic that became available to vernacular and Anglophone literatures in the early part of the century, replete with transgressive (both aesthetic and political) potentials, doesn't seem adequate for a contemporary protest literature. How and why did the "prescriptive militancy" of the social realist text become the de facto model for Dalit prose writing in the Hindi Belt? This chapter will consider the radical transformation that has occurred in the representation of Dalit consciousness from the period of high modernism to that of the realism of contemporary Dalit literature. As such, it will pay particular attention to the question of labor as the typical literary location of casteized singularity. In the decades since Anand's *Untouchable*, the historical trajectory—indeed, the birth and rise—of the Dalit movement has dismissed the modernist call to consciousness and its relentless focus on subjectivity and transformed it into a communitarian, collective ethos where "consciousness" is always already given, indebted as it is to the particular and exclusive condition of caste subjection. The juxtaposition of the Anglophone modernist anticaste novel of the 1930s with the contemporary realist Dalit short story demonstrates not only what I read as the articulation of a "particularist realism" that suggests a new temporal and spatial diagram of revolt but a critique of a progressivist universalism, long the dominant form of literary radicalism in India. The origins of a contemporary particularist realism must be read as a subalternist critique of the failures both of a Marxist-modernist humanism (of which Anand is one example) and of progressive thought, which is subject to its own forms of blindness on caste. This chapter will thus consider a series of constellated issues (modernism-metaphor-Marxism, realism-metonymy-consciousness) in order to ask of the contemporary Dalit text: Why realism?

THE LABOR OF METAPHOR

In the 1930s and 40s, novelists like Mulk Raj Anand (*Untouchable*, 1935) attempted to introduce the lives of the working poor in India into the novel. Faced with the burden of producing a fragile national consensus, novelists turned their gaze outwards: the peasant, the villager, the beggar, the untouchable. The democratic ethos that produced such a literary shift transformed the genealogy of the English novel in India, which was largely considered a middle-class, uppercaste affair, preoccupied with the domestic sphere. Novels were now to labor over an entirely different set of problems, including labor, caste conflict, and social movements. In the context of southern India, K. S. Venkataramani revalorized the rural in novels like *Murugan the Tiller* (1927), and Raja Rao excavated caste in *Kanthapura* (1938). In 1952, Bhabani

Bhattacharya published *He Who Rides a Tiger*, centered on the lower-caste Kalo and his Brahmin mimicry.[1] Framed by Gandhian and Marxist narratives, these fictions attempt to complicate the portrait of the Indian subject of modernity as it had been thus far fashioned by generations of fiction in English and vernacular languages.[2]

But early twentieth-century Anglophone writing was a bit of a moveable feast. Particularly in the period of the 1930s and 40s, romantic narratives of Gandhian nationalism flourished alongside peasant novels; texts experimented with orality and the vernacular in both modernist and realist modes. The work of the Progressive Writers Association (PWA), founded in 1936 and preceded by Premchand, is one strain of that cultural production, which mingled, via Anand and other bi- and trilingual intellectuals, with the Bloomsbury Group and the International Association of Writers for the Defense of Culture. Regional nationalism, Hindu revivalism, and organized communism formed other strains. In the spirit of anticolonialism and the call to conscience regarding the horrors of fascism and its initial elaborations in the colonies, Anglophone and vernacular literary production in this period often overlapped thematically, aesthetically, and politically. While Rao's oeuvre might characterize one direction, marked by the vernacularization of English, the rhythms of the oral, and the reproduction of the Hindu, the Brahminical, and the sacred within the space of the novel, Mulk Raj Anand shapes another. Cofounder of the PWA as a student abroad, Anand displayed a broad leftism that mingled avant-gardism with socialist realism. As such, he shared ideological spaces with both the late Premchand and the later Marxist Yashpal, as well as aesthetic predilections with the Hindi experimentalist writer Agyeya. All of this is to say that in the particular historical moment that was the 1930s in India, things were politically and also aesthetically uncertain. In the colonial world, literary aesthetics are compounded rather than teleological; the newness of the novel, the presence of indigenous forms of narrative, social and political radicalism, and various types of experimentalism meant that realism and modernism often functioned side by side and sentence by sentence.[3] What they shared, it must be said, was caste. Anglophone, vernacular, realist, or modernist: the *novel* in India was by and large the uppercaste novel, in language, ideology, and form.

Within this context, how did caste become a literary object of reflection—for which the untouchable, specifically, was the most salient metonym? In the variegated literary landscape of which Mulk

Raj Anand was one part, the nation was typically literarily derived using the metonymy of the peasant, who became the preeminent potential citizen. In the case of Premchand's *Godaan* or Venkataramani's *Murugan the Tiller*, this was a casteless figure, identified by his nativism, i.e., his relationship to land. And in the case of both of those texts, and several others, the model was a social realism overlaid by Gandhian romance. Mehta, *Godaan*'s philosopher-king; Ramu, the rural reconstructionist of *Murugan the Tiller*; and *Kanthapura*'s Moorthy would all trace their models to a potentially realizable Gandhian vision, which could only be referential in the case of both the intellectual and the beggar. Undoubtedly one of the most important literary influences of the period, Gandhian nationalism within the scope of prose narrative became somehow intertwined within the realm of the realist, whether through the optic of the hopeful (melodramatic) or harrowing (socialist). But Mulk Raj Anand's *Untouchable* (1935) was unusual in that it focused exclusively on the casteized subject, and also gifted him with an explicitly modernist subjectivity. Brutal description of the caste colony, and the various attempts at reproducing vernacular language cadences and meanings, mingle with a Joycean representation of subjectivity, as Anand himself has elaborated.[4] Described as "realist" and "documentary" by some, the putatively photographic elements of the text clearly compete with the aesthetic flourishes as well as the larger political philosophy of a cultural modernism that reveled in the singular individual consciousness. Anand's *Untouchable* can thus only be described as a staggering and unique experiment in the history of Indian Anglophone fiction, but it established a basic literary precedent in privileging the gaze, interiority, and subjective consciousness of the untouchable, thus presenting us with one model for the literary elaboration of caste. The problems of caste and untouchability were therefore translated via the swirl of English language narrative, international modernism, and Marxist compulsion into readable objects. What kind of transpositions necessarily occurred and how might they shed light on the contemporary elaboration of caste in Dalit fiction?

Untouchable, written shortly after the abolition of the category of caste in the colonial census (1931), is the story of one day in the life of Bakha, the sweeper in an army cantonment town of colonial North India.[5] As a sweeper, Bakha (and his family) are responsible for the removal of garbage from the streets and for the cleaning of latrines. Collapsed within the rigid chronological frame of the novel are the full range of problems they might encounter: material deprivation, including access to water; the molestation of Bakha's sister by the priest; the calling for *joothan*, leftover food, from uppercaste homes; the infamous scene of the "touching" of an uppercaste man; and the defiling of the temple. But caste enters this novel primarily in relation to untouchability and labor. This need not necessarily be so; the fictional world of marriage masks caste-as-endogamy. Though marriage is a crucial structuring device of the modern novel in India, most of these novels are not read, by critics or even metanarratively, as novels about caste, a reflection of a larger analytic problem. In the English context, however, it is the foregrounding of casteized labor with which we are initially concerned—i.e., caste as occupation.[6] In Anand's text, the problem of casteized labor structures our vision of Bakha (and the repeated elaboration of his physique) and occasions Anand's unique intervention, the construction of the casteized consciousness. Let's begin with labor then, and the kind of rhetorical and aesthetic deformations that caste makes narratively possible.

Very early on in *Untouchable*, the narrator describes Bakha's motions. "Brisk, yet steady, his capacity for active application to the task he had in hand seemed to flow like constant water from a natural spring. Each muscle of his body, hard as a rock when it came into play, seemed to shine forth like glass. . . . He seemed as easy as a wave sailing away on a deep-bedded river" (Anand 15). Coming as it does within the first few pages of the novel, this passage serves as an introduction to Bakha and his caste-ness; his labor distinguishes him from caste society while the way he *performs* his labor distinguishes him from fellow sweepers. Ringing with anticipation of the artistic doctrine of socialist realism adopted by the Congress of Soviet Writers in 1934, this image in Anand's text can be understood as part of the traditional Marxist adulation for the working body, suggesting a beautification and aestheticization of the labor process. Bakha has both become a *worker*, and is associated with *natural* spring water, rock, and a river wave. The text seeks to harmonize the working body with the elements of the natural world and to dissociate the repetitive motions of a manual and disgusting labor from the world of casteized work. This rhetorical feat is accomplished via the semantic device of metaphor coupled with the logic of reification. An exclusive privilege of the literary, metaphor is used to escape referential boundaries.[7] Making of Bakha a wave serves to naturalize his abilities; waves have no tormented relations with the work they do of the sea.

But can casteized labor be metaphorized via images of the natural, non-man-made world? Jonathan Culler argues that metaphor has become the preeminent literary device, "the figure par excellence through which the writer can display creativity and authenticity: his metaphors are read as artistic inventions grounded in perceptions of relations in the world" (*Signs* 191). As a history of structuralist criticism would demonstrate, metaphor has long been considered the guiding feature of the poetic, and contiguously, the distinguishing feature of the literary. Mieke Bal approaches metaphor from a different angle, understanding it as a "mini-narrative" that offers a glimpse not into "what the speaker or narrator 'means,' but into what a cultural community considers acceptable interpretations" (*Narratology* 35). Metaphor can thus work within an activist and artistic bent in order to allow the text to rewrite that "acceptable interpretation," while asserting itself as "literary" and therefore unbound by material reality. The metanarrative purpose of metaphorization in *Untouchable* is to detach labor from its context: the naturalization of the process of work, in the service of a socialist realism, demonstrates physical labor to be beautiful, nonmachinic, and nonindustrial. Typically functioning on the basis of distance, dissonance, and incongruity, the effect of which is to construct similarities out of dissimilarities, metaphor is also a way of knowing, an epistemological mode; it is to see something as something else (Culler, *Literary Theory* 97). Metaphor thus allows Anand to introduce Bakha to us as other than he is. And what he is, is worthy of heroic status: the status of protagonist. The labor that renders him untouchable is redeemed by its poetics.

In addition to revising certain forms of labor in the spirit of a capacious Indian nationalism, what can metaphor do for caste? Firstly, it is particularly in the shadow of industrial labor that metaphors of the natural are most evocative. Marxist conceptions of labor drawn from the factory and from the peculiar historical experience of urban industrialization are most evocatively and politically metaphorized as springs and waves—they draw on a binary between the man-made and the natural that inheres through high romanticism and the Victorian period.[8] Labor is not simply being read as an abstract category but it refers to a specific form of work in societies characterized by early industrialization. Secondly, in this casteized context, the narrative goal of metaphor can only be to delink this labor from Bakha's personhood. As the narrator tells us, "Though his job was dirty, he was comparatively clean" (Anand 16). The untouchable, who might be associated with dirt and filth, can be understood here via certain familiar tropes: rocks, rivers, waves. Labor is thus beautified because it is essentially detachable from Bakha's caste identity. In the context of a critique of capitalism, this would be called alienation. Alienation here functions not only in the rigid Marxian conception of the dissonant relation between the worker and his labor, as well as its product (though both would be relevant here), but also as a kind of abstraction, which thins the very concrete specificity of certain types of work. The curious rhetorical maneuver of *Untouchable* is that metaphor, as the preeminent sign of the "literary" (i.e., the nonfaithfulness to the material reality of latrine cleaning), dovetails with the Marxist. The rhetorical gesture that functions on the basis of comparison between two distinct elements is overlaid by a Marxist analytics in a period of capitalist transition.

Casteized labor, however, cannot be one version of a platonic and imaginary Labor, but is rather the collective labor practices engendered and demanded by the social and semantic structure of caste. Metaphorization of Bakha's work is an interesting narrative move because in the world of representation as well as the more material one, casteized labor is essentially metonymic: caste pollution is a product of power relations but also occupational *association*, what Roman Jakobson, from whom we derive the seminal analysis of metaphor and metonymy, would refer to as "contiguity." Bakha is untouchable because of the work that he does, and he does this work because he is untouchable—and thus not allowed to do other things. As Partha Chatterjee has pointed out, in the colonial period, "new forms of wage labor fit snugly into the old grid of caste divisions" ("Caste" 98). The crucial distinction here is that alienation, which in an industrial European context is the tragic outcome of high-capitalist labor relations, is here made desirable, for it decouples the body from the degrading work it is required to do. In the case of the novel *Hard Times*, for example, Charles Dickens refers to the workers as "the Hands," a poignant synecdoche. The synecdoche serves the ironic critique of the novel, in which the industrial working class is exploited for its productive capabilities. Metonymy works in *Hard Times* because the point is precisely the opposite: workers are much more than their hands, they have hearts and thoughts and politics and so forth; they are only reduced to their hands in capitalist labor relations. In Jakobson's well-known formulation, this is the realist prerogative; it is modernist poetics that rely on metaphor.⁹ In a world of fractured parts, where fragmentation is wrought by modernization, industrialization, colonialism, and now, caste, metaphor does the work of distillation and elucidation of the relations among things.

To associate the cleaning of latrines with natural beauty and the tropes of high romanticism or the pastoral is no idle gesture. Neither is water an idle vehicle. What Anand does is to represent casteized work, which is determined by a rhetoric of purity and impurity (as the most traditional ethnological analysis would have it), with a natural spring, in a novel in which the problem of water is regularly highlighted. What kind of a thing is water? Water is not only purificatory, but is the central scarce commodity in the novel, which organizes an entire scene around the difficulty of its procurement. Water has a casteized valence—it is easily polluted and ritually purifying—and it is also an inaccessible commodity. Only certain "things" as Elaine Freedgood has pointed out, ascend to metaphorical stature (10).

CASTEIZED MODERNITIES

Water is what Bakha needs but British clothing is what he desires. Bakha wears foreign clothing, the castoffs of the British Tommies, and suffers physical deprivation and the ridicule of his family and friends in order to do so. Trousers, overcoat, blanket, and broken cane chair: Bakha has gradually culled together the signifiers of an other's life. Contemporary critical language offers us only certain possibilities for this particular cultural embrace of the other: anglophilia. But Bakha's interest in such trappings must be read in terms of both the cultural capital and the liberatory potential they might signify. "The Tommies had treated him as a human being" (Anand 9). His anglo-filiation, rather, awards him not only certain privileges (the hockey stick), but more importantly narratorial admiration; Anand, and our narrator, prize Bakha specifically because he cannot be read as a social "type" in the Lukácsian sense, the dismantling of which can be counted as one of the central achievements of modernist narrative. Bakha's cannot, therefore, be a straightforward case of colonial mimicry despite the novel's best intentions; Bakha does not even speak English.¹⁰ The Tommies, decoupled from the logic of colonial occupation, demonstrate an egalitarian fraternity based on both their ignorance of and indifference to caste. More importantly, the so-called Tommies are often uppercaste Indians. It is a casteized perspective, I would suggest, that reads them as metonyms of a foreign, as well as native, elaboration of justice. Here anglophilia, mimicry even—constructs developed in ignorance of caste, and specifically suited to the comprador class—function as forms of Sanskritization. Sanskritization is the process theorized by M. N. Srinivas to explain the means by which lowercastes adopt certain cultural and religious practices and codes in order to mitigate or advance their actual caste status—the adoption of vegetarianism, for example, or the wearing of the sacred thread. Rather than resignification, or revalorization of traditional practices, Sanskritization assumes repudiation of the old in favor of the new, and the familiar in favor of the distant. It also locates the question of social mobility within the realm of culture. Critiqued heavily by later theorists who note the absence of an adequate theorization of power, Sanskritization, as M. S. S. Pandian has pointed out, delinks social mobility from modernization and Westernization, which becomes the exclusive enterprise of the uppercastes (1738). But mimicry, or anglophilia, in this context, cannot function without an account of caste, on which Bakha's ideologies of modernity, fraternity, and mobility are necessarily based. Bakha adopts the pantaloon, and by the end of the novel he abandons his broom, the sign of his stigma. The potential for threat and mockery implicit in a certain understanding of mimicry are here reserved not for the Tommies but for the uppercastes and Gandhi.[11] Westernization is thus a powerful mode of literary readability that masks caste mobility, Sanskritization, or other more legitimate means of assertion and radicalism; it is one vehicle by which fiction understands caste hierarchies—the symbol, the trapping, the detail. Bakha desires English and clean clothes, perhaps not those of the uppercastes of Bulashah but most certainly those of the uppercastes of the colonial army, whereby the army and its procedures signify modernity: a postcaste modernity. To casteize the critical concepts on which Anand's Bakha relies would be to ask: What kind of modernity does Bakha want?

Within the scope of the novel, these British army objects appeal to Bakha for another reason and that is the glow of the commodity he cannot purchase; Bakha's mode of social advancement and distinction is not simply culturalist but material. Severed from the context of actual warfare, imperial rule, and the nation to which he is forcibly attached by the narrator at the end of a Gandhian novel, these objects provide a dazzling seduction. "He had long looked at the shop. Ever since he was a child he had walked past the wooden stall on which lay heaped the scarlet and khaki uniforms discarded or pawned by the Tommies, pith solar topees, peak caps, knives, forks, buttons, old books and other oddments of Anglo-Indian life. And he had hungered for the touch of them" (Anand 11). If commodity fetishism consists "in the fact that the commodity reflects the social characteristics of men's own labor as objective characteristics of the products of labor themselves" (Marx 164), then Bakha's case might appear to be prototypical. But, like the colonial subject, the "untouchable" caste subject has to necessarily revise the relationship to the commodity as economists and anthropologists of caste would attest. Not only does Bakha have limited ability to purchase things (and this is not because he is poor but rather because he is compensated on a tip system), even in a time of transition and modernization, a casteized economy will function differently than the prototypical Marxian one—his relation to the commodity is explicitly unique. The narrative of the colonized subject to the products and objects of empire is one of envy—for that which he cannot buy and for alienation from that which he has helped to produce. But the objects of Bakha's gaze are "casteless," and therein lies their glow. This is not the desire of Thomas Babington Macaulay's mimic man to aspire to British culture, but rather a fetishism of Anglo-Indian life, which, infused by the British empire, no longer needs caste.[12] Books, which he cannot read; forks, which he does not use to eat; peak caps, which he does not wear—these are not only signifiers of the West but an India without caste. Arjun Appadurai suggests in *The Social Life of Things* a revision of the commodity from its strictly industrial logic; economic objects, he writes, "circulate in different regimes of value in space and time" (4). This narrative moment would compound his point; the Marxist conception of commodity fetishism, determined by bourgeois or uppercaste hegemony cannot fully apply to the caste worker, despite the framework within which the novel inserts Bakha.

When Bakha is finally able to spend, he settles on the sweet *jalebis*, bought from an uppercaste merchant in town (Anand 46). But the equalizing logic of the financial transaction is suspect. The coins must be transferred without touch, and must be purified with water upon receipt. The entire scene is tinged with shame; the *jalebis* are thrown, the money is cleaned. In the end, because of the infamous scene of the touching, whereby Bakha inadvertently jostles an uppercaste man and is assaulted, Bakha is unable to properly consume the object of his desire. Financial exchanges, in addition to social relations, are necessarily casteized throughout the text. The Gandhian recognition that all labors are potentially equivalent in Hinduism, what Marx would categorize as only possible via abstraction, is *that which drives the metaphorization of latrine cleaning* and makes of Bakha a "worker." But it is tragically unsustainable in the world outside; even the world of a fledgling modernity assumes caste recognition.

MODERNISM AND CASTE

Given this reading of caste and labor, what kind of privileges would the aesthetics of modernism offer an activist writer like Anand? The modernist novel is clearly not only of the world, but creates worlds in relation to certain social and historical circumstances. The nature of that relation, particularly in the period prior to the post-1945 canonization or museumification of modernist cultural production as high art, was, as Neil Lazarus puts it, "disconsolation" (432). Clearly drawing from its most famous proponents (Adorno, Brecht, and others), Lazarus emphasizes the aesthetic and social work that modernist writing sought to do: "namely, say 'no,' refuse integration, resolution, consolation, comfort, protest and criticize" (431). The imperial enterprise that undergirded that refusal and protest, the constitutive denial of which some argue to be at the heart of the modern, was dissected by writers in the colonized world. As Simon Gikandi puts it, in the context of the Caribbean, for example, the colonized writer masters "the form alongside its deformation" and seeks to appropriate its revolutionary linguistic capabilities while "renouncing the imperialism that underwrites the discourse" (*Limbo* 23). As many others have stated, modernist writing in the colonies was indeed produced by modernization, but also by its brute underpinnings in the form of the colonial power. As a result, critics like Aamir Mufti charge this early writing with "narrating the passage from primitivism to modernity" (184). It is between these poles— one of refusal and disconsolation, the other of the seductive aesthetic forms of European modernism and modernity—that one could locate the revolutionary project of Mulk Raj Anand, who refashions the fascination with "others" and with "suffering" that provided the impetus for so much of modernist art in the West, and couples it with its very immediate and local political imperative: the crisis of caste and its debilitating effect on the Indian nation. *Untouchable* falls between a modernist propulsion towards (and revulsion from) darkness and the "critical realism" cited by Aijaz Ahmad as central for the "even harsher critique of ourselves" (*In Theory* 119). The problem for *Untouchable*, however, was that the terror of the modern, the excesses of the real, and the new, were somewhat intransigent: untouchability was domestic, close, and intimate. In this text, the compressed chronology, a classically fragmented and decentered modernist subjectivity, the foregrounding of physiological and psychological sensation, all compete with the social realism seemingly demanded by caste. The novel works precisely by delinking the problem of form and content in modernist fiction, and solving it via a Marxist unification.[13]

Bakha is in some ways the most perfect novelistic subject: he has no leisure to make culture, and no money with which to buy it. He has few literary precedents and an elusive historical genealogy. His interiority, therefore, is the novelistic blank slate. This affective realm of casteism is one major contribution of a modernist lens on the caste question. The novel's one-day structure magnifies several forms of humiliation: sexual advantage, physical pain, indignity in a series of incidents, but also their contemplation. In *Untouchable*, the Dalit subject is poetic and pained; he is introspective, musing, wounded. The modernist reverie gifted to Bakha, however, is unsustainable, routinely interrupted by the world of which he is a marginal yet central part. In a protracted moment of self-recognition produced by a series of failures, tormented and alone, Bakha cries out: "For them I am a sweeper—untouchable!" Anand writes, "As he emerged from the world of that rare, translucent luster into which he had been lifted, he stumbled over a stone and muttered a curse" (34). Bakha himself may be like a rock, but he routinely stumbles over stone. The world of luster, and of water, is here internal, constructed, and subjectivist. But Bakha's subjectivity is the novelistic counterpart to his subjection. Why is this necessarily so? If caste enters as labor, then what restores man from dehumanization is his poetic sensibility. This kind of modernism, characterized by an individualist proto-existentialism that overlaps with a more collectivist-in-theory individualizable Gandhian one, is at some level ensured by a certain reading of caste: it is particularly when labor is alienating that the restoration of individual subjectivity, i.e., consciousness, is necessary.

This analysis demonstrates one origin of what has now become a kind of political truism: Marxist intellectuals often read caste in terms of class. But it also demonstrates the kind of aesthetic imperatives the translation of ideology into form produces. The point here is not to criticize Anand, or for that matter other Marxist writers on caste, who played a crucial role in making of it an object of literary interest. Rather, it is to demonstrate that this mode was one that allowed for a very particular literary readability of caste. Not only would adjudicating caste as one dimension of a leftist problematic be part of a legitimate political program, it would also subsume untouchability into something eminently rectifiable through consciousness and mechanization (the flush toilet that might replace the latrine cleaners is referred to as "the machine"). Both of these, in this case, allow Bakha a kind of universalism stymied by a casteist logic. Anand's own political and aesthetic predilections ranged from the Marxist to the nationalist; he is described as a Joycean and a quasi-Bloomsbury intellectual, or more recently as a "regional cosmopolitan" (Berman 142). Bakha too speaks a language of casteism but also pan-Indianism, existentialism, and individualism, thereby inserting himself in a range of discourses that have origins that might seem to be alien to him.[14] This language of universal humanism in the name of Indian nationalism and Marxism is one that many intellectuals in India during this period were speaking. Metaphor, that characteristic feature of modernism, allows them to speak it. Although this Jakobsonian thesis has its limitations, I would read metaphor here as symptomatic rather than broadly characteristic. To see something "as something else" was the project of both the Marxists on caste, and the modernist novel on caste worlds.

If it seems that the question of metaphor is being overdetermined here, let me add one final note. Metaphor, as Roman Jakobson has argued, is a contingent aspect of modernism, but it is the untouchable caste subject, in particular, who "needs" metaphor, precarious as his position is in the history of the novel. Metaphor massages him and makes him worthy of both artistic endeavor and novelistic enterprise. In English, *acchut* becomes "untouchable," *chuhra* becomes "sweeper"—terms sociohistorically delinked from religious, cultural, and economic valence of caste. To fit Bakha into a Marxist modernism requires him to be a laborer *and* a consumer. He is clearly those things, as well as a subject marked by a certain caste identity. To elaborate him as such would require a revision of abstract categories developed in the absence of caste. What route does the contemporary Dalit text take instead?

THE LABOR OF METONYMY: ARTLESSNESS AND DALIT SUBJECTIVITY

As Udaya Kumar has suggested in his studies of regional novels, caste *rearranges* the field of visibility. That is to say that caste is not simply the act of casteized labor, but rather a structural imperative, such that spaces are casteized, perspectives are casteized, as are gestures and languages.[15] What gets excluded when caste is equated with labor, and concomitantly, untouchability?

Appearing a few decades after Anand's *Untouchable*, Hazari's *Autobiography of an Outcaste* (1951) espoused an attitude quite similar to Bakha's. Moving from an infatuation with a British mistress to an English education to a conversion to Islam, Hazari's narrative showcases a range of strategies of social mobility; those that might be referred to as Anglophilia, colonial modernity, conversion, Westernization, nationalism. It is aspirations such as these—cultural, economic, and educational—that have led Dalit ideologue Chandra Bhan Prasad to pronounce Thomas Macaulay—whose famous "Minute on Indian Education" (1835) declared "a single shelf of a good European library was worth the whole native literature of India and Arabia"—as "the great visionary," the man for whom "the true god of Indians could only be modernity" (quoted in Ram Nath Sharma 81). Espousing capitalism, social mobility, urbanization, technology, Chandra Bhan Prasad, the controversial Dalit columnist for the English-language newspaper *The Pioneer*, suggests a new mode of Dalit aspiration, one in direct opposition to leftist-based casteist or identarian modes of assertion. As many Dalit autobiographies would demonstrate, the latter typically necessitates forms of religious, social, and cultural renunciation. A new debate has thus charged Dalit discourse in the last several years—that of the "Dalit middle class," and "the creamy layer."[16] In the quest for social mobility, destigmatization, and modernity, what, then, is Dalitness? As caste reproduces itself despite the movement away from "traditional" occupation, what are its new "locations"? The problem of casteized labor has become crucial to the literary reproduction upon which Dalit writing is reliant and by which it is defined, casteized labor being one prominent mode via which to explore economic and cultural Dalitness.

What do Dalit texts do with labor? Almost without exception, casteized labor is degraded rather than beautified. And almost without exception Dalit writers have chosen the language of specification over abstraction. Cleaning a latrine cannot be like riding a wave, not only because of the ideological impetus of the text, which is to eradicate such forms of labor on principle, but also because metaphor is resistant to specificity, precision, localization. These, I want to suggest, are the new values of the Dalit literary text. I focus here on two recent Dalit short stories from the mainstream of the Hindi Dalit literary canon that articulate a distinctively realist aesthetic and politics. This is, however a new realism: subalternist, referential, occasionally naturalist, and one that bears a strident critique of both the modernist and the Marxist. In Kurmendu Shirshir's 1999 story "Daangar" ("Carcass"), for example, the narrator details with precision the exact process of animal skinning and disposal of the carcass, with little rhetorical flourish. Forced to remove an animal after a grueling day of agricultural labor, Lotan's misery in the story is triangular: the work he must do, the weight of his wife Badamiya's critique who barely masks her opposition to Lotan's labor, and the fascinated disgust of his child, Debu.

> He tucked his *dhoti* to one side, tied a handkerchief to his head, and picking up the knives, sat down next to the carcass. First, from the tail to the mouth, then from above the hoof to the joints of the leg, four times he ran the knife. By the time he had made the four cuts on the legs, his hands were shaking. He was momentarily startled. He began to feel the fatigue in his legs. How many times that day had he run the plow, the yoked buffalos? At that time he had no idea that later the same day he would be skinning. Lotan was in pain. What was life? After death man becomes a vulture. (277)

And later:

> When Lotan returned he washed the skin with lime water and spread some straw on the ground. Even after rubbing the salt small bits of flesh remained, softened, rotting. The hair had been cleaned. Badamiya was disgusted, even from a glance. . . . Lotan wiped off the softened flesh with the straw. He rubbed and rubbed, to remove the hair. "Get me the *khurpi* so I can remove the lining," he called to his son. (279)

There are many such passages in the text, those that detail the nature of this labor with a careful eye such that no step in the process of skinning is missed. From the physical removal of the animal, the nature of incisions, the flaying of the skin, the tears made near certain joints by the vultures, the removal of the hair, the remainder of the flesh and so forth, the story is invested in a literal dissection of the process, its necessary vocabularies, and its gross particularities. And how different is Lotan from Bakha, lost in the unconsciousness of his task!

For György Lukács, description was a symptom of the collapse of realism's historicity, to describe was explicitly not to do. His critique was in response to what he describes as the exaggerated role that description as rhetorical device had come to play in naturalism and socialist realism.[17] Franco Moretti would clearly concur. He suggests that description indicates the static: only those characters for whom no change, no historical movement, is possible are relegated to narrative description (Moretti, *Signs* 113). But narrative description, a vexed category to begin with, has been crucial to the ethnographic, i.e., the narrative introduction of the "new"; Clifford Geertz made of "thick description" a form of anthropological analysis. "Thick description" was not description in the narratological sense at all, but rather the reproduction of the deep structure of a community/practice/individual. Lotan's labor in this text serves the purpose of elucidating both character and practice, producing what might have been formerly called "milieu." That is to say, passages such as these feed the narrative construction of the Dalit subject, as they do certain assumptions of uppercaste readership both of which desire the elaboration of Dalit "difference." It should be said that the depiction of labor, specifically, is crucial to that elaboration. In that sense a scene such as this functions as an appropriate example of the "bifurcated vision" of the Dalit text that, rather than being a straightforward illumination of an abstract identarian project, consistently has its face turned in two directions.

It would, therefore, be a mistake to read this as a kind of autoethnography, or simply ethnographically pedagogical, in part because these moments can be characterized as descriptive only when deliberately excised from narrative: that is to say, this is the *plot*. It is the context alone, as Seymour Chatman has elaborated, which would allow us to determine that these passages, in which "nothing happens," are actually the basis of narrative content (23). But the additional problem presented by an ethnographic or revelatory reading of the aforementioned passages is that ethnographic authority depends upon a stable informant and the assumption of an ignorant readership. This may very well seem to be true, in the case of "Daangar," but interwoven with the details of skinning is the sustained resistance of Lotan's wife and her revulsion, the way in which this work invades the peace of their home, as well as Lotan's son's visceral terror. They, rather than an abstract and fictive uppercaste readership, are the ones who are being "introduced" to this labor, and consequently horrified. Unlike the fictive narrator of the bourgeois novel who travels to the specialized locations of otherness, in this text it is intimacy that produces dismay, disgust, and eventually death. It is thus that the material specificity (rather than the metaphorical valence) of the work serves to drive the plot. And while this work is demonstrated as one of consummate skill, it is not an act of pride, rather one of distinction—i.e., that which distinguishes Lotan in the most unheroic sense, and that which others him from his own family. This is a realist text in which the most basic novelistic values on work are overturned, and inflected by caste crisis. Work here must be decoupled from Gandhian heroism, monetary gain, and ethical value: all the bourgeois pillars upon which narrative depictions of work lie.[18]

Description in this story might be understood as an analytic corollary to metaphor—the last resort of the modernist novel seeking to harmonize disparate elements. In the story "Daangar," description—strictly speaking, a narrativized description that involves the relaying of actions rather than persons or things—serves to cement a tight metonymic chain: carcass, hands, hooves, vultures, man, corpse. The metonymy here is not literal, but functions in the Jakobsonian sense, in which relations of contiguity rather than modes of substitution predominate. Lotan labors, incises, cuts, skins, the carcass gets all his time and care, the vultures are set to attack. The *khurpi* that is used to remove the lining of the carcass is also used by Badamiya to beat her son for helping his father. Lotan is evoked by the work that his hands do, Badamiya by her ailing body. The dead animal that gives the story its title is gradually reduced to carcass, flesh, joints, skin, and finally turned into economic value.[19]

"Daangar" could easily be read as working at a metaphoric level. If we take the example of Lotan's beautiful philosophical musing, "Man is a vulture," this seems like a classic case. The problem arises only because vultures play a crucial role in the literalism and symbolism of the text. Metaphor typically functions according to narrative distance; the greater the distance separating its constituent parts, "the more powerful will be the semantic effect and the disturbance to relations of contiguity" (Lodge 112). But vultures are not distant here; they are barely metaphorical. They actually precede Lotan at the site of the carcass, performing his labor for him. Lotan essentially continues the work the vultures have begun; he is saved, by them, the labor of removing the eyes. They tear the skin he later cuts with a knife. All of which serves to brutalize, indeed animalize, his condition. This text, like most, makes use of metaphor but I describe it as metonymic in that it continually reinforces relations of "contiguity and combination," even between men and beasts. If the basic opposition between man and beast is effaced, as it is in this Dalit context, then metaphor becomes metonymic.[20] Despite the putative "artlessness" of Dalit texts, which seem to rely on realist and therefore transparent metonymic acts, they clearly do travel in the symbolic. The strengths and weaknesses of the symbolic effect, however, are derived precisely from metonymic association that is spatialized within the text.[21]

The protagonist, therefore, does not lose himself in his labor, he does not emerge unmarked by it, he cannot remain immune to disgust. The purpose of the prevalence of detail about work is that it allows us to read Lotan: his caste, his hereditary occupation, the skills he has learned over a lifetime of subjection, all of which do not preclude a range of affective responses to this work. That is to say, despite his familiarity, this is "new" to him as well. The vultures that hover around the scene are symbolically weighted while confirming the real, both reality and reality effect. They indicate the abstract condition of the scavenger—the historical profession of the Chamar caste that is required to dispose of carcasses—while being legitimate actors (it is the vultures who remove the eyes), but they also confirm the truth-value of the Dalit text by helping to produce the prototypical horror of a scene of animal skinning. When man himself "becomes a vulture" we know that this means not Man but man: he who is afflicted by certain work. This existential mediation can only obtain in the context of Dalit reality. Metonymy, then, deuniversalizes and particularizes plight. Man is a vulture not metaphorically but materially; he too, must survive through scavenging. In this interwoven symbolic economy, Lotan eventually pays for the removal of his wife's dead body from the home with the promise of income earned from the next carcass. A carcass for a corpse: a nonmetaphorical substitution.[22]

CONSCIOUSNESS! OR SOCIAL CONSCIENCES

Let me now address the problem of labor in an entirely different modality, one wedded less to the detailed depiction of the conditions of Dalit work, and more to its continuing stigma. In Surajpal Chauhan's story "Sajish" ("Plot," or "Conspiracy"),[23] the protagonist looks to the bank for a loan. The first in his family to attend university, he is determined to start a transporting business, foregoing his community's traditional role as sweepers or pig raisers. However, cajoled, coerced, and eventually convinced by the bank manager's evidentiary logic (What would become of him in the case of an accident? What of his lack of experience?), our protagonist returns home with a loan for pig raising instead, easily and quickly approved. The Brahmin bank manager, fearing the entry and ensuing competition of educated Dalits in the workforce, and the potential resistance to "traditional" occupation, has surreptitiously made it a policy to only approve loans for Dalits that pursue the work historically allotted to them by caste.

Nathu, the protagonist, the dupe, goes home, only to face his wife's strident critique. Uneducated as she is, she easily reads the bank manager's ploy. Having convinced her husband of this injustice, she and her husband call on the Dalits of the town to organize a march in protest of the bank's policies. Nathu receives a loan for his transport business in the end. In many ways, this is a classic tale of modern Dalit literature, a paradigm of Dalit realism: grounded in the experience of casteism faced by a singular protagonist, seemingly artless in terms of narrative style, demonstrating a united platform for social change, and displaying Dalit *chetna* (consciousness). The story thus raises one of the most important questions of the genre as a whole—that of the call to the political—and here cites the wife as its harbinger. It is precisely her lack of education, we should note, that allows her to see through uppercaste "rationalism." In response to the manager's defense that he was simply thinking of Nathu's welfare, she replies, "That's enough Manager Sahib. We will consider our welfare ourselves, now. For centuries you have been thinking of us. Now you can relax" (Chauhan, "Sajish" 90).[24]

In addition to showing the extent of the complicity of financial institutions in maintaining social hierarchy and Dalit downtroddenness, "Sajish" illustrates the extent to which the *varnavyavastha*, the traditional fourfold division of Hindu society, has been actively facilitated, encouraged, and solidified by technocratic systems and unspoken policies. Such efforts, in an attempt to maintain a certain social and economic order that is dependant on the proper functioning of certain bodies, showcase the intense amount of labor that comprises projects of bodily regulation, suggesting again the extent to which such naturalization is precarious. The project of Mulk Raj Anand that we examined earlier in this chapter constructs rather than deconstructs this logic, concretizing as natural an association between bodies and labor that we have seen is highly constructed. The protest in "Sajish" is performed on the basis of such an abolition, as Dalits of several castes demand the freedom to move away from certain occupations. The crowd chants slogans: "Loans Must Be Given for Desired Professions!" and "Stop the Conspiracy to Keep People in Hereditary Occupations!" (Chauhan, "Sajish," 89).

The unity of the Dalit community, the prominent role of the woman in inciting social action, and the final scene of protest would all mark this story as a traditional example of the literature of protest. Fulfilling the basic requirements of fiction designed to raise consciousness, Chauhan's tale is both pedagogical and prescriptive. But the nature of Dalit radicalism here is of a distinct sort. The protest in "Sajish" is in the service of exacting a loan from a lending institution, peopled by a crafty uppercaste technocratic manager. The advance is necessary because entrepreneurialism is the only option in a job market closed to certain castes; Nathu has neither the proper caste background nor the financial means for bribery that would land him a coveted position as a civil servant—a ward of the state. The modern bank loan has now been made a feature of a genre, we must remind ourselves, in which much is made of indebtedness and the casteized moneylender is the object of a fierce critique. The social movement here, then, is directed towards a critique of capitalism and the disparities it produces but is explicitly non-Marxist and nongovernmental. In the story, Nathu and his followers demand not redress by the state in a classical Ambedkarite fashion, but rather individualized entry into new, and distinctly modern, economic formations. The most persuasive answer to the question of what constitutes Dalitness and its social location in this story is therefore neither culture nor occupation, political positionality nor atrocity suffered, but protest. I would thus locate the Dalit realism of this story in the final moment of organized action and, also, in its narrative antecedent: "but." In this short piece of fiction relayed almost entirely in dialogue, the focus of the text is on the verbal exchanges between Nathu and the manager, and then between Nathu and his wife. As the manager attempts to convince Nathu, persuade him, outreason him, in effect, Nathu interrupts by saying, "Lakin . . . ," "Kimtu . . . ," "Parantu . . . ," all of which might be translated as "But . . ." The tentative resistance to the managerial apparatus and its disarming logic is located in Nathu's rhetorical gesture, a narrative point that indicates profoundly the modernity and contemporaneity of this text. The "but" absolves the narrative of any epiphanic moment, which, I would argue, has now become obsolete.

To return for a moment to Anand's *Untouchable*, in which Bakha's consciousness of himself as an untouchable arrives serendipitously via the carefully articulated incident of the touching. Here, the moment of epiphany (as in the epiphanic mode of the modernist novel[25]) is not accidental; it clearly overlaps with the epiphany of the proto-Marxist: the moment when the working-class subject becomes conscious of his class position and his revolutionary potential.[26] This moment is supplemented by Bakha's call to political consciousness, which is spurred by a series of otherworldly intellectuals: the Christian missionary, the figure of Gandhi and then an apostle of modernity: the poet. Prior to this, Bakha is explicitly described as "unconscious": of his own stores of knowledge (94), of his radical potential (78), of Gandhi (138). The important point would be that there is a triangulation in Anand's novel among modernist epiphany, Marxist freedom from false consciousness, and the moment of Dalit awakening, which relies to a significant degree on the presence of an intellectual other.[27] But in these Dalit stories, how does the call to consciousness occur? In other words, what produces the narrative "but"? In both cases mentioned here, there is no epiphanic moment, only the relentless presence of others. And these others are explicitly not the Leninist vanguard in any sense, or Fanon's national intelligentsia, nor are they political compatriots. They are simply other caste subjects to whom is gifted the clarity of vision—typically via gender.[28] Although these two stories are not interested in the particular problems of Dalit female subjection, they are clearly invested in the revolutionary potential of the female subject who bodily suffers the effects of Chamar work; Lotan's wife becomes physically ill and dies, Nathu's wife experiences a threat to her home. Even when caste politics are portrayed as an ideological conflict to be worked out between men, women play a central role in the distribution of Dalit *chetna*. While Dalit textuality is still clearly reckoning with an incipient subaltern feminist critique, the crucial role played by the female characters in these stories acknowledge the condition of caste to be a gendered one: caste as endogamy, caste as social reproduction, caste as rape and other gendered forms of atrocity. These texts thus provide a kind of answer to the debates on revolutionary potential and the problem of consciousness-raising. Consciousness as such is not the problem; certain social conditions (communal, nonalienated) need to be in place for its social articulation. Utopianism, within the text, may not be utopianism at all, simply the possible. This is why Dalit realism is not simply an aesthetic and narratological program but an ideological, and readerly, commitment.

What does this mean for the literary text? A product of the newly configured space of Indian caste politics, Dalit literature necessarily reads political awakening differently. This would be the logical corollary in the case of a text like "Sajish," where no awakening is necessary—preceding the wife's intervention is the delicate "but." That new political reality, however, creates certain aesthetic imperatives. The novel, deriving from a bourgeois liberal individualism, has historically had a difficult time addressing community, movements, the crowd, the group, the mob—all the varied forms of political non-singularity. Dalit literature, I would argue, is finding new ways to address this very problem—one means of which might be the attenuation of the protagonist. The "relentless presence of others" is therefore compensatory, rectifying the excision of the Dalit from social life, his marginalization, while also deconstructing the tight relationship between liberal individualism and modern Westernized narrative forms. For example, in the case of "Daangar," the protagonist would typically be understood as Lotan, whose actions direct the arc of the story. Lotan is clearly the best candidate: he skins, he scolds his son, he worries over his wife, and the narrative is often focalized through him. But each of the other characters play such a strong role in determining the eventual unfolding of the story—Badamiya lodges her protest against Chamar work and promptly dies, the son is terrorized and disappears—that Lotan is the protagonist only insofar as he is the only one left at the conclusion.

"Lotan picked up the skin and placed it in his basket—all of a sudden the vultures broke loose. The wrangle of their wings and the collision of their beaks left Debu terrified. Holding his breath he bolted towards home. . . . Debu washed his hands and face and laid down on the cot. He kept rubbing his eyes, but even when the image of the flock of vultures darting towards the carcass faded he could not erase the sight of them clawing out its eyes" (Chauhan, "Sajish" 278). Lotan works, Debu suffers. Where is the space of the protagonist? What I would suggest is that the protagonist is rather a composite of all the possible subject positions in the text. This is not a narrative in which each character competes for the space of action, or where one is relegated to a subplot. The text also does not participate in a logic of major and minor characters. And though it is a short story, it does not function in the Lukácsian vein whereby the whole is rendered subjectively, a fragment dictated by the hero (Lukács, *Theory* 50). There is a fairly and unusually uniform division of narrative and affective labor in this story. Lotan also feels what his son feels, what his wife feels. In fact, Lotan *was* who his son *is* now in the present of the narrative, as one long analeptic moment demonstrates. The question that is raised by a fictional text such as "Daangar" is of the particular suitability for the protagonist to be defined as such, an assumption that goes unquestioned in realist and modernist texts alike. *Untouchable* goes to great lengths to demonstrate Bakha's unique sensibility, which justifies handing the narrative reins to a Dalit actor. Nothing distinguishes Lotan, or Debu, or Badamiya, however. They all seem equally fit or unfit to dictate narrative action.

The question of character (major, minor, singular, collective, individual, symbolic, allegorical) is a crucial one in Dalit literature; as we have seen in the previous chapter, Dalit critique is, within the realm of the literary, largely characterological. Character as representative, character as metonymic, character as symbolic, character as nonsymbolic. But what is this character, around whom an entire genre has been configured? The Russian formalists thought of character as device, not simplistically referential, but the central literary anchor of various strands and textures of plot. As Alex Woloch reminds us, the antinomy between the referentiality of character—its humanism—and character-as-device has been defining in the history of structuralist theory, which has yet to develop a proper theory of character (15). Citing the critique of character as "individual" and therefore indebted to certain bourgeois notions of personhood—that of Hélène Cixous, for example—Woloch suggests a model that considers character "distribution," "textual arrangement," and "character-system" (13). Character can thus be considered not only within its referentiality but in terms of its operation within space. "Novels touch history," says Woloch, "in the interaction of character-space" (20).

Characters in Dalit literature are always referential, never mere devices in the Russian formalist sense; to read them otherwise would invalidate the ultimate goal of Dalit texts, which is to function in the world outside them. But this does not mean, however, that that referentiality is not present in varying and intermittent degrees. The patchwork of character into Character is one example. In this case, referentiality wouldn't function on the basis of a one-to-one correspondence, but through a quilting, the composite of which provides an insight into Dalit reality and casteized life-worlds. The classic delineation between major and minor characters, protagonists and their enablers would, it follows, be slightly different in this context (and in the context of short fiction more generally). The minor character in these stories is hardly minor; in her is lodged revolutionary consciousness. Woloch reads the minor character as "functionalized" in the context of the nineteenth-century realist novel; he plays a utilitarian role in the narrative asymmetry of the novel, whereby the protagonist is followed and others are extinguished (27).[29] This seems appropriate in a genre attentive to problems of social class, social distribution, and hierarchy even as narrative asymmetry meant that historically, such a novel was not able to capture "plurals," or communities. Narrative privilege itself captured the problem of social stratification. But the naked partiality of the Dalit texts means that it is the uppercaste character who is "functionalized," "instrumentalized," in the service of evocation of Dalit reality. In a genre whose stated aim is the evocation of the hidden conditions of Dalit materiality and the prescription for its transgression, the character who provides the key can never be considered minor. The notion of a composite protagonist captures something of the collective politics of a stated literary-political text. Although this may superficially bear some similarity to a fragmented or fractured modernist subject, I hesitate to use such terminology here as it conjures a very different vision of subjectivity. The basic holism of the human subject that undergirds the modernist critique is an assumption that Dalit texts cannot by definition participate in, because the basic humanity of the Dalit subject could not be taken for granted. The *composite protagonist* has an opposite trajectory to that of the fragmented subject; he is constructed through several constitutive narrative parts. This, I would suggest, is one mode via which Dalit texts construct plurality, through a different construction of the narrative division of labor.

REALIST PARTICULARISMS

Many contemporary protest literatures speak a language of particularism, detail, distinction, and difference at the level of both form and content, while also harboring the impulse towards community, representativeness, and unity. The problem of labor in these texts is not simply a problem of literary content, but demonstrates itself to be at the origins of that particularism, even at the level of the nonmaterial. The description of skinning in "Daangar" could not be characterized as description in the way of Western narratology, whereby it either impedes narrative or provides symbolic content. The aforementioned scene rather organizes the logic of the entire story. It does so by reproducing in detail a scene new to literary Hindi, not only in the manner of exposé, but also characterization. In "Daangar" Lotan's labor distinguishes him even from his neighbor who exacts extravagant interest for lending the money for the corpse's removal. Labor isn't abstracted—it is the source of the nontransferable specificity of the caste condition. That particularism has been a driving force of contemporary Dalit politics in the Hindi belt. The politics of particularism in the literary text should of course be read as a necessary correlative to the fragmented political landscape of North India, which divides its electoral loyalties through a complex strategy of caste combination.

This might be read at the level of ideology but also form. An ideology of realist particularism becomes valuable precisely because of its ability to denote partiality, and specification—not, as one might think, its universalism. David Lodge, deriving from Jakobson, writes that the metonymic mode is resistant to generalization, functioning as it does via a network of subtle, dense, and always-insufficient detail (111). That textual web serves a metonymic function via its incomplete specificity; it indicates something larger but somehow contiguous. The particular, therefore, may become one version of the general. But the category of the general is of little interest in this genre of short fiction, as is indicated by the choice of genre itself; the short story rarely lends itself to a dissection of the problem of the totality in the way that the novel does. Aamir Mufti suggests that the dearth of the novel and the privileging of the short story in early twentieth-century Urdu literature indicates an ambivalent relationship to the project of nationhood (183). It is an interesting argument in light of the generic complexity of Dalit literature, which has chosen modern and Western narrative forms almost exclusively while also largely eschewing the novel. The materialist explanations of this are well documented: as many writers have stated, "Who has time to read a novel?" But if the foreshortened vision of the Dalit text, its version of realism, is organized by the problem of consciousness, then this is essentially a problem of duration. The formulaic, social realist, or predetermined utopias of certain Dalit texts are essentially reduced to this question:

Why is there no *gradual development* of consciousness? The answer is that these are neither detective stories nor bildungsromans, both constitutively dependent upon the unfolding of narrative time. Dalit *chetna* is always already present and doesn't require literary elaboration for its production. Realist metonymy here, rather than serving to indicate the social as a whole, or the careful elaboration of the subject, gestures towards the revelation of hidden meanings between things that can only be read via the lens of caste.

To quote Culler at length: "The privileging of metaphor over metonymy and other figures is an assertion of cognitive value and respectability of literary language, the accidental play of verbal associations and contingent juxtapositions is given an ancillary status so that it can be ignored. . . . Powerful forces are at work to make metaphor at once the opposite of tropes based on accident and the authoritative representative of figurative language in general, the figure for figurality" (*Signs* 199).

What are those "powerful forces"? Culler cites Umberto Eco, who deconstructs the fiction of metaphoricity by demonstrating the "third term": the term of contiguity via which two dissimilar things may be revealed as having similar essential qualities. Eco performs a literary analysis that resurrects the third term that has been "dropped out." Metaphor, he claims, is not simply dependent upon metonymy but works through invisible contiguities based on Culture, and the "Global Semantic System" (Culler, *Signs* 201). The interrogation of the problematic notion of a global semantic system would be the project of many literatures of protest, which derive their originary political impulse through resignification, and particularization, as in the case of the terms "black" or "Dalit." That resignification occurs in many ways, one of which may be the rereading of tropes as tropes. It is only the revelation of a casteized world that can demystify certain metaphors as metonymic. The equation of man and vulture isn't derived based on some essential qualities that privilege the creative and agentive abilities of author but rather the revelation that man and vulture are linked by relation to the *daangar*, the hidebound animal. The mystification of the third term, the invisibility of metonymic contiguity, helps to maintain the privileged role of metaphor in literariness, doing an extreme disservice to certain bodies of work such as Dalit literature, which attempt to make of artlessness something poetic.

In the case of the literary texts mentioned in this section, there is a basic reliance on the terms of social realism: language rarely draws attention to itself and is meant to be read as referential, dialogue and narration are largely literalist. The apparent artlessness of these texts is worthy of deconstruction: Where do their literary claims lie? Metaphor allows a certain rhetorical, but also ethical, freedom that serves both the exceptional figure of Bakha, who isn't required to move within a certain characterological grid, and also the activist and universalist claims of the literary production of a movement such as that of the PWA. It isn't that Bakha isn't particular or unique—he clearly is—but his uniqueness is his entry point into a greater humanity made available to bourgeois individuals by the novel; an untouchable has finally joined their ranks. Metaphor functions as the narrative location of this idealism. Dalit texts locate their idealism elsewhere, in a transhistorical utopianism.

In the Anglophone novel, caste may actually enter the novel using the rubrics of a different epistemology—i.e., those categorized broadly as Marxist.[30] Anand's text thus becomes anticipatory of a long tradition of Marxist scholarship on caste. Challenging ethnologists such as Louis Dumont, for whom the unity of caste as system was determined by a hierarchy of purity and pollution (and therefore static), historians of caste have sought to reinscribe movement, history, and economy into a reading of caste; the Marxist model has been one of the most influential. Historian Irfan Habib, for example, writes of caste as "a system of class exploitation" as rigorous as any other (172). Anand may not be representative—of early twentieth-century Anglophone writing, of high modernism, or of Indian fiction on caste. But his novel *Untouchable* is clearly representative of a Marxist imperative to read caste in terms of class. What kind of formal demands thus ensued? Metaphorization, for example, which here functions as a form of translation, is a process driven by several factors: the incommensurability of caste with English, a Marxist reading, and a basic literary humanism. A certain kind of literary history might demonstrate that there are certain analytical tropes to which caste analysis is subject. Metaphor may have become crucial to a certain process of translation by which a language, rhetoric, or ideology of caste can be transmuted or transcoded in the novel in English. Simon Gikandi writes of the late colonial, modernist text that "translates African phenomena into the cultural idiom of Englishness"—a central analytic feature of the work of Graham Greene or Joseph Conrad (*Limbo* 192). But what I am referring to is a microcosm of that process, whereby the problem of caste is translated into an English, novelistic, and modernist context in the service of a universalism.

A Dalit critique of a text like *Untouchable* wouldn't be launched exclusively at its modernist, expressivist subjectivity, as one might think. This was indeed Gandhi's critique of the novel, which featured, he thought, "an untouchable who speaks like a Bloomsbury intellectual" (quoted in Merotra 178). Some Dalit texts, such as "Daangar," make much of interiority; others like "Sajish" much less so. The heavy focalization of Anand's novel and its reproduction of a Dalit family have also been taken up in contemporary Dalit fiction. Most importantly, the radical shift in worldview heralded by *Untouchable* is one that has clearly been the defining marker of Dalit writing as a whole. But Dalit literature in Hindi has abandoned the trope of the universal for the partial, and the particularist. This can be read in terms of the basic distinction between class/caste and nation/region, but also in the development of new analytical rubrics. The casteization of concepts eventually gives way to new formal paradigms. When Dalit critics such as Omprakash Valmiki cite, as a central component of Dalit literature, opposition to the "Great Tradition" defined by the eminent Hindi critic Ramchandra Shukla, this is precisely what Valmiki means (31). The origins of Dalit literary "difference," as well as its realist turn, must be read both at the level of ordinary metonymy as well as political manifesto.

CHAPTER THREE

A Perfect Whole

Knowledge by Transcription and Rural Regionalism

Mother India dwells in the villages, in verdant fields, with bountiful crops. The border of her sari is soiled with dust. The soiled border! But now, in this season, her sari-border was golden. The east wind rippled the golden tassels of the wheat-filled fields. The villagers working in those fields looked like bathers frolicking in a waist-high river of gold. Those golden ripples, the rows of palms, the jungle of jharber, the bungalow garden, the lotus-filled puddles near the Kamla River—the doctor saw them all with new eyes!

—PHANISWARNATH RENU, *Maila anchal (The Soiled Border)*

In *Dalit sahitya ka saundaryashastra (The Aesthetics of Dalit Literature)* Hindi writer and critic Omprakash Valmiki lays out the basic conditions for Dalit *chetna*, or "Dalit consciousness," that crucial element for the production of Dalit literature. His list of thirteen items includes Ambedkarism, anti-capitalism, anti-brahminism, and anti-traditionalism in the realm of literary aesthetics. But after the elaboration of this list, Valmiki takes a moment to remind the reader of Ambedkar's comments on village life in India. "There is no place in India's villages for independence, equality, and brotherhood. For Brahmins, Indian villages are heaven, but for Dalits they are nothing short of hell" (*Dalit sahitya* 31). There is a complex lineage here, drawing on Ambedkar's exhortation to fellow Dalits to leave India's villages, move to the cities, educate, and agitate, which was itself in response to Gandhi's idealization of village life, his hope for the rural heartland and its political, social and economic development. "India," wrote Gandhi, "lives in her villages." In Hindi, the Dalit literature of the last two decades draws quite heavily on the rural experience in Bihar and Uttar Pradesh, as well as the regional district town, but only occasionally the city. In that sense it is crowning a long genealogy of literary texts that dissect the rural, the local, the vernacular, and the regional in the form of the village. Two of the most celebrated novels in the Hindi language, Premchand's 1936 *Godaan* and Phanishwarnath Renu's 1954 *Maila anchal*, derive their critical reputation in large part from a dissection of village economy, its brutalities, and its hallowed landscape. Though very different in tone, style, and politics, both novels are invested in the representation of the village as a stable site, the home of the peasant who is the village's most representative figure. The village, as Vasudha Dalmia writes, "is a defining feature of the Hindi literary landscape" (Introduction 58). For contemporary Dalit writers in Hindi, however, the anchor in the rural is only a stable position from which to launch a critique of the village as the most perfect realization of caste crisis; that stable position is, literally and figuratively, outside of the village. Dalit critic Sharankumar Limbale states, "Rural literature does not talk about the caste system. There is as much dissimilarity between rural literature and Dalit literature, as there is between the *savarna* society living in the village and the untouchable society living outside the boundary of the village" (29). Limbale's metaphor, drawing attention to locational politics and the spatialized production of text, serves to underscore a separatist position that derives from both the historical and material conditions of village life as well as the metanarrative problems involved in the production of Dalit literature. The village is a matter of thematic content but also produces certain kinds of narratives, one of the most significant of which may be the exodus from it. That departure becomes an organizing principle of the Dalit text and often helps to develop its narrative arc. This chapter traces the origins of certain narrative tropes—the village exodus, for example, and the figure of both the intellectual observer and the native informant—by examining the literary constitution of this site in the cultural movement of the 1950s called *anchalik sahitya* (regional literature). In its construction of the ideology of the regional, of the vernacular, and most importantly of rural realism, *anchalik sahitya* provides a model for the modern Dalit text, which lays no claim to the national, but also provides an opportunity for one instantiation of Dalit critique. Dalit writing is suggesting a realism that relies on a certain observational power but refigures basic notions of ethnographic knowledge that have been central to a putatively progressive canon. It is via this critique that we can derive a Dalit literary ideology that may—counterintuitively—be far more interested in form rather than content.

Premchand has largely been the focus of critical ire by the Dalit literary establishment. One of the early debates in Hindi Dalit literature, as discussed in chapter 1, focused on whether or not Premchand, as a socially committed writer, might be considered a legitimate part of Hindi Dalit literature's genealogy, despite his Kayasthaness. There have been exhaustive discussions of "Kafan," Premchand's short story that features two despicable Chamar characters, and entire issues of literary journals like *Hans* and *Dalit Sahitya* have been devoted to Premchand's relationship to Dalit literature. In contrast, Phanishwarnath Renu (1921–1977) has been of little interest. But Renu's oeuvre, rooted firmly in rural Bihar, continues a Premchandian tradition of microscopic focus on village life, according a prominent place to the various lowercastes and tribes of Bihar. It is Renu's famed *Maila anchal* (1954) that gives *anchalikta* (regionalism) its name.

Anchalik sahitya (regional literature) is a kind of forgotten literary movement. Largely overshadowed by the culturally dominant *nayi kahani* (the new short story) and its urban, middleclass, often nucleated domestic concerns,[1] *anchalik sahitya* was actually a crucial movement in the literary history of postindependence India. Associated with the representation of the rural, the peasant, the poor, and the geographically marginal, the fiction understood as *anchalik* was peopled by tribals, farmers, and fisherman in regions far from Bombay and Calcutta, and produced a number of novels in the first two decades after Indian independence. It differed radically in terms of narrative style from the novel as it had been shaped in India thusfar. It was not, for example, interested in psychological interiority, the development of character, linear narratives, or domestic crisis, nor any of the hallmarks of modernism and existentialism. In many of these texts, several narratives compete for primacy, several love stories are juxtaposed, several political conflicts emerge in parallel. *Anchalik sahitya* doesn't seem to have its roots in the eighteenth- and nineteenth-century European novel, the bildungsroman, the novel of formation or development, as did almost every other important novelistic trend in India. It is veritably untranslatable, moving from dialect to dialect, making careful note of vagaries in caste/class-bound speech, invested in the cadences as well as the politics of orality. Two of its most prominent practitioners, for example, Nagarjun and Renu, dabbled or wrote primarily in Maithili, considered a dialect and recognized as a distinct literary language only in 1965. Most importantly, *anchalikta* took location as its driving force. Renu's *Maila anchal* (*The Soiled Border*), for example, begins with an elaborate description of the region of Bihar and the Purnea district in which the village of Maryganj is to be found, assuming an unfamiliar audience: "To reach it, you go east from Rautahat station for about 14 miles, then cross the old Koshi River. Beyond the palm forest, the plains stretch for thousands of acres from the foothills of Nepal to the banks of the Ganges, a vast, barren border region. Even wild grass doesn't grow there. Just scattered sand dunes and an occasional ber bush. After crossing 2 miles of this plain, you can see a dark forest towards the east. Right there is the Maryganj bungalow" (Renu, *The Soiled Border* 5).[2]

The novel follows the political machinations of the village circa 1942 and the struggle for power between the Congressites and the Socialists for the political loyalties of village constituents, as well as various love affairs and caste conflicts. It is written in a mix of standardized Hindi, Maithili, Bhojpuri, and other dialects. It reproduces heavily the folk lyrics of Bihar, the poetry and the dance-dramas; in the text, one actually sees that the page is regularly broken up by the reproduction of lyric verse. *Anchalik sahitya* makes almost no reference to Delhi, Lucknow, Benares—crucial sites of literary textuality in India. And it very rarely moves outside the region that gives it its name.[3]

THE VILLAGE

Where do literary movements come from? What kinds of ideological shifts produced a movement like *anchalik sahitya*? These are questions that assume a certain importance in light of the larger intervention of this book, which is to establish an antigenealogy for the thing now referred to as Dalit *sahitya* (literature). Most literary movements are easily read as cultural extensions of political aspirations: this is indeed one version of the Progressive Writers Association, the cultural corollary of the Communist Party of India. But unlike the experimentalist writers of the 1940s, *anchalikta* is unmarked by the public embrace of a specific culturalist logic. *Anchalik sahitya* didn't produce manifestoes, protests, or the inevitable charges of obscenity and subversion. There were no conferences held or loud declarations made; flush with Nehruvian socialism, *anchalikta* arose in a different historical moment, characterized by postnational splinter and linguistic distinction. Many of the writers referred to became associated with the *anchalik upanyas* (the regional novel), almost unwittingly; Nagarjun, the communist poet, famously wrote several regional novels without any overt acknowledgment of the genre. Renu and Shiv Prasad Singh were *anchalik* writers who were also associated with *nayi katha* (the new fiction) and *nayi kahani* (the new short story), the literary trends for which postindependence India is most often remembered.[4] Despite this, however, *anchalik sahitya* did produce a number of texts across the Hindi belt that broadly correlate with each other, demonstrating a certain aesthetic logic: primarily novels that circulate in peripheral spaces, demonstrating keen interest in the village, the marginal community, the scheduled tribe, the inaccessible locality. Beginning in the 1950s with scheduled castes and artisan communities only accessible via the rural, writers then moved further afield, drawing on an ethnographic impulse to reveal the polyandrous tribe, the obscure custom, the raggedy edges of the new nation. The ideology of regional literature was that of discovery; literary elaboration presented itself as one powerful means for articulation of the new and different. *Anchalikta* thus participated in a radical decentering of the literary sphere, locating characters, plots, ethics, and politics in what had been considered nonliterary spaces while also fulfilling a desire to answer certain questions pertaining to the status of the nation via a rural realism. Rural realism wasn't simply the project of representation of the village but a sustained reflection on certain narrative practices and their suitability for high culture: the entire question of the folk. It was heteroglossic—paradigmatically so—mingling registers, languages, and tones. Most importantly, rural realism as a form was one means of providing narrative justice to nonhegemonic subjects and spaces. Many of the *anchalik* writers were committed activists; Renu and Rajendra Awasthi participated in Jai Prakash Narayan's antigovernment movement; Nagarjun, also a Narayan follower for a time, was a committed independent communist and Naxal sympathizer. Regionalism, despite its failings, was thus an intellectual harbinger of the rise of the subaltern and a critique of the national that would shape intellectual life in the decades thereafter. I would thus like to situate *anchalik sahitya* between two sensibilities: the political construction of a village India, and the recovery of a lost tradition.

In 1935, at the annual meeting of the Hindi Sahitya Sammelan, Gandhi appealed to writers to "go back to the villages." For urbanized, educated intellectuals, the village was to be understood as real India, and going "back to the village" clearly implied going back in time. For writers engaged in a critical realism, or the rural realism of *anchalik sahitya*, Gandhi's exhortation underlined that real India was village India, and that the real—inevitably meaning the authentic—was a kind of timeless space, a haven from the intrusions of modernity. "I would certainly advise you and those like you who love the motherland to go into the interior that has yet not been polluted by the railways, and to live there for six months; you might then be patriotic and speak of Home Rule" (*Hind Swaraj* 70). If centuries of colonial rule had produced the village as an administrative unit in a vast scheme of taxation—the "revenue village" or "microterritory of public authority," as sociologist David Ludden calls it—the Gandhian reading re-produced the village as a space of culture for the popular (urban) imagination. The interior of India was remote but better for it, primitive but ethically superior, impoverished but grander on a civilizational scale. This idea became so prominent in the following decades that the novelist Rajendra Awasthi, who would emerge as a crucial *anchalik* writer in the 1960s, would write, "the various regions are the only symbols of our country. The cities have never influenced our culture, and on the basis of cities a vast current of culture could never be formed. . . . The cities can be the centers of artificial cultures, but real culture is not born there" (Introduction 5). Awasthi's claims were made possible and defensible by Gandhian persuasion, which exalted the village over the cities—the cities being "civilized" only in the manner of the British, and therefore viewed as "plagues" (*Hind Swaraj* 68).

Gandhi's writings on the village, its harmonious functioning and its economic independence, are well-known and have been thoroughly deconstructed by Ambedkar and many after him. However, one of Gandhi's most radical cultural contributions was his rereading of the village as a potential site of social experiment, a laboratory: for *swadeshi* (self-sufficiency), for trusteeship, for a Hinduism without untouchability. If the rural interior was, for Gandhi, a space safe from civilization and modernity, it clearly wasn't meant to be a static enclave. Trusteeship, for example—Gandhi's revision of economic morality by which the wealthy served as the "trustees" of the poor—was reliant on the construction not simply of the benevolent *zamindar* but the ethical one. Sensitive to the hostility with which this theory of spontaneous ethical transformation might be treated, he writes: "Absolute trusteeship is an abstraction like Euclid's definition of a point, and is equally unattainable. But if we strive for it, we shall be able to go further in realizing a state of equality on earth than by any other method.... That possessors of wealth have not acted up to the theory does not prove its falsity; it proves the weakness of the wealthy" (*India* 69).

Gandhi's convictions regarding nonviolence notwithstanding (socialism's call for land redistribution required the putatively violent dispossession of the landlord and land redistribution), the consistent demonstration of the impossibility of trusteeship could not deter him philosophically because the village was seen as the site of such ethical experimentalism. The entrenchments of caste and class still left room for new configurations and relationships, and the potential revision of social relations.

Writers of *anchalik sahitya* attempted valiantly to produce a very particular form of the real—one, however, that capitalized on the village's actuality rather than its Gandhian potentiality. Bridging the divide between Gandhian idealism and a Nehruvian developmentalism, novels dealt with socialist revolution in the village, but also its failure; with the abolition of *zamindari*, but also the further destruction of the peasant in its wake; with the rise of Gandhianism, but also the damage that its disenchantment produced. Of course, many of these writers were committed leftists, disillusioned by the Congress Party and disgusted by the failures of *zamindari* abolition; their political project was to showcase those failures. The work of Nagarjun is an exception; in his novels revolutionary men and women occasionally succeed.[5] But *anchalik sahitya* seemed to have little space left for the idealistic realism of the early Gandhian Premchand and more for the postindependence disillusionment that characterized the discourse of many postcolonial intellectuals. The Gandhian village, then, became for the *anchalik* writers a site of literary rather than material and social experimentation, since in the intervening years Gandhi's village India had been dramatically altered.

What was this new post-Gandhian, post-Partition village that was taken on by the rural realists? Following the crisis of Partition, a crisis that marked the idealized village space with a brutality still lingering, the village was remade once again. Ludden writes that the postindependence village was seen as a "natural social order to be modernized by market economy and protected by state politics" (220). Protection and modernization required both a mummification of harmless tradition and a transformation of primitive tendencies, but above all a careful documentation of the citizens and regions of this new entity called the nation. In the 1950 census, constituents noted their age and religion but also their mother tongue. In preparation for the first general election in 1952, districts were named and numbered, bridges built to reach the electorate in the hills, and vessels sent to carry ballots to Indian citizens living in the ocean's islands. As historian Ramchandra Guha points out, the news media marveled at the vast participation in the electoral process (144). Two years later, the State Reorganization Commission traveled across the country, visiting towns and cities and conducting interviews in order to document and analyze the linguistic division of states. And in 1955, in support of Prime Minister Nehru's second five-year plan, his statistical advisor established the National Sample Survey, which collected reliable data on wages, employment, and standards of living and consumption (Guha 207). Protection, modernization, and reorganization demanded a knowable object, captured by ethnographers and statisticians, analyzed by anthropologists and sociologists, archived and preserved by historians. It is in this context that we might view critic Indu Prakash Pandey's observation that *anchalik sahitya* focuses on communities that are "recognizable as distinct entities" through "concentration and particularization" (Pandey, *Regionalism* 8, 14). Literary regionalism in Hindi was produced in a period of political regionalism; in Bihar, for example, the Adivasi Mahasabha established the Jharkhand Party to articulate demands for a separate state for tribal people and to contest "Bihari imperialism." There are novels that take as their project the elaboration of the peoples of the Kullu Valley, the Gonds of Madhya Pradesh, the Bhils, certain criminal tribes, and other indigenous communities. Rajendra Awasthi's 1976 novel *Jangal ke phool* (*Flowers of the Jungle*) focuses specifically on *ghot*, the Gond tribal practice by which young women choose their partners. All of these texts have a strong ethnographic and anthropological drive, reminiscent of Herbert Hope Risley's *The People of India* project and its focus on categorization and codification, as well as a kind of regional sensibility rooted in the vernacular dialects. What kind of ideological work are these texts doing?

An immense amount of observational labor went into the production of the exhaustive detail of *anchalik sahitya*, in terms of description, "authentic" dialogue, and extraction of folk culture and obscure custom. As one critic says, the region was to be read as "evidence";

detail served to authenticate the social problem under discussion, and detail, here, was derived from the region. In his 1957 novel *Parati parikatha* (*The Story of a Barren Land*), Renu writes of the five-year plan for agricultural development and the real obstacles of illiteracy and caste conflict that hinder its implementation—specifically in Bihar. When Nagarjun wrote of the crisis of socialist revolution in his 1952 novel *Balcanma*, both his and the text's political credibility are derived from the particular and locally distinct, rather than the generalizable, condition of the downtrodden. That is to say, the failures of modernization, as well as the utopian possibilities implied in the text, are grounded by the concrete specificity of location. In addition to the political and social "work" that the novels were doing in terms of description, elaboration, and transcription, the genre was also creating a romance of discovery. The doctor who comes to Maryganj village in Renu's *Maila anchal* is reminded precisely of that by his sister. He bemoans, "But I've decided to announce that my research was a failure!" "No research is ever a failure, doctor! At least you've come to know this land . . . love of the soil and of the people . . . that's no small thing" (326). This last statement reads as metanarrative commentary, particularly because it appears in the novel that produced a genre. Exhaustive research produces lasting love, the regional novel's most valuable product.

Regional literature reads defensively; it should therefore be contextualized within a longer tradition of the social novel that sought to find truth in the outside—the habitat, in fact—the external circumstances of life rather than characterological or psychological inquiry. However, it should also be situated within the broad space of Gandhian politics and the hegemony of the urban. The strong sense of being sidelined by the urban establishment helped to produce a glorification of the village—the very village that had been so thoroughly deconstructed by Premchand—as a kind of poetic enclave. In *anchalikta* is reflected, first, the postcolonial disillusionment that set in after anticolonial euphoria, prompted by the failure of collective politics and blunt starvation, and second, the modernizing impulse, read not only in terms of land reform, electoral advances, and the abolition of *zamindari*, but in the abandonment of folk culture for film. Anand Prakash says the work of Renu "makes it a point to resist the 'nation-building' mission of the new rulers" (1). In this sense, the regionalists were caught in an ideological bind, being required by their political convictions to underline the extant misery of the village, while also challenging the domination of urban space by exalting village life. The writings attempted to reproduce the real condition of sidelined citizens in a postcolonial context of despair; for these writers—"the modern progressives," as the regionalists were often known—the village as a site of modernity, social experiment, and potentiality had been dismantled, and that hazy space had been hardened into something else.

ANCHALIKTA AND THE ROMANCE OF THE FOLK SONG

In his introduction to *Maila anchal*, Renu writes, "I consider this particular village of this particular region a symbol of many backward villages, and from this I have constructed the space of the novel" (*The Soiled Border* 1).[6] I focus on the text here as one instantiation—the most powerful, in fact—of *anchalik sahitya*, which produced almost no other texts of national or international repute. *Maila anchal* has thus maintained its standing as one of the preeminent representations of rural life.[7] Situated in a village in the Purnea district of Bihar, the novel takes as its object the various communities that inhabit Maryganj. Each caste/community offers up a significant figure: the *tahsildar* (tax collector), a Kayastha by caste; his unmarried daughter Kamli; Baldev, the Vaishnava Congressite who loves Laxmi, the *dasin* (temple servant) of the Kabirpanth; Kalicharan, the socialist who has emerged as one leader of the Yadavs; Ramkirpal Singh, the Rajput; and the tribal Santhals. Distributed among caste, political affiliation, class, status, and language, the narrative shifts among these various actors and follows several interlocking plots: love between Kamli and the doctor, between the Ojha and Phuliya, the struggle for political power between the Rajputs and the Kayasthas, and the factionalism that Congressites, Hindutvawadis, Socialists, and Communists introduce into the village. The novel thus succeeds in illuminating the crisis of nationalism from a localist perspective. That interweaving narrative structure becomes one powerful mode of constructing the literary village, via the equal weighing of various interests, each signaled prominently by particular strains of dialect. Katherine Hansen reads in this heteroglossia a sense of nonlinear storytelling, "antiindividualist history" and "indigenous time" (Hansen, "Renu's Regionalism" 290). Anand Prakash characterizes this panopoly as "a code, a critique, and a medium" (Prakash 16).[8] The polyvalent, polyphonic, multil`ayered aspects of the novel were responsible both for its reputation for radical innovation as well as its literary disgrace: if it was layered, complex, and polyglossic, it was also plotless, heroless, and backwards in terms of literary language.[9] The linguistic and narrative requirements of *anchalikta* had very clear structural consequences for the text. Alongside modernist avant garde literary movements like *nayi kavita* (new poetry), regionalism had to legitimate its very claims to the literary sphere. The singular feature of this novel that is responsible for its literariness, and can thus legitimate its claims to the literary sphere, is its narrative framework—the doctor's expedition.

The driving force that inaugurates and in effect *produces* the novel and the village as its subject is the arrival of the doctor in the village. An orphan raised along the border of Nepal who becomes a physician in the urban center of Bihar, Dr. Prashant is of questionable caste and class status and is therefore identified as an intellectual through his training and his scientific rationalism. As a harbinger of realist, semirealist, and also secular romantic values, the doctor rescues the novel's rural regionalism from a formal identification with folk genres and popular cultural forms. He is the reader's counterpart within the text; it is his gaze that we follow. The doctor's interest in the very foreign spectacle of local culture, for example, justifies the textual reproduction of the Vidhyapat dance drama, a regional folk form that Baldev and other locals dismiss as crass. Anand Prakash writes that it is the doctor who "disturbs the cultural equanimity and the ideological self-assurance of the village," which, we are to understand, was at equilibrium prior to the textual intervention of the doctor, or novelist (9).

I would like to suggest that the most noteworthy feature of *Maila anchal*, and Renu's oeuvre at large, particularly in the context of a discussion of contemporary Dalit realism, is the use of the folk song. This feature of Renu's work—his incorporation of Maithili legend and song, Vidhyapat dance drama, the Holi songs sung by the women, and the sowing songs sung by farmers—is one of the most important outcomes of the evidentiary logic of the *anchalik upanyas*, and is almost single-handedly responsible for the overwhelming sense of nostalgia in his novels and short stories. In the famous story, "Tisri Kasam," ("The Third Vow"), a cart driver takes a woman who works for a theater company to the village of her next performance. Along the way, he tells the story of Mahua Ghatvarin, the fisher girl with the evil stepmother, who is sold to a local merchant and loved by his servant.

This narrative song becomes the driving metaphor of the story—the cart driver likens himself to the servant; the woman likens herself to the fisher girl. "Twenty years or so ago, performers of the Bideshiya, Balvahi, and Chokra dance dramas knew all types of songs—*ghazals*, and *khemtas*. Nowadays people listened to strange tunes that blasted from loud-speakers. Ah, the good old days! . . . Where had those days gone?" he laments (Renu, *The Third Vow* 60). Mridangiya, the drummer of Renu's story "Rasapriya" (collected in *Racnavali*) evokes a similar sentiment: "In the rising afternoon, workers in the field no longer even sing songs. Who knows if soon even the koyal will forget his song?" (127). In these stories, characters become mouthpieces for nostalgia, loss, and a preemptive project of recovery. This was one of the major accomplishments of *anchalik sahitya*: to produce, in the nationalist spirit, a traditional India, but also to locate what was traditional in traditional *culture* more specifically. This "required"— in the various and elusive forms of artistic constraint—an emphasis on artisan communities and farmers, singers, dancers, potters, etc.— almost all of whom were Shudras who, in their embrace of Ram, Sita, and other pan-Hindu figures, qualified as different and yet nationally representative. When and why does the work of the novel become the recovery of tradition via the translation of certain cultural products? And what does it mean for those cultural products to be read as vehicles for nostalgia?

In many respects, Renu's *Maila anchal* diverges dramatically from Premchand's *Godaan*—the model of the implied sympathetic-but-guilty reader so well deconstructed by Alok Rai doesn't obtain. *Maila anchal* does not produce the in-depth characterization that leads to readerly sympathy; it moves among several plots rather than investing in a few singular protagonists. This is one of the typical criticisms of regional literature, which does not work within a model of the individual transcendence of certain finite social conditions.[10] It therefore seems to potentially challenge the discourse of pity and the concomitant liberal-reformist model discussed in chapter 1. Unlike the body of work described as "progressive," the adjective most often used to describe Renu's oeuvre is "experiential." What this typically means is that it is driven less by authorial commentary than by observation—a type of naturalism, in effect, where naturalism indicates not the elevation of description but a certain use of language.[11] Critic Shivakumar Mishra, for example, objects to the characterization of Renu as a realist tout court. In an insightful Lukácsian analysis in which Premchand is the preeminent example of *yatharthvad* (realism), Mishra claims that the *anchalik*s cannot be Premchand's legitimate heirs because they are naturalists, committed to the introduction and observation of the new and the strange.

Naturalism, in the context of rural regionalism, is not an idle term; it is clearly related to an abstract nature, the documentation of which is one project of this genre. Nagarjun's work, for example, is replete with untranslatable species of indigenous fish and plant life, and occasionally its preservation. In the ideological commitment to the everyday as well, naturalism is an apposite term for rural realism, the aesthetic justification for the mundane aspects of peasant life.[12] After elaborating on the peasant economy, whereby the whole year's earning is produced during two months of threshing and goes towards the fulfillment of previously incurred debts, the narrator of *Maila anchal* points out, "The cycle would go on from harvest. Oxen were used to separate grain from straw on the threshing ground; oxen with muzzles on their mouths. The peasants' condition was just like that of those oxen.... Their mouths, too, were muzzled.... Ah, but still the magic of threshing season! That couldn't be broken" (*The Soiled Border* 76; ellipses in the original). Let me first point out that this is an atypical passage; the novel much prefers dialogue and narrative to rousing description such as this. But the passage is such a powerful indication of the dueling mandates inherited by the text that it is worthy of discussion. A fragile ellipsis unites the imperatives of rural realism with a musing romanticism.[13] Magic here is a code; it evokes not only romanticism and nostalgia but also a critique of rationalism and the relentless march of the electoral, bureaucratic, and financial—i.e., soul-crushing apparatus indicated by political modernity. The condition of the peasant is subordinate to the "magic of the threshing season," a magic in which the *entire village* participates. And herein lies the complication: the exaltation of the village requires a revindication of certain basic tenets of humanism. The brief focus on the plight of the thresher functions as an opening by which we are introduced to the ballads of Lorik and Bijaybhan.[14] For the condition of the peasant to be narratively subservient to the preservation of culture suggests a certain kind of reading of the subaltern. Although the mouths of the peasants are muzzled, the "magic" of the season is located in the land and the specifically oral culture emanating from the muzzled mouth. It would be easy to dismiss Renu and the regionalists as simply not radical enough, particularly in the space of an anachronistic

Dalit critique. But what is necessary here is a rereading of not only the historical limitations of *anchalik* literature, but its privileging of certain locations of culture. A novel such as *Maila anchal* celebrates lowercaste cultural forms not exactly at the expense of the peasant, but *as* the peasant.

The focus on the folk song is not idle, I would argue, because rather than an abstract indication of intertextuality, it has the potential to indicate a radically different epistemology.[15] If we take the folk song as a trope of a world-view that has historically eluded the novel (communitarian, anti-individualist, provincial, regionalist, oral, vernacular), then its inclusion in the regional novel certainly performs an intervention of sorts, what D. R. Nagaraj would call that of "lowercaste cosmologies" (65). The question, of course, is of what the novel, or rural realism, does with such a "text." Rajendra Awasthi's 1976 *Jangal ke phool* is illustrative in this respect, as a kind of synecdochal offshoot of a novel like *Maila anchal*. Although the novel does not take the village site as its object, it performs a similar set of functions: the elaboration of a particular community (Gond) and their unique practices (*ghotul*), the reification of their cultural traditions (tribal music, marriage ceremonies), all in the context of the national struggle. The central conflict in the text is the struggle among British revenue officers, tribal communities of Bastar (located in present-day Chattisgarh), and the rulers of the princely state of Jagdalpur. When the tribe prevents the death of a British officer embroiled in a local conflict, they are "gifted" a tract of land and given lease papers. A fierce discussion ensues at the meeting of the tribal council. "This land belongs to us! These jungles belong to us. The hole of this earth belongs to us. The Lingo, who made this earth, has made us too. Who is this Tehsildar to gift away two acres of land?" (Awasthi, *Jangal* 47). By now a familiar narrative of tribal exploitation and resistance emerges, one that takes its place alongside the better-known modes of anticolonialism. *Jangal ke phool* is a moving text that underlines subaltern contributions to the project of nationhood as well as its resistance to cultural hegemony. But the initial section of the novel is grounded in what can only categorized as romanticized ethnographic description.[16] Although there should be no easy conflation between the peasant and the tribal, there is a certain fluidity in their textual manifestations by *anchalik* writers, whereby the tribal may become another example of a marginal particularism that requires specialized ethnographic attention.[17] *Ghot*, the social practice by which young women choose their partners, for example, presents an opportunity for the narrator to exalt the freedom to love and to describe arranged marriage as bondage. While reveling in the beauty of the landscape, the novel functions on the premise of cultural difference. Gonds worship these gods, they perform these rites, they have these forms of self-governance, these notions of property. The act of translation of these cultural practices is performed by the native informants (in this case, Kartami the Gond peon) as well as the native attendant to the British officials (who describes the Gonds as "primitive")—both of whom are compounded by the narrator. The stability of the viewer, the narrator, and the reader, from whom the Gonds must necessarily be distinct, is in effect taken for granted. And the tribal song, in this text, plays a crucial role in cementing that difference, emerging in the very first paragraph of the novel, with onomatopoeic subversion, and again throughout the text. The reproduction of sound and verse, in particular, bridges the gap between representation and transcription, and affords the novel particular ethnographic privileges. I am going to refer to this intellectual operation as "knowledge by transcription"; it is in transcription that the rural realism of *anchalikta* appears most effective. Transcription is borne out of an ethnographic desire, but it seeks to deny the literary framework of its impulse. Within a novelistic space, transcription alternates with aspiration, romanticism, fascination, embellishment, and utopia. But the work of the text is also in the constitution of certain particular moments as "transcriptive," in the persuasion that transcription is the preeminent mode of knowing the other. *Jangal ke phool* thus presents a more dramatic version of *Maila anchal* in articulating regional difference and highlighting it via the cultural artifact, but also in cementing the normativity of an urban, elite, uppercaste readership, even while the broader project of *anchalik sahitya* was clearly to destabilize it via a pedagogy of the rural. To transcribe thus ensured that culture was located within a quantifiable retrievable product rather than within the ephemeral space of action.

"IT IS NOT ENOUGH TO REUNITE WITH THE PEOPLE IN A PAST WHERE THEY NO LONGER EXIST"

What I would like to suggest, as I continue to trace an antigenealogy for Dalit literature, is that it will offer us a different theory of culture than that proffered by rural realism. I turn to Franz Fanon's analysis of national culture in order to better read the ideological impulses of *anchalikta*, one locus of a reconstructed Dalit critique. In the search for a palpable sense of historicity, one dramatic failing of the colonial and postcolonial native intelligentsia is its misguided desire to recover the past.[18] In the chapter "On National Culture" (in *The Wretched of the Earth*) Fanon bemoans the desperation of the intellectual, living in another language for so long, compelled, Fanon writes disdainfully, to "unite with the people" (158). But in the realm of art and artistic production this historical moment produces a distinct epistemological crisis. "The colonized intellectual ... is content to cloak these instruments in a style that is meant to be national but which is strangely reminiscent of exoticism. The intellectual who returns to his people through works of art behaves in fact like a foreigner" (160). After independence, the translation of this desire confines him to "the detritus of social thought, external appearances, relics, and knowledge frozen in time ... a point-by-point representation of national reality which is flat, untroubled, motionless, reminiscent of death rather than life" (161). This intellectual plunge into a working-class tribal or peasant culture produces "an inventory of particularisms," "a visible veneer," "stereotyping details" (161). "Culture," Fanon writes, "rarely has the translucency of custom" (159). Fanon's analysis functions as a critique of the hollowness of negritude, which he saw as an ideological dead end, as well as a critique of the social position of the Leninist intellectual, who can only speak "for" the people. While this move "backwards" was a necessary dialectical response to the falsehoods of colonial historiography, it was based on a distorted and essentially bourgeois notion of recovery that would eventually require revision. But the beauty of this analysis lies in the collation of a series of interlocking terms: people, culture, detail, custom. This is an inverted ossification by which the abstraction of the "people" is gradually read in the particularisms of custom.

Though specific to the condition of the postcolonial African intellectual caught in a backward glance while attempting to shake off the cultural origins of the petty bourgeoisie, Fanon's analysis is relevant to us particularly in its insightful reading of the intellectual operations that are not only characteristic of but indeed productive of literary movements. That "inventory of particularisms," for example, must be traced to a desire for a comprehensive source of ethnographic knowledge, necessary at historical moments as varied as that of anticolonial culturalist agitation, and postindependence national inventory. In the context of the regional writers, the employment of the "backward glance" might also be read as a sideways peering; in *anchalikta* the village emerges as the site of that past, and culture is read in terms of transportable artifacts worthy of documentation, categorization, and analysis. And while *anchalikta* accomplished a considerable expansion of the literary sphere, both thematically and linguistically, this expansion also had the effect of allowing us to read culture as a product rather than a fluid, multifarious, and malleable process—something *anchalikta* shares with a certain strain of colonialist anthropology. In Renu's *Maila anchal*, for example, there is a significant detailing of the rise of Kalicharan and the Socialists, or Baldev's Gandhianism and the newly established Handloom Center in the village. The struggle for the ideological heart of the village, represented by the various conflicts between political parties, is one of the central anchors of the text and a large part of the novel is concerned with the microscopic localisms that foil these political communities. But the novel itself doesn't read these as "cultural" processes. By this I mean that the moments of resistance of the village to various forms of political modernity are indeed cultural, though they don't appear that way. For example, the wrangle over the succession of the religious leadership in the Kabir temple, a debate that has a long lineage in the history of the village, actually prefigures the downfall of Baldev, the Congressite leader (Renu, *The Soiled Border* 98). Similarly, when the socialist leader Kalicharan intervenes in a decision that has been imposed from above to install in the temple a *mahant* (spiritual leader) from another region of Bihar, he does so by introducing the document, the vote, and the principle of localized administration. These precedents of Maryganj actually set the stage for a particular reception of the Socialists or the Congress Party and they form the basis of a legitimate political culture. But culture, in the novel, is read differently. The Holi song, with its unusual meter, is the perfect local emblem of an indigeneity, desirable precisely for a particularism that is ethnic, linguistic, and cultural, a particularism that prefigures to some extent the rise of Dalit literature and the sociopolitical critique that it presents.

Foregrounding the folk cultural product, even those folk genres that clearly engage with the problems of contemporary politics, is only one means of knowing and representing "the people"—"knowledge by transcription." But the making of politics in the novel, and a political culture in the text, takes many forms, particularly when it remains uncompromised by a penetrating narrative voice. To take one example from a conversation between the Brahmin *pandit* and various inhabitants of the village:

> "When two buffaloes fight, the grass beneath them gets crushed. The Congress and Socialist Parties are fighting with each other. Both of them are seeking new members. The poor people will be ground between the two grindstones."
> "No the poor people won't be crushed. In fact they'll benefit," was someone's reply.
> "Things aren't accomplished by one party alone. It is the competition and rivalry between two groups that benefits the public. It's like that time when some dancers came from another village to the Rautahat Fair. They danced half-heartedly, and not a song they sang was well done. But on the third day of the fair, a group of Balvahi dancers arrived, and the two groups challenged each other to a contest. . . . They sang an incredible number of *ghazals, kawwali, khemtas* and *dadra*, and both groups kept right on dancing until dawn." (Renu, *The Soiled Border* 129)

This conversation goes unattributed, as does a significant portion of the dialogue in this text, distributed among various anonymous villagers. This is in and of itself a significant point as it indicates that the only character that this dialogue is responsible for constructing is that of the village itself. The creation of the village as a character or a unity is one problematic feature of *anchalik* literature that will later be deconstructed by Dalit texts. As D. R. Nagaraj writes, "Non-Dalit society desperately tries to keep intact the construct of the unified village and they do so by invoking and using the cherished ideals of 'harmony and brotherhood'" (37). But this moment also clearly indicates one powerful hermeneutic of culture. The analysis of whether or not contemporary votebank politics will offer some benefits to the villagers is clearly indigenized and localized. A Fanonian analysis would insist that it is the abolition of *zamindari*, and the struggle for political hegemony on behalf of the various electoral contingents that is the real culture-making agent of the text. Here, the *khemta* and the *dadra—untranscribed—*serve an entirely different function. They are pedagogical—in their very form—without being objectified.

What kind of theory of culture does *anchalikta* present us with? For Renu, culture meant folk culture, and folk culture was politicized—particularly during times of crisis—but not necessarily an act of politics; it was expressive of an indigenist spirit that connoted difference. If the Kisan Sabha (Peasant Union) and the Handloom Center are acknowledged to be the kinds of political activity that *signify* modernity and produce a modern subjectivity, then the village is preemptively foreclosed from that kind of cultural sensibility. The rural, or regional, realists were thus working with the village as a translatable object, one to which the novel provides a kind of unmediated access, and the transcription of the folk song plays an important role in its readability. Juxtaposed with the political wrangling that occupies the major portion of the text is the folk "text"—containable, insertable. Intertextuality—and formal intertextuality—specifically the mingling of the folk and the novelistic, the oral and the literary, serves in this case to reify a certain cultural difference rather than emphasize its continuities. Fanon, again, writes, "The educated circles go ecstatic over such careful renditions of truth, but we have every right to ask ourselves whether this truth is real, whether in fact it is not outmoded, irrelevant, or called into question by the heroic saga of the people hacking their way into history" (162). In the name of totality, the hackers are displaced as the central object of rural realism. The second section of this chapter will deal with hacking—the historical eruption—and the question of Dalit literature.

HACKING INTO HISTORY

I begin here with three citations that will anchor this discussion of the Dalit text.

> A national culture is not a folklore, not an abstract populism that believes it can discover the people's true nature. It is not made up of the inert dregs of gratuitous actions, that is to say actions which are less and less attached to the ever-present reality of the people. A national culture is the whole body of efforts made by a people in the sphere of thought to describe, justify, and praise the action through which that people has created itself and keeps itself in existence.
> (Fanon, *The Wretched of the Earth* 168)

A discussion of national culture may seem like an anachronism in any discussion of Dalit particularism, casteism, or essentialism but it allows us to better apprehend their origins, all of which begin with the national's prototypical theoretical unit: the village. "What is the village but a sink of localism, a den of ignorance, narrow-mindedness and communalism?" (Ambedkar quoted in Guha, *India* 107). A Dalit literary critique of the village as a site can only be understood within the context of an Ambedkarite critique; as D. R.

Nagaraj writes, "Ambedkar rejected the village as the basic unit of justice" (31).

In contrast to *anchalik sahitya*, Dalit fiction in Hindi and in other vernacular tongues, presumably, is devoid of nostalgia, glorification of tradition, and the ideological bent that underlines a project of recovery. Less obviously, its ethnographic detailing of traditional caste practices often illustrates its apartness, its inability, as well as lack of desire, to qualify as national. The few celebrations of Dalit culture in the mode of Negritude focus on cultural products and practices like music and dance only rarely, and more often on egalitarian social interactions and modes of resistance, as befits a protest literature.[19] Committed to exposing the underbelly of Brahminical domination, Dalit fiction has spent comparatively less energy, it seems counterintuitive to say, turning its representational gaze on itself. The production of a "Dalit experience" has thus necessarily produced a rereading of uppercaste culture. This has required a careful attention to the space of the village as an entity that, in the intervening fifty years since *Maila anchal*, has clearly transformed into something unrecognizable, even impossible, literarily, in the Renuvian sense. In "The Disappearance of the Village," Nagaraj writes,

> When terror and violence are released against Dalits, a very fundamental question surfaces: does it mean the disappearance of the village as a distinct emotional entity? The answer is yes, but it will have to be qualified a great deal. The old village seen as the expression of consensus and indirect coercion is certainly dead because a significant section of its structure has said a firm goodbye to the old constitutive rules. (*Flaming Feet* 39)

The fictions perpetuated by rural realism are no longer tenable.

I am going to consider the site of the village and the production of a Dalit theory of culture by discussing a short story written by Mohandas Naimishraya entitled "Apna gav" ("Our Village"), published in 1999.[20] Naimishraya, like Omprakash Valmiki, is a well-known and prolific author, widely respected in Hindi Dalit literary circles, and anthologized routinely.[21] He has also been particularly influential in the construction and articulation of a Dalit literary history, creating a genealogy for Dalit literature in the pre-Ambedkarite period, unearthing lesser-known untouchable caste poets, and other crucial figures of the Dalit movement in the North. In the story "Apna gav," Chamiya, a young woman, is disrobed and paraded naked through the village by the local *thakur*. She is being punished for refusing to work in his home (i.e., to consent to sexual relations with him) in repayment for the debt owed to him by her husband. In a miserable flashback that appears after she comes home to the shamed faces of her family, who have been completely powerless to help her, she recalls a chance meeting in the forest with another woman who was also there collecting firewood. The woman, having learned that Chamiya's husband has left for the city after taking a loan from the *thakur*, reveals to her the way that this debt will be paid. She, too, it seems, was forced to repay a debt in this way. This foreknowledge doesn't help our protagonist; she is determined to maintain her sovereignty when the *thakur* calls. But a kind of perverse tradition emerges, a secret knowledge that has trickled down to the present generation. We learn, for example, that this is why young women in the village, girls actually, are married and sent to their in-laws at a young age—in order to avoid the lecherous landlords. The origin of this tradition is clearly entirely different from the uppercaste genealogy of child marriage, structured around the cult of virginity.[22] In this case, the families of the Dalit community in the village fear not only the loss of virginity but rape. When, towards the end of the story, it is revealed that Chamiya's father-in-law's wife, and perhaps even her grandfather-in-law's wife, suffered similar assaults, the Chamar community decides to abandon the village. Without any sense of irony, the community dislocates and moves on, in an attempt to undo this most recent tragedy and its potential repetition. The exodus is here articulating a demand for justice that cannot be obtained in the village.

There is a tradition being archived in this story, passed down, continuous and abhorrent. The *thakur*, for example, uses the incident to educate his sons in debauchery; his eldest is known in the village for the same ferocity that characterizes his father. And the story works with tropes of discovery, revelation, and detail that are metanarratively similar to *anchalikta*. But this is not a tradition worthy of nostalgia. The utopian conclusion, the decision to walk away, is an attempt to *erase* the past rather than to preserve it. And culture here is inspired by a Fanonian sensibility; it is less a product than a process, difficult to isolate and transcribe. Fanon writes compellingly, "It is not enough to reunite with the people in a past where they no longer exist. . . . National culture is no folklore where an abstract populism is convinced it has uncovered the popular truth. It is not some congealed mass of noble gestures, in other words less and less connected with the reality of the people" (168). With the exception of the word "national," this analysis is particularly relevant in the Dalit context, which seeks to embrace modernity by advocating a clear cultural break with the past rather than a reification of it. Naimishraya's story would thus challenge the typically romanticized connotations of tradition, folk, and culture in order to present the naked power differential that in fact produces the folk song, the dance drama and other cultural forms, separated not by privilege but by segregation. The tradition to which Chamiya is subject is its necessary corollary. That is to say, not only is the "folk" as a category organized by caste, and therefore subject to deconstruction by contemporary Dalit writers, but its difference, particularism, and localism is ensured by the same conditions that generate atrocity.

What produces the literary impetus in "Apna gav"? By this I mean, how could we derive the source of its fictional drive? In *Maila anchal*, it is the arrival of the doctor and the malaria clinic that make the village an object of literary analysis: the doctor, his romantic gaze, his benevolence, puts the village on the literary and figural map. In "Apna gav," too, an outsider comes to the village—a journalist arrives to investigate the aforementioned incident. Dressed in Western clothes and smoking a cigarette, she is an object of fascination for Chamiya's family. The journalist—i.e., the foreign intellectual—comes too late to the scene, and doesn't have the necessary analytic skills to properly transcribe the incident. She fails to do justice to the victim and the community, a commentary on the complicated politics of viewership the text interrogates. This incident is embedded in the story, however, and not its driving force. It is the atrocity that demands narrative articulation that directs the course of events in the text.[23] Finally, it is the marvel of village exodus, an unprecedented act of resistance, which requires retelling. And this utopianism is distinct from its Gandhian counterpart, which saw the village as a site of reformist potential. "Utopias," writes Nagaraj, "carry helplessness in their very interstices and Gandhiji could escape the inherent powerlessness of utopian projects by offering the village as a form of life that could be retrieved from the dark sewage of history" (39). In other words, Gandhi's vision of the village was unsustainable, revealing the desperation behind the utopian vision; Dalit exodus is a testament to this. But the Ambedkarite vision of Naimishraya's text is deliberately nonreformist and moves towards the new rather than revising the old. "Apna gav"—"our village"—is thus both critique and utopia. In the early part of the text the question that is raised is: Is this our village? And in the latter part, with the founding of a new settlement near a stone quarry, the answer has become: *this* is "our village."

Exodus, utopia, and even nomadism are all terms that carry within themselves a certain sense of dire possibility, which may help us properly theorize the Dalit text. Firstly, in the context of modern India, any discussion of exodus would conjure the specter of Partition migrations; this exodus might then once again register a casteist disassociation from the national, a politics that surfaces in almost every text discussed here. But self-exile is also a complex sociological revision of being outcaste, "cast[e] out"; it speaks to a material and metanarrative politics of segregation.[24] The utopianism of this gesture is therefore distinct from any vision of technological futurism and classless society but rather speaks to a place of castelessness. That is to say, the vision that I am characterizing as exodic and utopian is particular for being not urban—an eminently possible trope—but rather rural, a settlement a short distance from "apna gav," and its distinguishing feature is not the anonymity of urban India but a different kind of "castelessness." It is made transformative only by its affective vision. Utopia here would seem to be distinct from the Jamesonian version, taken from modern American science fiction and Russian futurism, where "the effort to imagine utopia ends up betraying the impossibility of doing so" (Jameson, "Progress" 153). The realpolitik vision of the entire text (derived, incidentally, from a real incident that took place in a village outside of Allahabad), the various potential solutions to this crisis that are then discarded (Burn the *thakur*'s fields? Abduct his women? Leave for the city?), all demand that the utopian be read as realist. And yet, the abrupt conclusion of the story, which ends before the hard labor of the establishment of a new community, is what also characterizes its utopian vision: the text concludes with an idea, one that most readers would only see as an impossible romanticism.[25] The carving out of a separate space, one not coerced through casteized segregation, is the crucial element of any utopian vision, but it isn't given narrative elaboration, or, in other words, narrative time.

What then is the relationship between the village of Naimishraya's story "Apna gav" and the village of the *anchalik sahitya* writers? In the Dalit story, there is a binary logic of a war between Dalits and the landowning caste. In *Maila anchal* there is vast complexity of competing interests and ownerships. In the Dalit story, the Chamar is at the edge of destitution—there is no interest in the politics of landless labor and ownerships, while Renu's novel allots equal space to several conflicts, earmarked by song. There is a vast ideological gap between these two villages and between their respective politics of representation. In Renu's story "Rasapriya," for example, Mridangiya the drummer suffers an insult when he is forced to conceal his caste. But this detail receives one line in the story, which is largely concerned with the lost tradition of the Rasapriya song. The construction of Mridangiya the drummer might be read as an elaborate narrative structure, in the Russian formalist sense, designed to valorize Rasapriya. More importantly, the caste structure that would produce nonhegemonic, countercultural, and little-recognized musical traditions is simply unreadable in the text. We have reached the realm of myth, in fact, and it is only an urban critical establishment that could characterize this mythicism as rural or regional "realism."

Dalit literature is of course necessarily weighted towards the representation of certain castes. But this has also required a dismantling of the ethnographic gaze, and its reign of romantic "objectivity."[26] The particular form that Dalit literature has taken, then, must be read as a critique of the problem of totality that rural realism aims to recuperate. This has consequently produced certain forms of narration and like other literatures of modernity, Dalit fiction has been influential in deconstructing fictions of omniscience and shifting narrative power elsewhere. To take one example: in Jai Prakash Kardam's 1994 novel *Chappar (Roof)*, the narrator is a young Dalit student living on the outskirts of an urban center.[27] The novel actually follows the oscillating structure of Premchand's *Godaan*, as discussed in chapter 1, moving back and forth between the lives of the parents, Dalit landless peasants in the village, and their son, a student living in a *chawl* (tenement building). But the ethnographic lens that the novel employs is not that of an impartial, distantiated observer-intellectual, but the son himself, and its object is the slum dweller, the city folk, who are subject to his social critique. Reversing the trajectory of the intellectual who brings enlightenment to the village, a crucial trope in the development of the novel, Chandan moves to the city, and "sees" with new eyes. What he finds is that misery is distributed evenly between the village and the city but it takes new forms: the cruelty of the *zamindar* has been replaced by the swears of the *malik* (boss).

> The people living in the shantytowns had none of the self-seeking individualism of the middle classes, neither their professional attitude

A Perfect Whole

> that was typically coupled with cunning. Their passions extended only to song and music. It could be said, though, that they were outside the major currents of life, tossed around by it, barely hanging on. Social changes, the country's happenings: they had no knowledge of these things and no interest in them. From morning until evening, back-breaking labor, at night, exhausted, a bit of something to eat then falling to bed, only to awake and once again work in order to secure the most basic necessities. Their entire lives were caught in this maze. (Kardam 16)

Chandan's meditation on the life of the *chawl* dweller is reminiscent of the nineteenth-century bourgeois novel, in its knowing psychosocial reading that establishes Chandan's fitness to properly narrate. Moving from ethnographic realism to romanticism to social critique, Chandan-as-narrator adopts a range of positions throughout the novel. And despite the bifurcated structure of the text, it is his secular materialist vision that predominates. Take, for example, this flashback to the moment when Sukha, Chandan's father, is accosted by Pandit Kanaram for permitting his son to go to the city to study. Our narrator supplies Pandit's vital details.

> The priesthood was his hereditary profession, so Kanaram learned a few things that way. He even memorized a few Sanskrit *shlokas*. After his father's death he decided to make a living in the same way—what else could he do? He wasn't very educated, and couldn't find a job, and physical labor or any other type of work was out of the question—because he was a Brahmin, this was a question of self-respect. Had he been born into any other caste he surely would have died of hunger, this Pandit Kanaram, but thanks to India's social arrangement a Brahmin can never die of hunger. From his birth to his death, the Brahmin finds a way to collect his taxes. (Kardam 35)

This analysis should be described as a materialist critique of caste (distinct from a Marxist one) and it makes of the narrator a rationalist, postcaste observer. Apart from the nuances of the nature of this focalization, is of course, its very fact; the narrative power of the gaze is one analytic that a Lacanian-influenced postcolonial theory has bequeathed to us. Fanon, for example, would argue that looking, in and of itself, connotes and incurs a certain power. A narrative that gives the Dalit observer the power of social critique, and crucially, *a reformist gaze*, advocates a basic subalternist vision: there are certain things that only some can see. We must note, for example, that *this* narrator-observer does not seem to be interested in the aforementioned song and music.

But there is one moment when the narrator's materialist resolve breaks; after an exhausting day, he sits in one corner of the slum to hear the nightly music going on outside. This is what he observes:

> Even when these people sang *raag-raagini*, they had their own distinct style. When a singer sang with complete passion and rhythm, he did so with one hand on his ear, and the other gesturing to the people. As he picked up the speed of the song, his style became more effusive. And with the rhythm of the song, his hand would rise above his head, or fall to his chest. In those moments he seemed as small as one who had scaled the lofty peaks of mountains. As his voice rose with fervor, his hands and head too rose; as the song came down its slope and its rhythm became more faint, his hands and head would bow down. And sometimes while singing, he would make dancing gestures—his entire body moved with the rhythm of the song, bent double, his forehead kissing the ground. (Kardam 36)

I would suggest that this narrator's interest in song and the cultural artifact is entirely distinct from that of the *anchalik*s, which functioned in the service of an ethnographic project of recovery. Firstly, and most apparently, there is no transcription; this viewer is not interested in the *content* of the song, but in its affect and the transient world of bodily gesture. The reader's eye is geared towards the performance, and all those affective qualities that are effectively unpreservable. That is not to say that the perspective here doesn't do ethnographic work, or is disinterested; it is clearly very romantic. And yet, Chandan's vision is determinedly presentist and antirevelatory; his observations tell little about the particular community of slum dwellers, or their "culture." The impulse to describe the way "these people" sing, in other words, is born not from a desire to transcribe the folk, but from a different ideology.[28]

We must then ask: Why would a modern realist text be interested in the form rather than the content of the song? It is true that Chandan's materialist and secularist vision could never allow for the kind of orientalist gaze exhibited by earlier readers of the social other, simply because culture itself can not do that kind of signifying work, and cannot occupy that kind of ideological power. The modernizing impulse of the Dalit text is such that one is required to leave behind all forms of stigmatized culture rather than to reify them; knowledge by transcription becomes obsolete.[29] Should this then be read as an attempt to disavow casteized forms of knowledge and culture? I would suggest, rather, that Dalit realism lays claim to a different kind of referentiality in that it steers from the archivable, transcribable, and factually knowable in favor of those fleeting affective realities that have been historically underserved, made impossible, by the category of the literary. To take Gayatri Spivak's point, "sometimes the basis of a truth claim is no more than a trope" (*Critique of Postcolonial Reason* 147). Naturalist knowledge is appropriate for obsolescence, for that which may soon become extinct, but for the culture in flux—i.e., the putative "identification" of the Dalit community/individual—naturalism falls short. The work of Naimishraya and Kardam thus present us with two narratives of village exodus that disobey the rules of regional realism: one is a narrative of rationalist individualist self-fulfillment, the other of a communitarian utopianism. The village as an intellectual site can only become the repository of certain sufferings and it is with its abandonment that Dalit literary narrative begins.

REALISM AND REVELATION

Regionalism, like provincialism in the English novel, was not without its critics. Mohan Rakesh, a modernist novelist and playwright as well as a seminal figure of the *nayi kahani* movement, argued that village life should not be glorified because urban centers were the true sites of progress. Other critics attempted to read the urban-rural divide differently, justifying the exclusion of urban content and the more generalizeable downtrodden, from *anchalikta*: "Urban life is different from regional life with its purity and simplicity, and is full of filth and complexity, therefore its presentation is not acceptable to us as regional" (Yadav 5). While the word *anchal*, means "region," the related *aanchal* literally refers to the sari border, specifically the portion that covers a woman's breast. As such it is responsible for a number of associations with femininity, proper behavior, and motherhood. *Anchalik* as regional, therefore, connotes several things, not least a particular type of region—marginalized, impoverished, and primitive, certainly, but also pure, clean, and nourishing. The word *maila* means "dirty" or "soiled," but has less literal connotations: polluted, foul, offensive.[30] The final lines of Renu's novel reiterate a loose association between the *aanchal* of Mother India, and the village that is her truest representative. The notion of the village as a distillation of purity and simplicity harbored by regional realism would necessarily be revised by Dalit literature.

The contestation over the imaginative boundaries of *anchalik sahitya* suggests that one genealogy for the movement was a kind of fight for possession: What is the village? And who has a right to determine its "content"? David Ludden mentions the success with which the Bengal *bhadralok* projected their cultural identity over agrarian Bengal (216). Via the novels of Bankimchandra, the rural heartland was viewed through the cultural lens of the *zamindar*. There is a certain vantage point, therefore, that has helped to produce the aforementioned comment regarding purity, drawing on a long tradition of the peasant as simple, hardworking, and benighted; the village is the home that produces such a figure, cultivated under the shadow of the regal, crafty *zamindar*. Kannada novelist A. R. Ananthamurthy wonders if "the authentic Indian peasant who relates to nature organically" is himself not an "imported cult figure of the western radicals who are reacting against their materialistic civilization" (quoted in Mukherjee, *Realism* 156). No one, then, who equated the village with the *baniya* (merchants) or the caste *panchayat* (council) would write of it as the home of the pure and the simple. But putting the peasant at the center of the village narrative economy, with the folk song as his cultural product, has produced contradictory outcomes: a reading whereby the prototypical villager is to be read, pitied, and analyzed by the knowing narrator—a mode shared by many *anchalik* texts—as well as a reading that demands nostalgic recovery. In *Maila anchal*, two voices dominate: that of the narrator, who does the complicated analytical work necessary for readerly comprehension, and the doctor, the outsider whose life is charmed, enriched, and challenged by the villagers in his drive to cure malaria. Between these two figures, narrative labor is divided; the liberal doctor uplifts and gleans, the narrator pities and explains. "The villagers didn't understand even the basic principles of economics. They were overjoyed that the price of grain was going up, and better yet, the value of jute was on the rise!" says the narrator, who then reminds us that "people were going half-naked, for lack of clothing" (Renu, *The Soiled Border* 124–25). And the doctor, who forcibly vaccinates his patients with the help of socialist party thugs, inevitably falls in love with the village headman's daughter and the village culture that produces her. The crisis of these texts, that which spurs the nostalgia, romanticism, and exoticism that often mark them, is that of modernity, which inevitably means loss rather than progress.[31]

Juxtaposing Dalit texts with the rural realism of *anchalikta* thus demonstrates certain gaps in the realist imaginary, particularly in its reading of the village, the scheduled caste, and the indigenous tribe, but also explains certain formal tendencies of Dalit realism. *Anchalikta* emerges as a powerful means by which to articulate difference and to contest nationalist hegemony, whereby the region is only loosely yoked to the nation, but it betrays the drive towards ethnographic recovery and containment that is a crucial feature of the literary progressivism. The ethnographic gaze in the context of distorted power relations "is meant to be national but is strangely reminiscent of exoticism," writes Fanon (160). In this case those relations are determined not by the settler and the native but the urban and the rural, the literary and the oral, the hegemonic and the folk. The important phrase in the previous citation—"meant"—indicates the inability of a romantic culturalist project to inaugurate a new political logic. The inclusion of the caste subject, the focus on a rural space—a space that speaks a different language—all indicate an intentionality, a potentiality that was envisioned by rural realism and triangulated through visions of the *ajuba* (curious, strange), *vilakshan* (extraordinary) and *an-pachan* (unfamiliar) in the form of the region that had escaped the metropolitan view. But the anthropological curiosity cannot fight its own battles. The resistance to the ethnographic gaze, articulated in a range of genres (autobiography, first-person narratives, memoirs, and both realist and postmodern fiction) is that of the cultural insider who rewrites a transitive orientalism. One crucial transition that thus emerges from the juxtaposition of *anchalikta* and Dalit texts is the movement from the ethnographic gaze to a putative native informant—from the doctor to Chandan.[32]

The use of the notoriously unstable first-person narrative might in and of itself seem to be one indication of this, as would the limited and knowing, heavily focalized third person. And Dalit literary criticism asserts again and again that only the Dalit subject can write the Dalit text. The debate between Omprakash Valmiki and Marxist critic Namvar Singh, cited in chapter 1, is paradigmatic in this respect. In all of these texts it is the Dalit subject who emerges as the carrier of a specialized knowledge of suffering that is often untranslatable, other than metanarratively. This is what the bifurcating structure of a novel like *Chappar* demonstrates philosophically: no one, not even the hero of the text, has a firm grasp on the condition of the Dalit other. Chandan is separated by vast distances from his parents and thus cannot—ontologically—narrativize their plight, which is effectively cordoned off from the true trajectory of the novel. But Dalit texts, I want to suggest, would propose that the native informant is not the only means by which the subject can "hack his way into history." Between the ethnographic gaze of rural realism and that of the native informant theorized by Gayatri Spivak—where texts perform or are read as performing a kind of auto-ethnography reduced to data collection precisely because they are cut off from the ranks of true subjecthood—between these two poles there is a vast space to be mined. Dalit literature is rewriting a narrative mode of seeing, which has required either a distantiated narrative observer, a position available to only certain castes, or a native informant, a position equally restricted by caste but more so by its potential for knowledge retrieval. Straddling the space between what would be characterized in postcolonial studies as an orientalist distance and the intimacy of the native informer, the Dalit observer is imbricated in a different kind of description, in a kind of knowledge that can evade transcription and information retrieval. The irony here is that Dalit texts, those texts that are mined for their ethnographic content precisely because of their unadorned realism, may be less interested in content than form.

Lukács's understanding of bourgeois realism as potentially capturing the dialectic of history, the situation of man socially, as "synthesis" and "three dimensionality" (*Studies* 5–9), is an anchor for Dalit literature as well as a foil. Dalit literature by its very presence acts as a disturbance to notions of totality, wholeness, and organicity. Its incessant focus on the Dalit, as an act of historical revisionism as well heroic inspiration, is indicative of a separatist logic, which vindicates the Dalit from the erasure to which the holism of progressive realism has confined him. And yet, if Dalit literature is to fulfill its understated mission of revealing the structural underpinnings of caste, it must demonstrate the "complete human personality" who is produced in these texts as a subject of caste discrimination, oppression, and atrocity. This requires a necessary literary and metaphysical engagement with the *socius*. It is because of this dual burden that readings of Dalit subjectivity and textuality can be easily misread as exclusively ethnographic—i.e., what I would call *pure revelation*.

This analysis thus offers us one explanation of not only the emergence of the Dalit text, which cannot be made distinct from its political movement, but the particular form that its literary incarnation takes. In the previous chapter, we have seen the origins of what Fanon would call that "will to particularize" (173), which has become a central ideology of form for the Dalit text. The context here is not, of course, colonial, but casteist. In this chapter, the relationship between the Dalit text and regional fiction would demonstrate why a rehabilitative ethnographic particularism, such as that of the regionalists, cannot be the solution. And yet to read Dalit literature as unselfreflexively reproducing a nativist informer is also problematic, though it is routinely read as such. A model of *pure revelation* would collapse upon the careful withholding of content, as in the case of the song, because the entire structure upon which revelation lies would be thrown into question.

The impulse to transcribe and to iconize the folk is deeply embedded in and perhaps inextricable from a progressivist literary culture indebted to the village as a construct for its literary radicalism. The village as a literary construct has seemed to be accessible via description—both in the traditional sense of static writing in a certain tense[33] that stops narrative time as well as via a repetitive doing, the gerund rather than the indicative—and transcription; these are crucial narrative contracts that have introduced the Dalit to the literary sphere. That introduction has been made possible primarily by description, displacing the privilege to upset narrative action onto other figures. But narrative justice cannot be produced via inclusion alone. In the radically different context of the nineteenth-century novel of the urban metropolis, Franco Moretti theorizes description as that to which certain characters are subject. As mentioned in the previous chapter, Moretti claims that the city is accessible via narrative shifts in time and temporality, and in vast social networks that bring people together—narratively, description serves this very little (*Signs* 111–12). Rather, description is left for those who are irrelevant, who do not change, who are immobile; it is those who cannot be described, who can only perform narrative acts that the novel follows. Granting the fact that the classic realist novel is a historical particularity, this is a sobering argument for protest fiction, which has staked its transgressive claims precisely on radical forms of description that can somehow *do justice* to its subject. Dalit writing will insist that description is never enough: characters must act, even when to do so breaks the haze of the realist—i.e., the conventions according to which Dalits are written. In the case of a text like "Apna gav," which contains almost no descriptive elements, the final act, which would conventionally be read as challenging the realism of the text with its utopian impulse and its sense of wish-fulfillment, should also be read as insisting on narrative action rather than description, which is where the textual drive of protest literature often lies. In this sense, the realist is here again capturing a transient affective desire, the literal and metaphorical will of the community, capitalizing on a form of utopian wish, delicately obviating its content. Of course, this also raises the larger and more pressing question of the expansion of narrative time to the utopian: the fictional proper. This is a problem of perspective: the Dalit text is asking that the utopian be read as realist, thereby raising the central questions of the realist enterprise—those of time, history, historicity, and literary chronology. If Dalit literature shifts the narrative focus such that the departure from the village becomes an organizing principle, and, in fact, the very moment (and space) of literary articulation, it then refuses introduction to the literary as simply an appendage of the rural. Narrative will be required to make time for the Dalit, rather than ceding space. This is the question I will take up in the final chapter.

CHAPTER FOUR

Casteless Modernities

The Contemporary Anglophone Novel and Its Invisible Interlocutors

And that was how, to my mortification and sorrow, and with every kind of grief for my father and our past, I became part of the cause of the backwards.

—V. S. NAIPAUL, *Half a Life*

In a Dalit autobiography from the 1950s, Hazari's *I Was an Outcaste*,[1] the narrator writes: "I could not make up my mind, whether to fight for the freedom of India or to fight for the freedom of untouchables from the degradation of the caste system" (92). The Dalit perspective that emerges from the narrative notwithstanding, the narrator has isolated one of the central crises of nationalism in India; castelessness was the modern imperative. In the polarized atmosphere of North India in the 1920s, the movement for the uplift of the untouchables was seen as irreconcilable with the major anticolonial struggle against the British Raj. Caught between two conflicts, symbolized by the figures of Ambedkar (the father of the Dalit movement in India) and Gandhi (the father of nonviolent resistance to the British), the proto-modern subject could follow either the former and be marked solely by caste identity or the latter and remain unmarked—or rather, marked by a secular casteless nationalism.[2] Modernity, particularly in the form of national citizenship, required the shedding of old affiliations of ethnicity, religion, language, and—importantly—caste. Historian Dilip Menon writes, "One part of our pursuit of that obscure object of desire—modernity—has meant a repression of the persistence of the primordial" ("An Inner Violence" 60). The primordial may be ethnicity or religion, but also refers to caste, understood as the last impediment to the creation of secular modernism. In Mulk Raj Anand's 1935 novel *Untouchable*, discussed in chapter 2, the latrine-cleaning protagonist Bakha becomes conscious of his caste identity, only to turn his face towards Gandhi in the end. Though his desire for education, his love for a girl from another caste, and the repeated insults he suffers for crossing physical boundaries would seem to make him a candidate for Ambedkar's movement and its call for "education, intermarriage, and interdining," the novel gives him no such opportunity. Bakha turns to Gandhi not only because of the complete absence of Ambedkar in the novel, but additionally because of the general absence—in a novel about Dalits—of any real Dalit politics. As North India was moved by Swami Achutanand, the Adi-Hindu movement, and a number of other untouchable-caste movements, the novel marches Bakha on towards Gandhi, whose position on caste and untouchability would be excoriated by subsequent generations of Dalit intellectuals. Gauri Viswanathan points out that this type of Gandhianism, and more importantly a similar elision of Ambedkar, is reproduced in another novel, Shanta Rameshwar Rao's 1976 *Children of God* (223). But the elision of Ambedkar in these two texts is only symptomatic of a more general disinterest in, and elision of, caste in an Anglophone literature determined to be "modern." Vivek Dhareshwar writes, "A large part of our intellectual discourse has in fact been an autobiography of the secular—read: upper caste—self, its origin, its conflict with tradition, its desire to be modern" (115). This provides an apt intellectual explanation for the contemporary evasion of caste in which Indian Anglophone fiction participates. Dhareshwar points out that this is a greater problem of the English public sphere in general, which has "imposed its secular categories on the social world" (116). M. S. S. Pandian writes that the discussion of caste in the public sphere is always "transcoded"; the discourse of modernity allows it to take shape only in terms of the division of labor, or as a question of hygiene. The burden of caste therefore falls on the low (Pandian 1737). Pandian draws from upper-caste autobiography to situate his claim, working within the context of contemporary Tamil Nadu. He doesn't stress, however, that this is a deduction made from uppercaste autobiography in English, a fact that appears almost self-evident. The normativity of uppercaste identity in contemporary Indian Anglophone writing notwithstanding, the refusal to read caste, or its sublation into a national problematic, is as indicative of caste positioning as a position of fierce partisanship. This is the posture that the Anglophone literary sphere has encouraged.[3] In fact, the liberal parameters of this sphere, which faithfully ensure the production of a national paradigm, may be—as Hazari suggests—preemptively closed to any serious contemplation of caste. In this chapter, I suggest that Aravind Adiga's Booker Prize–winning first novel must be read as the most recent in a long lineage of novels that elide caste questions. Despite featuring a non-Brahmin, non-urban, non-Anglophone, non-upper-class protagonist, and despite exposing the brutal underside of New India with a relentless *class* critique, *The White Tiger* (2008) confirms a genealogy of texts that crown the casteless figure of modernity. In broad brush strokes, I will first outline some of the central complications of this body of literature—namely, the erasure of caste, its concomitant conflation with class, and the genre's participation in a privileging of communalism.[4] I then want to suggest that the production of Dalit literature in Hindi, often Anglophone fiction's unconscious other, might be read as a response to the kind of analytical simplicity that characterizes Anglophone fiction in relation to caste.[5] The rise of Dalit literature in the North, occurring in parallel with the burgeoning of diasporic Anglophone Indian writers such as Salman Rushdie, Amitav Ghosh, and V. S. Naipaul, as well as Aravind Adiga, Raj Kamal Jha, Siddharth Deb, and the many others who write from India, raises the crucial question of the relation of the vernacular—and the "vernacular" vernacular—to the Anglophone literary sphere. Dalit writing attempts to unwork the unwritten caste logic of a certain body of work—a logic maintained through many stylistic and aesthetic contortions—such that caste is once again foregrounded as a phenomenon of structural consequence. My reading of the Dalit insistence on a new realism, then, must be understood as complicating the desire to unearth the buried facts of Dalit life, and as a critique of the failures of social realism, modernism, and even a contemporary postcolonial realism to inaugurate a new analysis of caste.

QUALIFYING CLASS

In *The Politics of the Urban Poor*, Nandini Gooptu describes the rise of the Congress Socialist Party (CSP) in North Indian cities like Allahabad, Benares, and Meerut in the 1920s. Determined to break from the uppercaste, elite image of Congress and its resistance to land reform, the CSP made strenuous efforts to court newly migrated Dalit communities and asked for their participation in trade unionism and in the resistance to industrial exploitation. Its efforts, says Gooptu, largely failed. Even in the case of small-scale participation in unionist activity, it was the Adi-Hindu movement that swept North India in the 1920s and that provided the space for lowercaste political assertion. Once it became clear that CSP politics required the collapse of caste under a class-based politics, Dalits returned to the Adi-Hindus and Swami Acchutanand. The Adi-Hindu movement in the North was one of the earliest Dalit movements, preceding even Dr. Ambedkar, and it argued for a Dalit identity based on "original inhabitancy" in India, advocating a Dalit pride of place alongside a policy of general uplift. It marked an early instance of the occasional overlap as well as deep tension between caste-based and class-based ideologies—a tension that still underlies Dalit literary form today. As Hazari's statement at the beginning of this chapter suggests, the parallel development of nationalist and casteist movements sometimes masked the underlying ideological conflict between certain political categories.

In Arundhati Roy's *The God of Small Things* (1997), the Dalit character Velutha is sacrificed by the Communists, his broken body a testament to the failure of the often-Brahminical left to accommodate the Dalit worker. On the website *Dalit Voice*, writers refer to Naxalites as "Manuvadi Marxists"—a critique of the almost uniformly uppercaste leadership of the Naxal movement in several states. Dalit writers in Hindi have also been stridently opposed to Marxist and soft-Marxist approaches in both the construction and criticism of their work. Prominent Dalit writer Omprakash Valmiki, for instance, critiques Marxism for its links to the long history of a romantic literary vision of the village that was produced by peasant sympathies. Economic exploitation, he writes, is characteristic of the village because of the social stratification of village life that is, in turn, necessitated and determined by caste (*Saundaryashastra* 76). To be Dalit was to be constitutively deprived of property rights, to be required to perform forced labor and/or labor without systematized wages. Leftist movements organized around class struggle have been unable to accommodate such paradigmatic experiences, and in fact have remained blind to them. Valmiki then cites a poem by Dalit Hindi literary critic Dr. Dharamvir that decries, "Ranon ke pahad/ byaaj ke saagar" (Mountains of debt / oceans of interest) (*Saundaryashastra* 77). Mountains of debt isn't a cliché in Hindi as it may be in English; in the poem, the romantic landscape is transformed into a metaphoric placeholder for the real problem of economic crisis. For Valmiki, predictably, only caste is determinate; the lack of capital and the question of labor are both a function of caste oppression.[6] For many Dalit writers in Hindi, this position must be contextualized as a critique of canon as well. As discussed in the previous chapter, the peasant has been a standard motif in Hindi fiction, a literary modality that has helped to produce a certain progressive reading of canonical texts. However, Valmiki's comments might also suggest the intellectual conundrum that has haunted casteless fiction more generally. The valorization of peasant life as the preeminent example of both mass nationalism and subaltern culture requires the glorification of an abstract *panchayati raj*—a self-governing politic less ravaged by British colonialism and the Western modernity of the Indian elites.[7] The debates (described by historian Ramchandra Guha) between Ambedkar and N. G. Ranga, the Telegu freedom fighter and father of the peasant movement, concerning the framing of the new nation's constitution (1946–1949) are illustrative in this respect. Ranga responds to Ambedkar's critique of a potential *panchayati raj* and his tirade against the village by saying, "All the democratic traditions of our country have been lost on him. If he had only known the achievements of the village *panchayat*s in Southern India over a period of millennium, he would not have said those things" (Guha 107). The celebration of peasant culture, of the democratic institutions of the village, and of the formal practices they engendered, as well as the figuration of the peasant as the preeminent potential citizen, often semantically required the elision of caste critique in the name of a nationalist and socialist sentiment. Crystallizing an intellectual position Dalit leaders were to level for the next several decades, Ambedkar writes, "Nobody now accepts the economic interpretation of history as the only explanation of history" (*Essential Writings* 177). This is a product of accumulated historical experience, but also, I would add, of the epistemological failure of the class-based approach to produce literary radicalism on questions of caste.[8]

Dalit critique, then, exposes the irony that inheres in a certain progressive reading of the peasantry—the peasant as the prototype of the poor relies on a kind of tragic abstraction. It is in this reading that uppercaste vernacular fiction and the Anglophone novel often converge (both rhetorically and critically). Mainstream fiction—what the Hindi Dalit critic would call *savarna* literature, of which Anglophone fiction is actually only one small contingent—has been instrumental in creating a literary sphere that is putatively secular and therefore often casteless, or caste-constrained. The effect has been a glaring but influential deferral of responsibility that leaves caste politics to be dissected by Dalit writers. The rise of the Anglophone novel in the last two decades might be read as the most significant and systematic disclosure of this failure, producing a type of hegemonic casteless fiction.

A LITERARY HISTORY OF THE ELISION OF CASTE

It is an analytical challenge to demonstrate pointedly an elision but I proceed here from M. S. S. Pandian's point on "transcoding" (i.e., that caste appears as something else), as well as the assumption that reading beyond what appears in relief also yields certain ideological bents.[9] I would also suggest, as Susie Tharu does in her work on the Dalit widow, that to feature caste literarily in an uppercaste literary sphere now made conscious of caste is to "make an intervention" on this issue (187).[10] In "The Caste of the Indian English Novel," Makarand Paranjape does a brief survey of Anglophone writers and their caste origins, asserting Brahmin caste status "as a metaphor of dominance and privilege" (57).[11] Biography, however, is much less compelling than self-reflexivity, whose literary function is often to probe complex features of lineage, history, and identity both inside and outside the text. The self-consciousness of a body of work that has interrogated such categories hasn't properly been extended to caste lineage, caste histories, and caste identities. Concomitantly, the complex genealogy by which uppercasteness has been perceived as secular "castelessness" is itself difficult to unearth, though Menon, Dhareshwar, and Pandian all gesture towards it: caste as inimical to the project of secular nationalism, caste repressed as primordial and therefore backwards, caste as a religious or spiritual problem rather than a political one. Caste, then, is reserved for certain bodies and certain discourses, themselves marginalized by generic demands.

If the serious discussion of caste in English fiction has been transmuted into a problem of lowercasteness, then an analysis of elision must move beyond the question of biography. Rather, I suggest we begin to unearth such an elision by considering the broader realist imperative, which has been responsible, in many genres, for the introduction of unsavory material into the fictional sphere. There is a precedent for social realism in the Anglophone novel, though it never develops into a fully established tradition. Social realism in the tradition of Premchand, particularly the strain that declared the novel a vehicle for the explicit, reportage-style critique of the social conditions of poverty and the liberal discourse of "uplift," never gained a solid foothold within Indian Anglophone writing, whose primary concern has been with the legacy of colonialism, increasing urbanization, and the forces of migration.[12] The most salient example[13] of this tendency is the aforementioned *Untouchable* by Anand, who used English to bring to light the plight of the Dalit in India. *Untouchable* traversed the path of social realism by elucidating the misery of social conditions, but perforated the positivist lens of authors who sought to dignify and magnify the poor by granting the protagonist Bakha, the latrine cleaner, a modernist consciousness worthy of Stephen Dedalus. Anand glorifies and beautifies the labor of latrine cleaning and directs Bakha towards modernity via the innovation of the flush toilet and Gandhian reconciliation.

Other than Anand's forays into modernism, however, the dissection of poverty has historically required an investment in the tropes of realism. For a certain readership, satire, irony, and magic have become the privilege of the bourgeois, who are free to engage in aesthetic contortions. The "slum's eye view," as critic Ashis Nandy calls it, of the social films produced in the India of the 1950s acquired a certain sociological currency precisely by avoiding such narrative experimentalism, and Dalit writers (on whom the literary burden of the dissection of poverty often lies) who experiment with form have been criticized as fraudulent and inauthentic. This is entirely predictable since, as readers, we were first introduced to the rhetorical "slum" via the realist novel, which often smoothed our transition to the specialized locations of poverty by sending us along with an affable, middle-class narrator, or at least, middle-class positionality. This is as true of the novelists Sarat Chandra in Bengali and Premchand in Hindi as it is of Vikram Seth in English, who, in the Austenian *A Suitable Boy*, paves our way to the untouchable Chamar colony of leather workers in just such a fashion.[14] Rohinton Mistry's notable *A Fine Balance* uses the urban to meld those locations and brings the Chamar tailors into the middle-class urban apartment, creating them as one characterological anchor in a larger realist design. The careful depiction of poverty and the analysis of complex social conditions are understood to be what realism, of all aesthetic forms, does best. But the various aesthetic paths taken by Anglophone fiction—from the more traditional realist, to the neorealist, to the modernist, to the experimental—have also been concomitant with a broader indifference to questions of casteism, even as it might be tied to basic analyses of poverty. Paranjape points out that even when the poor are addressed, thematized, or prioritized, their caste is not mentioned, thereby preventing it from becoming determinate in any sense (59).

The exception to such a paradigm, almost predictably, would seem to be V. S. Naipaul, for whom caste is the beast of burden, the object of nostalgia, the marker of Indianness and of primitivity, as much of his travel writing demonstrates.[15] Naipaul, of course, should be cited for his own communal agenda, but caste in his fiction is a legitimate object of analysis. His 1961 masterpiece *A House for Mr. Biswas* deals peripherally with the translation of uppercaste custom in the wild of the West Indies: The protagonist briefly considers adopting his ancestral profession of the priesthood but is rejected for reasons of defilement of ritual purity. Produced by the unusual historical legacy of Brahmin indentured labor in Trinidad, Naipaul—whose grandfather retained the hereditary calling of the priesthood while his brother labored in sugarcane—demonstrates a strange interest in Brahminness, caste ritual, and Hinduism, of a kind not seen in the Anglophone novel since Raja Rao. Rao's *Kanthapura* (1938), titled after a fictional village in South India, treats the advent of Gandhism in the rural context and analyzes the figure of the Gandhian reformer. Caste in this novel is something to overcome, something that stymies the nationalist project. In the most poignant scene of the novel, Moorthy, the local and Brahmin incarnation of Gandhian leadership, demonstrates his goodwill and his investment in the national project by accepting a glass of water from a Dalit woman.[16] This is the complicated nature of Gandhi's position on caste, variously described as Hindu universalist and social reformist, which called for an end to untouchability but not to the caste system itself.[17]

For Naipaul, caste has been untwined from its Gandhian reading and reread with the harshness and critique, rather than the romanticism, of the diasporic gaze. In *Half a Life* (2001), the novel that most seriously produces a politics of caste, the protagonist is the blighted product of an intercaste marriage between the Dalit niece of a social activist and a Brahmin from a line of temple priests. The misery of Willy's life is read almost exclusively in terms of this marriage, the intimate "reality" of Ambedkar's public advocacy of intercaste marriage. His father makes this marriage out of a desperate desire to turn his back on his family lineage—[18] a perverse revision of activism—and regrets the decision his entire life. When public disclosure forces him to cohabit with the "backward" woman to whom he is betrothed, he experiences a kind of political crisis.

> Elsewhere in the country they were talking of Gandhi and Nehru and the British. Here in the maharaja's state they were shut off from

those politics. They were half-nationalists or quarter-nationalists or less. Their big cause was the caste war. For quite a time they did civil disobedience about the lawyer and me, campaigning for the lawyer's right to walk past the temple, and for my right to marry the firebrand's niece, or for her right to marry me. I had wished, after all, only to follow the great men of our country. Fate, tossing me about, had made me a hero to people who, fighting their own petty caste war, wished to pull them down. (29)

In *Half a Life*, a novel in which the local has no credibility of its own but is only a debased version of the national, caste is a local problem, a petty problem. Naipaul reads caste not as a web of purity and pollution paradigms with potential for transgression and punishment, nor as a materialist economic crisis, nor along an axis of knowledge and ignorance. Caste politics is a kind of provincial politics of grievance supplanted in the novel by the real crisis—that of colonialism. By the end of the novel, Willy has migrated to a fictional Mozambique and the political struggle between guerilla fighters and the Portuguese colonial establishment there, alongside the interracial relationship between Willie and Ana, supplants the petty politics of Indian localism. The colonial struggle that occupies the bulk of the text, referred to as both "big happenings" (155) and "jacquerie" (after the medieval European peasant revolts) (156), emerges as the "real" conflict worthy of analysis and imitation. Recalling the vexed choice of both Hazari and Gooptu's actors, Naipaul's characters—though they may never choose nation—never choose caste or nor any other kind of fellowship, not even love. The notion of a Dalit politics in the world of the Anglophone novel, then, strains the imagination. Within the framework of liberal secularism, where even the poor are casteless, a politics grown from caste identity would be eviscerated mercilessly.[19]

Naipaul's loveless novel, however, was preceded by Arundhati Roy's *The God of Small of Things*, which exploded in the literary landscape like a mine (Ahmad, "Reading Arundhati Roy" 118). Much commentary on the novel stressed its novelty in terms of language and theme as well as the political activism of the novelist.[20] This fact alone provides an important intersection with Dalit textuality, which does not properly distinguish itself from its political movement. However, the novel was primarily read as an intercaste romance—particularly given the contextual waters it rippled—though it also performed several other acts. Heralded in particular for its rhetorical style, the fixation on the relation between an uppercaste woman and an untouchable-caste man is the narrative anchor of the text. It is worth mentioning that beyond the intercaste relationship, *The God of Small Things* is often read as an act of environmental criticism, drawing on lush and complicated descriptions of landscape to suggest a potential eco-critique. The relationship between landscape—land, even—and the Dalit subject is an interesting and problematic one, as I've mentioned in the previous chapter. But the narrative drive of the text moves us from its passing glance outside towards its conclusion where the sexual act between the two is revealed. It is in this act that transgression, social resistance, and capitulation lie; as Aijaz Ahmad complains, "The novel does stake its transgressive and radical claim precisely on issues of caste and bodily love" ("Reading Arundhati Roy" 113). Aijaz Ahmad received some criticism for reading transgression in the realm of "private experience" as a failure and for challenging the proposition that "eroticism is that transcendence which takes individuals beyond history and society" (116). That the unfolding of matters of sex and love are rarely cordoned off to the private doesn't interest Ahmad; in Dalit literature the recurring topos of rape reminds us of that very fact. That being said, Dalit literature in Hindi only very rarely chooses the route of interrogation of the Love Laws on which Roy's narrative architecture is based. Love has only recently become a trope in the Dalit text, which has historically privileged nonromantic, nonconjugal, and nonconsensual acts as well as coercion, and violation. While Dalit feminist writers like Kusum Meghwal and Sushila Taakbhaure have considered the particular crises of the Dalit female subject and occasionally the structure of caste influence over "private" intimate lives, the Dalit text has been home only to certain very particular forms of love.

However, Roy's novel is also instructive for its infamous caricature of the Communist Party (CPI-ML) and its ideological failures, described by Ahmad, heatedly, as "burlesque" (116). An important and underread aspect of the novel—the portrayal of the Communist Party—suggests a critique of the organized left in favor of an ill-defined, but certainly individualized, politics of hope. The decoupling of the realms of caste (private, domestic) and class (public, institutional), which Ahmad suggests occurs in the novel as a result, actually prefaces the following reading of *The White Tiger* and the discussion of Dalit fiction that follows. I will return to Roy's novel and this very question at the end of this chapter.

The subservience of a caste politics to a world *politik* model, in which the clashes between civilizations, between the colonizer and the colonized, are perceived as central and determinate, may be highlighted by Naipaul, but have long been in circulation in Anglophone fiction with its origins in nationalist thought, social reform, and Christianity.[21] The confluence of a secular politics with the privileging of national over local rests on a postcasteist assumption and has contributed to the strange configuration of a "casteless" Anglophone sphere. M. S. S. Pandian, as mentioned, traces this phenomenon through the uppercaste autobiography in English, in which caste is never articulated as caste but "masquerades as something else and makes its muted modern appearance.... Caste always belongs to someone else; it is somewhere else; it is of another time" (1735). As such, caste appears but is depoliticized, becoming visible only in the realm of dining and modern questions of cleanliness; such concerns become can then be articulated as "castelessness." That is to say, without a certain type of microscopic investigation, other than the aforementioned salient examples, caste as a self-named object of inquiry would be difficult to read at all.

CAGING THE WHITE TIGER

It is in this light that one must read the "novelty" of *The White Tiger*, which, when viewed within the purview of the recent Indian Anglophone novel, is apprehended immediately. Its protagonist is not urbanized, affluent, or uppercaste, and—somewhat unusually—he hails from a village, has little access to consumer goods, and bears no nostalgia about his past. Village life is not idealized, migration is forced by material circumstance, and the romance of the rural is entirely absent as is also romance more generally. All the tropes that have come to characterize the majority of Anglophone fiction from South Asia—produced by generations of readings of the work of R. K. Narayan, Anita Desai, Salman Rushdie, and Amitav Ghosh among others—are less present here. Hailed as exposing the "shadowy side of booming India," *The White Tiger* is a novel about economic and social impoverishment, and its protagonist is identified almost exclusively by his class critique: "Do you know about Hanuman, sir? He was the faithful servant of the god Rama, and we worship him in our temples because he is a shining example of how to serve your masters with absolute fidelity, love, and devotion. These are the kinds of gods they have foisted on us, Mr. Jiabao. Understand, now, how hard it is for a man to win his freedom in India" (Adiga 19). Historian

Sanjay Subrahmanyam calls Balram Halwai a "subaltern"; critic Pankaj Mishra calls him "a shrewd member of India's globalized lumpen-proletariat."

Since the early 2008 release of Adiga's novel *The White Tiger*, described as "brutal," "blunt," "stark," and "harrowing," there has been a revolving critical discussion of realism, fidelity, authenticity, and the potential of the novel-as-genre. This is standard procedure as far as the reception of Indian Anglophone fiction goes, which historically has often proceeded from the defensive position of requiring particular ideological justification for writing in English. In this case, this justification has been made on the basis of realism: "There are some things," says the protagonist Balram Halwai, "that can only be said in English" (Adiga 3). Sometimes English offers privileged access to unmined territories.

In *The White Tiger* this territory is referred to as "the Darkness": India's rural world, deprived of money, education, water, electricity, goods, services, equity, and equality—a world full of misery, poverty, feudalism, corruption, men who've become spiders in their servitude, and women who've become witches out of desperation. Balram Halwai is a former inhabitant who has made his way, like so many others, to the city of Delhi and has become a driver for a wealthy family there. As a social entrepreneur with class aspirations that exceed the Darkness, Balram is required—he would say—to engage in unorthodox methods of careerism, leading to the eventual murder of his master. English, the language in which the protagonist chooses to write a series of letters to the Chinese premier describing his ascent, is also the language that demonstrates that Balram has arrived. The premier is representative of a new interlocutor; the Chinese have replaced the British other with which this genre has so often been in dialogue. The text unfolds via these letters in a strange monologic version of the epistolary novel. Letters are written but no one responds.

Adiga's novel is unusual for an English language text in that it participates, at least superficially, in caste questions by advertising its protagonist Balram Halwai *as* a Halwai, a member of the "sweet-making" caste in Bihar. The novel's critique, however, proceeds from an entirely different orientation than that of Dalit fiction, where caste specificity produces a character's entire trajectory. Halwais are middling castes that don't suffer untouchability, atrocity, or social segregation. At the same time, they have been left out of the middle class aspirations that globalization has fed the urbanites and are also ineligible for the meager privileges awarded by reservations[22] to the truly backward classes. Balram does not identify as a Halwai in general, but only insofar as it is possible to use such categorization to his advantage. He has no sense of caste consciousness, the basic condition for Dalit literature. The difference between the village and the city in this novel isn't based on any notion of casteized tradition, rural culture, or values; it is the difference between a bicycle and the Egg, Balram's master's car. As Balram points out quite poignantly, "In the old days there were 1,000 castes . . . in India. These days, there are just two castes: Men with Big Bellies, and Men with Small Bellies" (64). By the end of the novel, he has become the former. In *The White Tiger*, one thousand castes are two classes.[23]

Adiga is clearly indebted to Naipaul in a psychosocial and aesthetic sense; even the term he uses for the village, the Darkness, is Naipaul's term for the slums in his *Guerillas*. The following observation made by the narrator of *The White Tiger* reads as a metanarrative confirmation of the premise of *Half A Life*: "India is two countries in one: an India of Light, and an India of Darkness. The ocean brings light to my country. Every place on the map of India near the ocean is well-off. But the river brings darkness to India—the black river" (Adiga 14). Rivers are petty, but oceans—which connect, correlate, and compare India with other nations, globalizing it, in effect—are sources for Big Men. One of the cleverest features of the novel, one that complements the river/ocean dualism, is the trope of the rooster coop, the allegory of servant culture in India.

> The greatest thing to come out of this country in the ten thousand years of its history is the Rooster Coop.
> Go to Old Delhi, behind the Jama Masjid, and look at the way they keep chickens here in the market. Hundreds of pale hens and brightly coloured roosters, stuffed tightly into wire-mesh cages, packed as tightly as worms in a belly, pecking each other . . . —the stench of terrified, feathered flesh. On the wooden desk above this coop sits a grinning young butcher, showing off the flesh and organs of a recently chopped-up chicken, still oleaginous with a coating of dark blood. The roosters in the coop smell the blood from above. They see the organs of their brothers lying around them. They know they're next. Yet they do not rebel. They do not try to get out of the coop.
> The very same thing is done with human beings in this country.
> (174)

The rooster coop is the ideological explanation for Big Men monopoly and Small-Bellied failure: men are pawns terrorized by a feudal oligarch. But the servant culture cited here can also be read as a metaphorization of the occupational distribution of caste hierarchy, which functions along the de facto assumption of service and the ensuing maintenance of the purity of the uppercastes. The entire question of servitude could also be read as derivative of caste structure. Instead, modern misery is here presented as individual shortcoming as much as institutional culture. It is a an allegorical reading, yes, but one immune to the nuances of a tree-like social hierarchy of caste—a hierarchy that is forgiven or made acceptable by the more general binary logic of the novel. In a sea of false consciousness, therefore, Balram Halwai emerges as the chicken who sees the truth of his social conditions. Echoing a familiar conceptual paradigm, Balram writes confidentially to the Chinese premier, "Mr. Premier, I won't be saying anything new if I say that the history of the world is the history of a ten-thousand-year war of brains between the rich and the poor" (254).[24] The collapse of class and caste has a long lineage in the genre of Anglo-Indian fiction; there are many plausible explanations.[25] However, what I want to argue is that to write in the tradition of Anglophone fiction from India effectively requires—at a metatextual and figural level—reading caste in a certain way, and both the realist and postrealist strains of such fiction have displayed a very uneasy relationship to caste questions.

Let me state clearly that Adiga's novel doesn't function according to a highly sophisticated Marxist understanding of class; rather, it is the allegorical form of the text that demands an economic binarism under which caste is subsumed. But the conflation of caste and class, or the effortless favoring of a class analysis by Anglophone fiction is ironic, particularly in light of the last several decades of Dalit movements in India that have fought, on principle, such an intellectual conflation and—more to the point—challenged any abstract and grandiose notion of "the poor." Dhareshwar explains, "For secular liberals as well as leftists, thinking in terms of caste is morally distasteful; for leftists, thinking in terms of class is a normative requirement as much as an explanatory one" (119). The Ambedkarite movement and its followers in several regions of India have asserted again and again that, despite sympathies with a kind of proletarian humanism, class is not caste. Dalit literature, in several languages, has articulated a critique of the traditional left as well as Marxist literary movements for their failures to truly accommodate questions of casteism—a problem that Roy's novel *The God of Small Things* tackles fearlessly, if simplistically. Dalit writer and critic Sharankumar Limbale, following Ambedkar's critique of Lenin, writes, "Indian Marxism cannot evolve without taking into consideration the unequal social order created by Hinduism, because inequality in Indian society is not the consequence of capitalism alone. It is a much more complex disparity, and there can be no movement forward unless the place of caste, morality and truth in Hinduism is evaluated" (62). Limbale reiterates Ambedkar's well-known sentiments, "The caste system is not merely a division of labour. *It is also a division of labourers*" (Limbale 63). Limbale effectively presents a two-pronged critique of both historical materialism and the critical impoverishment of the Indian left, insisting that Ambedkarism and caste analysis are the essential supplement to Marx. Who, then, is responsible for the bars of the white tiger's cage?

IN SEARCH OF THE REFERENT

What would happen if we take seriously, for a moment, Adiga's referent—i.e., the cultural formulation that invalidates caste as a distinct problematic? The irony of the novel is that Bihar, the state from which Balram has escaped, is almost synonymous with caste complexity and caste crisis. One of the most rural states, Bihar is also described as one of the most economically backward, and one in which, arguably more so than in other regions, caste determines class status. As Anand Chakravarti argues, "Agrarian class relations in Bihar are embedded in caste, because whether a person controls land or not is conditioned by that person's caste status" (1449). Like many contemporary scholars, Chakravarti suggests a revision of the traditional Marxist analysis that locates caste in the realm of superstructure. This is also, I would argue, the metanarrative argument made by Dalit literature more broadly; caste, like race in the Fanonian conception, is determinate. This is particularly relevant in the case of the lowest castes, for whom there is often a very strong correlation between caste, occupation, and economic opportunity, but the inverse is also true. If Balram has migratory potential, this flexibility can also be read in terms of his caste status, which allows him a range of possible service opportunities unavailable to others. As a Halwai—an upper middle caste that is occasionally, but not often, a landowning caste in Bihar—Balram would harbor a particular resentment against the monopoly of land ownership by the few castes at the very top, despite land reform.

The novel appears to circumvent this problem by seamlessly moving from the caste grid, which is one of the major determinants of village life, to an urban grid, where caste distinction is putatively no longer relevant. However, as is ethnographically typical, Balram is employed not by just any owner, but by the very feudal landlord whose clutches his family would, in historical terms, attempt to escape. If we contextualize Balram as a Halwai—neither as a Dalit nor an OBC (other backward castes[26])—his class critique reads as a class *ressentiment*, a consumerist envy rather than a desire for structural readjustment, thereby warranting a rereading of every conflict in the novel. The conflict, for example, between the novel's master and servant represents not only the hatred of the low for the high, a genuine class critique, but a caste rage, for a Halwai should have done better than a rickshaw-puller's means. But it is not a caste rage grounded in the ethical superiority of the Dalit movement, produced by structural exclusion, violence, and poverty on the basis of caste. Balram's is a caste rage provoked by the falsity of meritocratic rhetoric that has preemptively gifted certain uppercastes. The Halwais suffer neither atrocity nor injustice, but they have failed at the meritocratic dream produced by the 1991 "opening" of the Indian economy. In the end, Balram's other is Ashok, his liberal Anglophile master and consumer of English liquor, not the "authentic" feudal landlord for whom he exhibits a cynical, grudging, respect. In the same vein, the narrator's sarcastic reading of the Great Socialist, the politician that dips in and out of the text (likely directed at Bihari MP Lalloo Prasad Yadav), is not merely, as one might think, the gaze of the weak at the falsities employed by the exploitative, but also the caste hostility of the Halwais towards the OBC Yadavs who, having garnered petty benefits and political power for their community, rule the state as a fiefdom of their own. Balram is not critiquing the corruption of the Great Socialist, who woos the people and wastes them; he is wishing this were a privilege of his own. The irony of Balram's position is that, despite what the framework of the novel implies, he has "traded down." From his father's ownership of a rickshaw to his family's ownership of the tea stall, he has become a servant, the urban equivalent of the landless laborer. It is urban life that has proletarianized Balram, who unlike his father does not even own the vehicle he drives.

The White Tiger, therefore, despite its radical protest, is a culmination of a literary tradition that demonstrates a deep discomfort with caste and therefore may be better realized in English. The prevailing impression of the novel as an epic Hegelian contest between the master and the servant, the first and the last, is produced by the circumvention of the "real" problem of village poverty and the refiguring of the last as a Halwai. The novel's ethical authority, in fact, proceeds from Balram's construction of himself as last. Of course, Balram's family is indeed impoverished: his father works as a rickshaw puller who dies of tuberculosis for lack of medical care, his uncles are day laborers, Balram is pulled out of school as a young boy to work in a tea shop and extend the family's meager income; his brother suffers the same fate. But the narrative voice is imbued with a bitterness (not a despair, it is important to note) that reads all these failings as personal and social rather than structural—the fault of the grandmother's cunning, the father's abjection, the landlord's corruption. Balram is one of the "last" *despite his caste status*, not because of it. All these engender Balram's eventual break with his family and a very different kind of revolt.

To read the misery of the Darkness as one anchored in a dialectical struggle between the haves and the have-nots, rather than or alongside a caste one, is a kind of reading that is produced most successfully in English, subject as it is to the kind of flattening out of complexity that the genre of the Anglophone novel demands. Heir to the first generation of Anglophonists like Anand and Rao, and indebted (not least of all for its mordant wit) to Naipaul, Adiga has constructed a figure of modernity—a New Man, as the protagonist himself says—strangely stripped of caste. By the end of *The White Tiger* Balram Halwai has become his own master, unscrupulous, corrupt, and very wealthy, with the police in his debt and beautiful women in his bed—a master in the tradition he despised. He has taken a new name and his most singular marker is wealth, that of the big-bellied in the New India.

THE ETHICAL CONUNDRUM

What does such a reading of caste *do* to the novel's hero? What are the effects of anchoring the protagonist in such a formulation? Balram's "castelessness" in the novel produces (and is produced by) a total detachment from his family and his wicked grandmother that has sinister (literary) implications: it problematizes the allegorical reading that is favored in analyses of poverty. There is no easy linkage here among Balram Halwai, his village, his province, and his nation. Rather, there is a direct indictment of any communitarian impulse and any collective politics. This is true on a literal level (Balram abandons his brethren in the village) as well as on a literary level (he is, seemingly, deliberately unrepresentative). His anomie, uprootedness, indifference, and misogyny make him vaguely reminiscent of a modernist antihero, the novel's "realist" desires notwithstanding.[27] Anticipating the reader's horror at the monstrosity of his murder of his master, which will undoubtedly provoke revenge and plunge his family into terror, Balram says, "Now, who would want this to happen to his family, sir? Which inhuman wretch of a monster would consign his own granny and brother and aunt and nephews and nieces to death?" (67). Balram's indictment of familial relations gives him an ethical "freedom" that he invariably turns to his advantage. The most compelling confirmation of this is Balram's complete indifference to the Naxalites, the Maoist guerilla movement that circles around the edge of the novel and that has turned a rage like Balram's into its proper ethical authority. Balram wants no part of that, insisting on a narrative "I" and never a "We." This is an "I" radically different from that derived from the claims of *atmavad* (experientialism), the philosophical premise of Dalit literature where the basic assumption of communitariansim puts a radical pressure on singular subjectivities.

The integrity of this narrative "I" is never compromised in this text, even by sexual relationships or unions. In one strange and poignant moment that challenges the isolation of the text, Balram sets off for the red-light district where he eyes beautiful women. But: "From my waist down, nothing stirred. *They're like parrots in a cage. It'll be one animal fucking another animal*" (251, original italics). In a weak moment of solidarity Balram exercises his rage on the pimp and the resident *paan*-seller. But this moment of apparent political sympathy with the animalized aside, this is a sexless novel. That sexlessness should be contextualized within a generalized misogyny that dogs the novel shamelessly. Beyond the caricature of the wicked grandmother and the disgraceful wife of the master, village economics is read as fueled entirely by the dowries of daughters and cousins of marriageable age, and Balram's own wedding is read as an opportunity solely for sex and exploitation of the girl's family. When thinking of his marriage, the narrator says to his reader, the Chinese premier, "Now, it had been a long time since I had dipped my beak into anything, sir, and the pressure had built up. The girl would be so young—seventeen or eighteen—and you know what girls taste like at that age, like watermelons" (192). This shared intimacy between our narrator/writer and the Chinese premier underlines an important ideological point: class struggle in the novel is written as a violent contest between men and men alone. Misogyny creates manhood and manhood requires murder. "All I wanted," says Balram, "was the chance to be a man—and for that, one murder was enough" (318).

The absence of any feminist critique, any feminism, or even females, is an important point in one of the few Anglophone novels since the 1930s to take on a subaltern politics. While Dalit litterateurs in Hindi are often accused of being masculinist and dismissive of both the particular situation of the Dalit female subject and the gendered and genderizing condition of caste reproduction, Dalit writing is no monolithic entity; rather, it is fractured by the self-difference of region, politics, aesthetics, and, importantly, gender. Dalit writers in general, including women, have been attentive to the casteized aspects of the social, the space of the domestic, and gendered forms of humiliation and atrocity. As such, there has been sustained attention paid to the relations between the public and private spheres and to the dismantling of these categories that, it is argued, never properly inhered.[28] By doing away with caste, and the kind of familial and social constraint it produces, even in the city, the novel is free to present Balram as a monstrosity, thereby articulating a political ideology that challenges the tradition of the leftist movement in favor of a more liberal discourse of individual rights and privileges. Freed from all ethical constraints, Balram is gifted with a privileged grandiose vision. "Of course, a billion servants are secretly fantasizing about strangling their bosses," he notes, but none have Balram's determination to travel alone (104). While other drivers read trashy murder magazines, or leave their desires to be fulfilled by the Naxalites, Balram acts, remaining disturbingly unallied, haunted by frightening images, but determined to take no one with him.[29]

The novel is therefore forced to take the clichéd modernist route, having unmoored its protagonist from caste, community, location, and all the other analytical categories of belonging; it is required to resort to the idiosyncrasy of psychopathology. For Lukács, this is one of the defining features of modernist ideology, whereby individuals fall outside the bounds of normally accepted social types. The eccentricity of characters in the realist tradition is transmuted into a perverse pathology by modernist writing where, according to Lukács, it becomes "an immutable *condition humaine*" (*Meaning* 31). *The White Tiger* doesn't necessarily go this far, but it does suggest that a murderous pathology is necessary to become a Man with a Big Belly, particularly if you have been a Man with a Small Belly: "*The Indian family* is the reason we are trapped and tied to the coop. . . . only a man who is prepared to see his family destroyed—hunted, beaten, and burned alive by the masters—can break out of the coop. That would take no normal human being, but a freak, a pervert of nature. It would, in fact take a White Tiger. You are listening to the story of a social entrepreneur, sir" (176). In a literary space unaccustomed to caste as a structural category, family is its code, its symptom. Its abandonment—caste abandonment—is what engenders new men. This is a trope in Dalit literature as well—village exodus, as we have seen, is a very typical narrative arc. It is always, however, couched in structural necessity. Once monstrosity becomes the norm, the new economy simply requires that one must learn from the elite rather than overthrow them, and only a singular individual is capable. There is a reason that the novel is entitled *The White Tiger*, not *A White Tiger*.

Balram isn't properly "last," neither in the Darkness, nor in the Light, where he benefits well from his liberal master but refuses to distribute the wealth; he has no sense of camaraderie with fellow drivers or servants; he grudgingly drags his nephew along for the ride; even narrative authority is wrenched away from a storyteller who might temper his ferocity, or his agency. But the most troubling aspect for progressive readers of all sorts is that it is the liberal master who ultimately suffers by his hand, not the patriarchal, feudalist characters Snake, Mongoose, or Stork, all of whom seem so deserving of a whisky bottle to the head. Master Ashok Sharma, whose name Balram will eventually take as his own, is kind, generous, and sympathetic to Balram's difficulties. He is also shallow, indifferent, and condescending. *The White Tiger* reveals liberalism for what it is. The vague sense of concern for the servant, the moralizing on family and rural values, and the lazy ignorance of or investment in inequity are shown to be what they are: a tragic and temporary emollient for rage. *Ressentiment* is not the same as rebellion. Balram does not rail against social conditions, he rails against the master. He wants to inhabit his master's position, sleep with his master's wife, drive his master's car. But this is a Sartrean reading rather than a Fanonian one. Balram's crisis is his own failure, or the failure of his father, to be what a Halwai could be. Not a feudal landlord, of course (a position reserved for the uppercaste Bhumihars and Brahmins), but certainly a player in the new Indian economy. "My father's father must have been a real Halwai, a sweet-maker, but when he inherited the shop, a member of some other caste must have stolen it from him with the help of the police. My father had not had the belly to fight back. That's why he had fallen all the way to the mud, to the level of a rickshaw-puller. That's why I was cheated of my destiny to be fat, and creamy-skinned and smiling" (64). This is ironic conjecture but confirms that the social critique presented by the novel isn't of hierarchy per se, but of one's failure to confirm his rightful place, of the world that sullenly refuses to conform to his demands.

All this produces a hero concomitant with the times, atypical of the "angry young man," the "man of the people," or the "antihero," all of whom engage in a range of ethical uprisings from vigilante justice to covert subversion to democratic challenge. Balram is engaged in a very different type of revolt. *The White Tiger* endorses a theory of social entrepreneurship that eclipses its roots. He has none of the amorality that characterizes the misanthropic vision of the world popularized by Naipaul; rather, he has a fierce critique of injustice, but—fortunately or unfortunately—only his very own. In the end it is he alone who drives off with the master's car. Unmooring Balram from the past, and caste, Adiga has produced a monster, but a monster whose ethical position is seductive, and clearly indicative of a generic politics. By occluding the complex backdrop of mundane poverty, the novel throws the protagonist into a literary and ethical relief for which it is forgiven, supposedly, because of the uniquely oppressed vision it showcases. This may be what happens when modernism tries its hand at caste.

VERNACULAR FICTIONS

Let me stress that this is not a critique about fidelity or authenticity, although these are categories still central to the criticism of South Asian literatures. The novel, as a genre, should not be faithful to the caste conditions of Bihar or others out of a misguided, and misunderstood, realist imperative. But the artfulness of the text—its allegory, for example—is precisely what contributes to its evasion of caste. This is the privilege of art, but also its right; it draws from the discursive and political space made available to it. Why, then, is caste analysis so rarely a question for aesthetics, and why does its refiguration require a translation into the language of pathology? Pandian's concept of transcoding suggests that the space of the literary, the Anglophone novel in this case, is, despite its allegorical and other freedoms, despite the diasporic cosmopolitanism to which it is often linked, indeed subject to the larger public, and deeply indigenist, discourse on caste. What rings *true* in a reading of *The White Tiger* is its desperate Manicheism—borrowed from Fanon who borrowed it from Hegel—the agonizing contests between the last and the first. In *The White Tiger*, the staging of the contest between the last and the first is misleading, however, because the real "last" (the referent, so to speak) has been preemptively written out of the competition. "These people were building homes for the rich, but they lived in tents covered with blue tarpaulin sheets, and partitioned into lanes by lines of sewage. It was even worse than Laxmangarh" (Adiga 260). Balram gets a brief glimpse of these vaguely figured last, but this isn't their story. And of those last who do not make it to the city, his brother, for example, very little can be said. Though Balram's success confirms that not only the first remain first, it also confirms that the last remain the last.

The subtle elocution here is that *The White Tiger* does shift the moral compass of the social world to the driver, as Lavanya Sankaran does in the recent story "The Red Carpet" (2005), or as Thrity Umrigar shifts it to the servant in the recent novel *The Space between Us* (2007).[30] More recently, Manu Joseph's *Serious Men* portrays a Dalit assistant to a Brahmin physicist who, by stealing exams, cons the scientific community into the belief that his son is preternaturally gifted. The original contribution of Adiga's novel, however, is the manufacturing of a kind of insidious consent, based on the shared assumptions of neoliberalism and a Darwinian meritocracy. Though Balram acknowledges corruption, complicity, and structural disenfranchisement at every level, the novel confirms his unique ability to overcome them. Even Balram's monstrosity makes him heroic. While several generations of novels before this one elided caste, Adiga presents a caste analysis but rhetorically persuades us of its anachronism via the worldview of a deprived and depraved character. Isn't it possible, the Anglophone novel rhetorically asks, that the last might be a position that is exclusively class determined, particularly in light of the opening of the Indian economy? Caste and class should not compete for causal space, states Dhareshwar (119), and in these fictions, they simply don't have to. The old binary, the paradigm of the settler/native dyad that has been so central to the development of the Anglophone novel as a genre, haunts the most radical attempts to push at its boundaries, dooming even the web-like complexities of caste to be read in a dualistic and overdetermined way. In this novel, the old other configured by the specter of British colonialism has been seamlessly supplanted by the new master, the Chinese, whose rapid ascent in the world of globalization and capital Indians can only aspire to. Catapulting over the indigenous other and master of the caste problem has been no easy charge; it continuously surfaces in strange paratactic ways. The intermittent hovering of the Naxalites around the edges of the novel is just one way to read such a surfacing.[31] In *The White Tiger*, the Naxalites are portrayed, barely, as one side of a dualistic struggle against landlords and the fact that this overlaps with a struggle between Dalits and uppercastes is somehow occluded. Caste continues to strain the realism of the Anglophone novel, which is challenged to accommodate it.

To juxtapose the kind of class critique that is occurring in the Anglophone novel, then, with the kind of caste critique occurring in vernacular language literature presents a sharp contrast. If, as Dhareshwar says, the elite have used English to "impose its secular categories on the world" such that caste becomes "repressed" (116), Menon confirms his thought: "This modern subjectivity, framed in English, has allowed caste to be approached only at one remove, as something restricted to the private domain suffused with the vernacular" ("An Inner Violence" 62). While the locus of that vernacular critique has been Dalit writing, canonized writers in Marathi, Kannada, Hindi, and Malayalam have also taken on caste politics in poetry, fiction, and theater.[32] In Kannada, the language that hovered over Adiga's upbringing, there is a vibrant Dalit movement, and writers like Mogalli Ganesh interrogate with complexity the notions of "community," "movements" and "leaders." This is equally true of Hindi, the language of Balram and his master. Dalit literature as a movement would have shifted the cultural production of the mainstream—i.e., uppercaste—literary landscape in several languages considerably.

In his introduction to *The Vintage Book of Indian Writing*, Salman Rushdie writes, "The prose writing—both fiction and nonfiction—created in this period [the fifty years of independence] by Indian writers working in English is proving to be a stronger and more important body of work than most of what has been produced in the eighteen 'recognized' languages of India, the so-called 'vernacular languages,' during the same time.... The true Indian literature of the first postcolonial half century has been made in the language the British left behind" (50). What particular kind of critique does vernacular fiction warrant? "The besetting sin of the vernacular language is parochialism. It's as if the twentieth century hasn't arrived in many of these languages and the range of subjects and the manner of the treatment of them is depressingly familiar: village life is hard, women are badly treated and often commit suicide, landowners are corrupt, peasants are heroic and sometimes feckless, disillusioned and defeated. The language is a kind of Indian equivalent of what, in the Soviet Union, was called 'Tractor Art'" (Interview 37). The vernacular, in Rushdie's account, is thus collated with an elementary critique of realism. But in the very same historical moment characterized by the rise of a global Anglophone literature, the social realism of the vernacular tongues that Rushdie so derides has been deployed in contemporary Dalit literature, demonstrating, first, that the literary type is clearly more flexible than Rushdie would allow, and secondly, that a realism of the sort cited by Priyamvada Gopal, Satya Mohanty, and Aijaz Ahmad demands a certain ability to acknowledge and negotiate the persistence of such literary typologies. As a literature of protest, Dalit realism is required by its insistence on caste as a category of structural consequence to negotiate the type as it has informed its own realist literary history. This loose understanding of realism might be better contextualized as a challenge to literary orthodoxy and convention in all its forms, alongside what Ahmad refers to as a "critical realism"—"a critique of others . . . in the perspective of an even more comprehensive, multifaceted critique of ourselves" (*In Theory* 118). Mohanty argues in *Literary Theory and the Claims of History* for a postpositivist conception of realism, one less anchored in the commitment to a certain referent and abstract notions of objectivity. Though Mohanty is working within a philosophical paradigm, his reading of the realist framework is one that leaves room for the implicit failure of the "objective" lens while retaining it as a utopian possibility. The elision of the caste problem in South Asian Anglophone fiction is actually a problem intertwined with the realist determination of a body of fiction fixated on questions of historical, social, and national consequence. The metaphorization of the slippery web of caste into the putative solidity of a class formulation produces a novel that, despite its radical intentions, reveals more about the genre of Indo-Anglian fiction than the reality it purports to bring to an Anglophone audience.[33] Part of the resistance, both aesthetic and ideological, on the part of Anglophone fiction, including Adiga, stems from a general aesthetic refusal to trade in the types Rushdie identifies and critiques.

The debates regarding the vernacular might be said to underline the fixation with an Indian worldliness that the Anglophone novel seems poised to investigate, articulate, and confirm. I would argue that, at a metanarrative level, an interest in the communal question, at the expense of the caste one, is in part what makes the Indian novel worldly. Meenakshi Mukherjee underlines the historicity of this point in *Realism and Reality: The Novel and Society in India*. Other than the pedagogical fiction produced specifically for early converts to Christianity, which was concerned with caste at some level, the novel in India, in Bengali, Hindi, and Marathi has been a place to sort out communal tensions and British colonialism (62). Informed as it is by the legacy of Partition, modern Anglophone fiction has followed a similar track. Postindependence Anglophone fiction has been fixated on Partition, as is attested by the work of Salman Rushdie, Shauna Singh Baldwain, Kushwant Singh, Bapsi Sidhwa (Pakistan), Mukul Kesavan, and others. Even texts that do not directly feature Partition circulate around it as the inevitable locus of trauma. The communal question then, is read as a direct outgrowth of Partition analysis and has produced a body of fiction of its own. This body of work has confirmed the assertion of Dhareshwar and Menon that, if a secular modernity in the form of an abstract citizenship is the goal, then "communalism can be read as the central agent of violence" (Menon, "An Inner Violence" 61). Menon sketches several intellectual tracks, the resulting assumptions of which have structured the undercurrents of such fiction. If, for example, to be modern is to be secular, then to proclaim Dalitness is to be casteist. If, for example, the secular self is one incarnation of modernity, then religion is the schismatic force; caste, ironically, becomes a sociological rather than a socio-religious phenomenon. This is not only in the manner of realpolitik, confirming that India, like America and Israel, has a "Muslim problem," but it also confirms a genealogy of fiction that works within a bivalent paradigm, and a basic structure of otherism.[34] It is this particular logic that has made the Anglophone novel what it is today. If the Indian novel has, as a whole, made caste a question for the very poor by taking it out of the realm of public space, as Dhareshwar asserts, its Anglophone constituency should be read as an integral part of that, not as an inauthentic, diasporic usurper; in terms of this question there has been a remarkable continuity—even more evidence that a proper study of Anglophone fictions can never occur severed from the vernacular context (112).

The White Tiger doesn't disavow the caste question entirely but it elides it by denying its centrality in modern consciousness. Balram points out to a fellow Halwai that a mutual acquaintance is a member of "the pigherding caste"; later, his master asks him about the rites of his caste—these moments remind us continually of this structuring principle of daily life. Balram himself has an analysis of caste as a social phenomenon: the well-ordered zoo, he calls it, destroyed by Independence and the advent of democracy. But this becomes a cosmetic embellishment in a novel determined to demonstrate that the struggle between the rich and the poor has been the most important one, and more significantly, the only paradigm by which one can understand modern life. Caste is the flourish that decorates a relentlessly classist analysis, thereby becoming solely a problem of the very poor.[35] In India, it may seem that one's economic position buys one's way out of a caste paradigm, but that castelessness is itself a feature of certain castes—those singled out as representative or dominant by the Indian Anglophone novel. If literary constructions of caste are always read by Anglophone texts as a dualistic contest, this is in part a leftover of an anticolonial nationalism and a contemporary fixation on the communal. When Roberto Schwarz argues slavery to be a kind of rhetorical thorn in the realist side of the nineteenth-century Brazilian realist novel, he suggests the strange ways in which the occluded never becomes symptom or surface, but nevertheless betrays its structural impact. Caste may be the problem that is revealed by the aesthetic contortions contingent upon use of "borrowed form." *The White Tiger* might be exemplary, but also the pinnacle of such an achievement, for it creates modernity as a casteless acquisition—not through disavowal, but though active devalorization. And the Halwai, of course, becomes a Sharma in the end.

CASTEIZING THE LITERARY METASPACE

Dalit literature is about Dalits, in its single-minded focus on the creation of the Dalit literary subject, and it may also be for Dalits, as so many writers claim, but this is the most ungenerous reading; Dalit literature also inaugurates a kind of analytics of oppression, grounded in caste. It too has often been accused of a binary logic, of coaxing its characters into the rigidity of certain subject positions. If one strain of Indian Anglophone writing has been engaged since its inception in the broad deconstruction of the colonial romance, then Dalit writing shares with it a literary-political imperative, engaged as it has been in the challenge of another form of romance. Dalit literature is a movement, of course, and as a protest literature differs from other forms of writing. However, I want to suggest that in its active reworking of a hegemonic logic on caste, Anglophone writing has become its silent interlocutor. More recently, the impetus for translation of Dalit texts from vernacular languages into English, precisely in order to reach a more worldly (not cosmopolitan) audience, and more rarely, the actual writing of Dalit literature in English, have thrown into relief that unspoken relationship.[36] Rashmi Sadana suggests that the terms vernacular and regional are somewhat diminished by the continual juxtaposition of "regional literature" against "global literature (written by Indians in English)" (310). That isn't my intention here. I would rather make the argument for overlapping spaces, which are often mutually constitutive. The very heteroglossic nature of the Dalit text, which moves through several registers of Hindi as well as its regional variations, often conspiring with English (as can be seen in the work of Ajay Navariya), suggests this. In Hindi's exceptionalism, its function as a regional lingua franca, its national aspirations, and its putative cosmpolitanism derived from a now–transnational Bollywood, it circulates in a globalized world. It is in these senses that I would say that Dalit literature shares a literary metaspace with Anglophone writing, although without any political acknowledgement of that fact.

Ajay Navariya's fiction may be most emblematic of those shared spaces of concern. Navariya's work stands out in stark contrast to the field of Hindi Dalit literature but it seems to be charting the direction in which that field is moving.[37] Navariya is a young, eclectic, and outspoken writer, also a professor of Hindu Ethics at Jamia

Milia Islamia University in Delhi, and like many other Dalit writers, he moves generically among short stories, poetry, and novels. But characters in his work give little indication of caste identity; they almost never experience the moment of caste consciousness or caste realization that is a standard feature of the most well-known and important Hindi Dalit writers, like Omprakash Valmiki and Mohandas Naimishraya. Rather, Navariya's characters have long abandoned the village and navigate the vicissitudes of urban life, exhibiting a kind of postcaste consciousness; they often speak in English. Importantly, however, they are the first generation to do so. If this fiction seems "casteless" in its embrace of the modern, technological, and urban, then it is deliberately, strenuously, and anxiously so, rather than unconsciously—a feature that distinguishes it from the non-Dalit literary field that surrounds it.[38]

In Navariya's 2004 story "Usar mein kasht ki" ("To Plow a Barren Land"), a young woman circumvents the suffering of a miserable marriage through an affair with her sister-in-law's son, a young man her own age. Ten years later, after the affair has fizzled, the story follows a new romance, with a distant colleague of her husband, a young Dalit man who asks her to marry him. The condition of crisis in the story is not only that of the casteized subject but the gendered one; "Woman is a worm, a tape worm," says the narrator in an intimate, revealing first-person narrative (7). We are given no official indication of the protagonist's caste (though we are to assume she is a Brahmin), but we are given many of her social class status. Her story is peppered with English-language phrases including "French kiss" and "mixie," and the initial meeting with the second lover of the story takes place at the cake-cutting of her daughter's thirteenth birthday party for which elaborate preparations are made.

All of this strikes the reader as unusual if he is at all familiar with the basic paradigms of Dalit literature. Despite the critique of the rural romance cited by Valmiki, and confirmed by many others, much Dalit writing in Hindi is firmly situated in the village, as the previous chapter maintains; that is the location that provides its ethical license for revolt. But in Navariya's work the teleological drive to escape the village is so palpable, so unquestionable, and its endpoint is a celebratory uncritical modernity. In that sense, one of the central problems of the story "Usru" is somewhat similar to that which Arundhati Roy refers to as "the love laws" in *The God of Small Things*. What have honor, social convention and custom done for women? And what are the tragic ways in which these things dictate their emotional and economic lives? Sukanya ("good girl"), our protagonist, is no rebel but she wrestles with the conventions of bourgeois middle-class, uppercaste morality in long moments of psychological realism. What would people say about the abandonment of a marriage after so many years? It would be as if she were spitting on her honor, her traditions. The real source of blame is her father, who married her dowryless to a much older man. These questions may seem familiar; indeed, they have been present since the very origins of the novel in India. The protagonist of Premchand's *Nirmala*, as discussed earlier, is caught in a very similar conundrum: married to a much older widower due to the family's sudden loss of fortune, Nirmala becomes a step-mother to a boy her own age. But in *Nirmala*, these psychological conflicts are cast within a secular space and a language of tradition and values, as well as individual emotion. What Navariya's story does so brilliantly is remind us, by the imposition of the low-caste character at the end, that these questions are questions of caste. The possible transcoding, then, by which caste manifests as something else, cannot sustain itself; in a text that locates itself within Dalit literature when a self-identified Dalit character offers his caste history and caste analysis (at the very end of the story, I should add), Sukanya's tragic reverie must be reread. As Dhareshwar has pointed out, one of the effects of the strident secularism of the Anglophone public sphere has been the subtle equation of caste with lowercaste, almost exclusively. But "Usru" insists that the maintenance of caste hierarchy is not only read through the burden born as a result of atrocity or indignity, but also the daily dance of decision-making by uppercaste individuals who read social norms, social structure, and individual provenance in a certain way. Caste crisis is not only a Dalit problem.[39] Even more to the point, the material trappings of a certain class positionality—the mixer, the birthday parties, and the fancy cake—do not invalidate a caste analysis; the inverse maybe actually be true.

Conjugality and sexuality are central vehicles via which caste becomes an object for fiction, in Premchand's *Godaan* and in Renu's *Maila anchal* as well as in Roy's *God of Small Things*. But in commenting upon the latter, Aijaz Ahmad remarks:

> What is most striking about that final, phallic encounter between Ammu and Velutha is how little it has to do with decision and how much it takes the shape of what the recent title of a movie calls fatal

attraction. Now the difference between decision and "fatal attraction" is that whereas decision, even the decision to accept suffering and/or death, is anchored in praxis, in history, in social relationship, chosen and lived in a complex interplay of necessities and freedoms, fatal attraction can never cope with such complexities and must be acted out simply in terms of a libidinal drive. ("Reading Arundhati Roy" 116)

Ahmad is clearly influenced here by the Lukácsian analysis of potentiality and possibility in the realm of fiction; conscious decision-making is the requisite of history-making. Fatalism, that characteristic so close to modernist nihilism, would be read by Lukács as the decadence of a modernist aesthetic that revels in the fantasy of pure subjectivities. As a result it misreads the "real," that realm of historical totality. In "Usru," there is a passionate drawing together of uppercaste woman and lowercaste man, and the brief catalogue of sexual detail. But the coupling is so relentlessly deconstructed that there can be no ethos of fatalism. The story addresses this problem via interiority, which reveals one character's consciousness of that "social relationship" and "interplay," but also by presenting the moment of sexual union in passing; the crisis appears in the problem of how to proceed in the social world.

Navariya's work is unusual in that it locates the question of causal supremacy within individual action; his fiction works within the modernist trope of individual agency and alienation. The question of broader political claims, then, is always triangulated via character; the alienated subject, unlike Adiga's in *The White Tiger*, is produced by caste. The self-difference of the Dalit project, however, is such that this mode exists alongside several others. In one story, "Antata" (1997), Rana Pratap stages realistically the choice faced by a middle-aged factory worker whose loyalties are being claimed by both the Mazdoor Sangh, the workers organization, and the Harijan Sevak Sangh, the untouchable-caste uplift society.[40] The protagonist is in a bind, as his daughter's Brahmin tutor/employer has made inappropriate advances and fellow community-member intervention is required, but his time is demanded by the union in its attempt to challenge new regulations. "This is not the time for all of this," says the union leader of his daughter's potential marriage, attempting to placate the protagonist (Gupta 204). Marriage (a problem of caste) should be deferred to the realm of the social; the material crisis at hand requires immediate attention, his comments imply. The protagonist Ganesi the Chamar disagrees. He seeks out the help of his fellow caste members who insist on marriage and a "conversion" ceremony for the Brahmin, one that shames him deeply. The story might therefore read as a typical parable of identarian solidarity. It comments without irony on the broad disinterest in traditional leftism in Dalit literature, as is evidenced by the few fictional works that engage with such movements at any level. It also suggests that these political forms are ideologically incapable of accommodating the problems of the social. In that sense, Ganesi's experience is emblematic of an underlying trend in Hindi Dalit writing that insists on the inclusion of the social as a means to introduce caste into the public, and therefore political, sphere. This kind of heavy-handed decoupling of rubrics of caste and class, I would suggest, is precisely the point.

In different ways, more "traditional" fiction like Rana Pratap's and more experimentalist work like Ajay Navariya's are laboring under the burden of a heavy critique. Using both realist and modernist aesthetics, challenging and confirming the type, Hindi Dalit writing is producing a canon of writing that insists on caste as a rubric of analytical value, as well as one that produces certain aesthetic forms. In the case of Navariya, for example, the modernist tendencies that he exhibits—the insistence in his writing that pleasure be a value alongside more immediate needs; the prevalence of love as a thematic of the Dalit text; the author's own commentary that the proper context for these stories is "the dream"—all of these aspects do not undermine the work's central contribution: it restores caste to its location of structural power (*Patkatha* 7). The varied aesthetic paths taken in the field of the Dalit text coalesce around this singular ideology.

To return to the broader question of this project: How might we read contemporary Dalit texts like Navariya's dialectically with the Anglophone production that is more recently attempting to make interventions into the problem of caste, as well as that of region? *The White Tiger* does not accidentally draw from Bihar, one central locus of intranational migration. The trope of the abandonment of the village for the city, of which Adiga's Balram is one instantiation, is a literary trope; it is the narrative arc of both the European bildungsroman and much of Dalit literature. Let me explain the nature of this trajectory in one Navariya text, "Patkatha" ("Screenplay"), published in 2004. In this long short story, three generations unfold in three distinct parts, three "scenes." Each section follows one man and his wife or girlfriend; in each section some dramatic instance of caste conflict is staged. In the first, Kalyaram, a Khatik who sells skins, recites poetry to his wife Sugni every morning. Having saved enough money, he buys her a sari embroidered with stars, to be worn for the Teej festival. This is perceived by others as social affront, and Kalyaram is badly beaten by the local *thakur* at the urging of the village priest. The day of the beating, however, is the same day that Gandhi is to speak, proclaiming the Quit India movement. Tending to her husband's battered body, Sugni calls on fellow villagers to challenge such inhumane treatment and the following year, all the women of the village wear spangled saris for Teej.

In the second section, Kalyaram's son Mohanram has become a teacher, one of the few educated lowercastes who have remained in the village. It is 1971; Pakistan is mentioned, recalling the war, but only to locate the date. Mohanram has moved from a hut to a house with his wife and two children; books are scattered all over his home: Tolstoy's *War and Peace*, Gorky's *Mother*. Thakur Isuri Singh has replaced Thakur Harnaam Singh, who is, incidentally, suffering from paralysis. Pandit Triloknath, who incited the beating of Mohanram's father, has been replaced by Pandit Ramnarayan. There is a symmetry here, but things have changed, as the narrator mentions. One no longer kneels to address the *thakur*. And one might also protest. When called in by the *thakur* to discuss his organizing of the Khatiks and Chamars for the upcoming *panchayat* election, Mohanram, anticipating a blow, punches the *thakur* in the face. The family then leaves the village.

In the third section of the story, Mohanram's son Bhaskar has finished an MA in animal husbandry, is working towards his MBA, and soon finds employment in a marketing firm. It is 1993, and history irrupts in the form of communal riots, which color the subsequent narrative elaboration of caste justice. When the congenial manager of the firm learns Bhaskar's caste, Bhaskar is let go; in a telling moment, he exits the lift of the multistory office building, and "became one part of the crowd" ("Patkatha" 133). Bhaskar is politicized by this, and shares his new ideas on resistance with his girlfriend. The two choose in the end to abandon an offer to work abroad in order to work towards social change at home. All these tales are interwoven by, first, the problem of caste conflict that takes new and different forms as one transitions from a village to an urban economy, and second, love—the romance of the couple undergirding each story and functioning as a nascent political solidarity.

Three generations, three men, three crises: Kalyaram gives way to Mohanram who presents Bhaskar. In each story, the space of the home is constructed not literally, through proper description, but through the relations between the couple. These are also narratives of evolution: Bhaskar presents himself to be savvy, introverted, and artful, in comparison to his father and grandfather, and in response to new and less overt forms of casteism. By the third section, the village is very far away, metaphorically speaking. And problems of casteism are not sorted out between individuals but via structures. With each generation, caste is remediated and appears as something else, from a proscription against finery to the prevention of promotion. In each there is a bystander—the observer, the gossip, the friend—who circles the narrative arc of the protagonist in order to distinguish him. And in each section it is made clear that there is a lineage of resistance: Bhaskar's politics are made possible by his father's opposition and his grandfather's transgressions. One generation inherits the crises of the previous one, and devises new means to attack new political problems; causality is produced in the very act of juxtaposition. This isn't just a question of representation, I should stress, or of a certain presentation of the intergenerational lowercaste family, which clearly is narratively available. Rather, this is an analytic that demands that Bhaskar's political commitments be read as the narrative outgrowth of the work of several generations. The gesture here is also not analeptic—a feature much more common in Dalit texts, which often narrate a moment of crisis via flashback once the protagonist is socially situated, adult, and has gained the kind of contextual authority that can provide him with narrative authority.[41] Analepsis is still rooted in the present of narrative time, and anchored in the individual protagonist, solidifying his vision. What I refer to here is the compartmentalization of the text according to generation, which immediately brings us into a different register. It is a highly, and strictly, compressed generational saga, the aged structure of a certain type of realist novel, retrofitted.

I take here Lukács's point that aesthetic forms are determined and categorized not on the basis of narrative technique but ideology. The text's allusion to cinema and theater, and its formal features seem like the kind of play that distinguishes this text from more typical examples of Dalit realism. But the text's ideology seems rooted in the notion of the essential fragment of human life, the problems of intergenerationality, totality, and historical time. I would categorize this as realist for another reason as well: the text plays with the knowledge conventions associated with a type of writing that was determined to introduce and confirm. There is a movement in this text between that which is already familiar, and that which is new and potentially shocking. In Premchand this often occurred through narratorial conspiracy—knowledgeable generalization and detailed specificity. The peasant mentality was new, but knowable, and confirmed what "you" yourself might have "seen." In Navariya's compressed story, this occurs at a narrative level rather than a narratorial one. The entire first section of the story performs the prototypical understanding of caste violence as well as Dalit literature; it fulfills the basic conditions of expectation in terms of how casteism is portrayed and how Dalit literature operates—there is the village space, there is violence, there is emasculation of the male, and threat upon the female body. This section then functions as a preparation for the more subtle caste critique, and caste context that will be raised in section three.

Much of Hindi Dalit literary production, particularly the short stories, function as snapshot, a momentary gaze. Anchored in a single individual and the contours of his, sometimes her, life, they clearly embody their own sense of historicity but move along a narrow timeline. A story raises many interesting questions of possibility, potentiality, and even utopia, just as a modern social realist novel would, but it is clearly a selection of the most salient or representative moments of a literary life. There is no point, I mean to say, of speculation regarding the protagonist's childhood, his or her domestic life or family. It is not that kind of realism. The story contains—"contains"—all the information needed to prepare us for the central act, and its retaliation. Many Dalit texts thus magnify, microscope, and select the moment of atrocity, or caste consciousness, or political revelation that is most crucial. "Patkatha" is no different in that sense—it is conscientiously and reflexively selective. The grandfather's life is marked by his excessive love for his wife, which leads to the purchase of a transgressive sari. The father is a rationalist and his transgression occurs through political channels; he too ends up abused as his father before him. And Bhaskar, the final protagonist, gains a kind of political consciousness after his failure to succeed according to the logic of a putatively caste-blind Indian corporate meritocracy. But the juxtaposition of generations, however synechdochally it is done, is a significant literary trope. Literary Dalits are lateral—i.e., they have been traditionally portrayed as historyless. In the history of the Indian novel in both English and Hindi, the casteized figure is only very rarely granted any sort of historical depth. But Dalit literature, too—focused on the problem of journalistic disclosure and the narrative scope of one life produced by the autobiography—has also confined narrative to a kind of presentism, to synchronicity. Producing a textual genealogy—even in the service of a demonstration of a political transition—is no slight gesture.

I will gesture here briefly to Baburao Bagul's story "Mother" (1969) as it is discussed by critic Susie Tharu. In her incisive analysis of widowhood, Tharu juxtaposes two widow stories, one upper-caste and liberatory (Gita Hariharan's "The Remains of the Feast"), one Dalit and tormented ("Mother"). In this analysis, caste as it appears in the story "Mother" is justly analyzed as familial horror: the mother is assaulted by her husband's hands, her son's suspicions, the overseer's desires. Tharu writes that the narrative of untouchability presents as "extraditions that are revised and renewed by a brahmanism that is constantly updating its patriarchy, as desire in the scene of the family, as bodies that are compelled by, but disallowed contact into the feminine or masculine . . . always deficient, always in excess. In brief, as terror in the domain of the citizen-subject" (202). Terror is clearly the experience of the first generation in "Patkatha," though its locus isn't domestic. The domestic emerges, rather, as the source of love, and a kind of bourgeois focus on the couple is one strain that runs through each generation of Navariya's story. The mother of Bagul's story, says Tharu, "in order to find bodily life, as woman-self, must die as mother" (201). In comparison to the Brahmin widow, whose liberationist gestures are those of consumption, the Dalit widow's liberation requires a kind of psychological and ethical treason against the son. The desire in this family is that of the mother who has become a prostitute, the father whose jealousy incites bodily violence, the brother-in-law who stares lustfully, and the son who judges. It can only demonstrate its distance from the normative, and Tharu's own juxtaposition, placing the Dalit story after the Brahmin one in her critique, can only serve to emphasize that fact. But the mother of Navariya's "Patkatha" is of Gorky's *Mother*; the idle detail of the book on the shelf is neither reality effect nor symbol, but metonym. In the first section the mother launches collective action, and the following year all the women of the village appear for Teej in star-covered saris. In the second section the mother sanctions her husband's resistance. And in the third, in a casteist retrogression perhaps characteristic of the times, the future mother threatens to kill herself if Bhaskar goes abroad. There is fiction in the Hindi Dalit canon that shares the despondency and terror of Bagul's story, written in Marathi, but "Patkatha," produced almost forty years later, is not one of them. The casteized family space is not one of terror, as it is in *The God of Small Things*, *The White Tiger*, and Bagul's "Mother," but rather—in a narrative shift that according to the critical paradigms available would only and very problematically be called bourgeois—is a sanctum. In classical European realism, as Jameson has argued, the home is infused with desire, a manifestation of dreams of property (*Political Unconscious* 143). In "Patkatha," that desire is produced, but only through the subjectivities of people in political union; the home is something never fully constituted, the house is something left behind.

REALISM AFTER MODERNISM?

To take us back to the analytical track of contemporary Anglophone fiction against which Dalit literature can be fruitfully positioned, let me recall the protagonist of *The White Tiger*. The pathology of the modernist antihero, of which *The White Tiger* may be one instantiation, isn't revelatory in the sense of Anglophone fiction's engagement with the Dalit (this it expressly does not do) but rather because it indicates a casteized *socius*. Balram Halwai moves in a world by now *made conscious* of caste, unusual within a solid corpus of casteless fiction. The kind of space that is now literarily possible is as much a product of the democratization of the literary sphere of which Dalit literature is one essential part as it is a product of post-Mandal Commission politics and other sociohistorical contingencies. Identarian literary movements do not simply close in on themselves but expand the cultural sphere to certain meanings. For hegemonic—in this case, English language—cultural products like the novel to engage not simply "the specialized locations of poverty," but hegemonic spaces in which narrative actors move within a web of casteized social relations is a phenomenon intricately tied to its intimate other, Dalit literature, which rejects the structural principles of national belonging, postcoloniality, and a progressive class-based ideology in favor of values that are largely anathema to the Anglophonists: essentialism, particularism, and casteized exclusion.

If the contemporary novel now functions in a consciously casteized world, however, it does so by relying on the conventions of an existential modernism that, interestingly, is dependent for its function (that of the text—which unfolds in an epistolary format thus requiring Balram's isolation—as well as that of the protagonist's, whose success must be singular) on the deliberate excision of that *socius*. For Lukács, pathology is the hallmark of modernism precisely because it dislocates the individual from his relationship to social life. Reacting against Heidegger's "thrownness-into-being," Lukács cites the ahistoricity of the modernist experience: "the hero himself is without personal history.... He is 'thrown-into-the-world': meaninglessly, unfathomably. He does not develop through contact with the world; he neither forms nor is formed by it" (*Meaning* 21). The white tiger, that endangered species, may not be historyless, but is determined to read himself this way, and strives for the clean slate that will offer him opportunity, at the clear expense of any sense of the social, whether construed as sexual relationship, family, or political community. It is comforting to read this as pathology because the other possibilities, of a genuine realpolitik for example, are politically very disheartening. The crucial point is that the ideology of naked individualism and ethical pathology that colors the novel relies for its functioning on the excision of caste-as-family.

In Dalit literature, the restitution of the Dalit protagonist to social life, isn't a restitution per se—his condition is socially determined. But in order to privilege a Dalit epistemology and a Dalit subjectivity, narrative excision—the social isolation of the protagonist—might have become necessary. Ajay Navariya's story does this as well, but by producing a political genealogy it simply doesn't allow for a pathologizing of the protagonist's political perspective, however radical—precisely what occurs in *The White Tiger*. Navariya's figures cannot be "thrown into being" because they are linked by lineage. This is what might be called a modified realist structure. There is an implicit assumption of historical referentiality, but structurally, the story is segmented on the page, and draws on the metaphor of theater and film via title and epigraph. The father doesn't appear in Bhaskar's story, the grandfather doesn't appear in the father's. The lineage here is actually a repetition; that repetition is based on caste conflict. This is presented very explicitly as *reproduction of caste* rather than reproduction of class. Bhaskar's MBA studies, the corporate environment, the liberal meritocratic achievements, his individuality—precisely what frees *The White Tiger*'s Balram, and indeed what allows Bakha of Anand's *Untouchable* a subjectivity—do not narratively interfere with the newly configured, subtly masquerading, forms of casteized logic. Exceptionalism cannot be the solution.

Dalit literature might be broadly read as a corrective to a body of work determined to claim nationally representative cultural status. By asserting not only the use of the vernacular, but the deconstruction of class/caste and the formal tropes of a broadly conceived modernism, its presence, in addition to its declaration of a certain analytics, serves as a critique of the Indian literary canon as it is generally understood. In "Patkatha," for example, Navariya writes: "From afar, Kalyaram looked at Sarpanch Harnam Singh seated on the terrace. First, he removed his *pagdi* from his head, folding it under his arm, then he removed his shoes. Placing one on top of the other, he pressed them to his other side. Even from a hundred feet away, his shoulders were bowed as if they were broken, and his neck, toppling forward, had fallen on his chest like a slaughtered goat" (122).

This passage might be a concrete example of what is referred to as a kind of premodern literature characterized by an aesthetic and a vantage point of social realism, in that it indicates a palpable village hierarchy and the trope of the broken man: the peasant. But this story was published in 2004. Rather than the assumption of literary historical belatedness, I wish to suggest another metaphor for the management of the very varied and multifarious space of Indian literature. A story like "Patkatha" is coeval with *The God of Small Things*, just as is Omprakash Valmiki's work with that of Aravind Adiga. Though the hierarchical nature of their reception in the West might lead us to believe that such an aesthetic praxis is striving on an evolutionary path towards postmodernism, evaluation of Dalit literature suggests a revindication of certain aesthetic principles of social realism in the name of a kind of presentism. "Belatedness"—what in Roberto Schwarz's formulation of Brazilian national culture in the face of the West becomes "backwardness"—might also be strategically necessary. When a literary sphere that shares spaces, languages, histories, and cities creates entirely different aesthetic paradigms, the determined posture of that chasm is worthy of deconstruction. Why has a newly emerging Dalit literature remained wedded to certain categories of realism, a modernist and modified realism even, certain of its aesthetic principles, certain of its philosophical assumptions? What, alongside other vernacular and English spaces, does this allow it to do? Dhareshwar argues, "Explaining caste without taking into account its logics of representation (in all its senses, including that of the representational politics of democracy) has the consequence of mystifying caste" (119). One critique that might be raised by a literary commitment to realism, albeit in new and modern forms, is the failure of literary radicalism and aesthetic experimentalism to consistently engage and shift caste worldviews. This may be because the paradigm for literary radicalism has been largely dictated by ideologies of secular leftism. What does a Dalit radicalism look like? It may, in fact, not *appear* to be very radical. But this is a question that will be taken up in the concluding chapter.

CHAPTER FIVE

Some Time between Revisionist and Revolutionary . . .

Reading History in Dalit Textuality

> Dalit autobiography has become important not because of the vast expanse of experience but by its violent bonsaization. Massive trees, like the suicide of an uncle, are dwarfed. Bonsai trees are cute, true, but they can never be a substitute for the giant woods.
> —D. R. NAGARAJ, "Against the Poetics of Segregation and Self-Banishment"

In one telling moment, the narrator of Omprakash Valmiki's *Joothan*[1] (one of the many Hindi Dalit autobiographies) recalls a Brahmin teacher who has instructed his students to rip out several controversial pages on Dalit history from their school primer. Officially sanctioned by the textbooks of postindependence schools that have opened their doors to untouchables for the first time, the pages on Dr. Ambedkar's movement remain on the floor. For the narrator, this incident is a sign indicative of the hostile atmosphere in which the Dalit community must live. But it is also a reflection on historical erasure and excision, which is consciously being textualized. Beyond the role of the state in the construction of official historical narratives, the passage underscores the many ways in which such narratives are challenged and dismantled; in this case, however, the resistance is not on behalf of a radical revisionist history but rather in support of a retrograde casteist logic. In addition, we might read this moment as a metanarrative comment on the writing of *Joothan* itself, which functions as an originary textualization, a meditation on the act of writing. As the narrator recalls the unfolding of the incident, and the eventual publication of the torn pages in a newspaper, he places his text alongside other torn pages whose destruction was not necessarily publicized.

The notions of both history and historicity theorized by Dalit writers and critics differ significantly from the critical apparatus on which *savarna* (uppercaste) and Western academic criticism is based. Stripped of liberatory overtones, the historical chronology that frames Dalit literature bears little sense of triumphant nationalism and does not privilege modernity despite being "postcolonial." As Dalit philosopher Gopal Guru writes, Dalits are "still in search of an inclusive civilization that would ensure them at least a sense of decent time and space" ("Dalit Vision" 758). For obvious reasons, Dalit writing doesn't bear traces of nostalgia or the glorification of the idyllic past,[2] and it only occasionally projects utopian visions of the future; it is also by and large bereft of the signpost historical moments that would allow it to participate in a national historical chronology. Yet despite the continual assertion by writers and critics that the individual figured in Dalit texts is always representative of a collectivity and that Dalit humanism is essentially transposable across various Dalit communities, the writing is marked by a conscious historical and cultural specificity hardly interested in the timelessness and spacelessness that characterize other forms of futurism. Dalit literature therefore insists on its own historicity by other means. This sense of historicity is one that is tied up with conceptions of authenticity and lived experience, and articulated through an allusive referentiality as well as a formal, yet iconoclastic, realism.

This chapter will disentangle the slippery problem of reading history and historicity in Dalit texts. If Dalit literature is often read as an ahistorical, ethnographic expression of Dalit identity "at home,"[3] then it is now being read alongside postcolonial and Third World literatures abroad. But these texts articulate a historical consciousness that is determined to complicate both critical frameworks. Neither explicitly revisionist nor explicitly revolutionary, the unraveling of narrative time and the reading of historicity in Dalit literature are difficult to situate; they differ in significant ways from both *savarna*, or uppercaste, readings of the historical, as well as from the more Westernized conceptions of history circulating in postcolonial fiction. I argue here that it is what Dalit texts *do* with the narrative construction of history that makes them difficult to accommodate to an external critical apparatus. The importation of an external critical map as an evaluative frame therefore seems to doom the Dalit text to failure. When, for example, a Dalit text like Mohandas Naimishraya's *Apne-apne pinjare* (*Cages of Our Own*) elides Partition, or a text like Hazari's *Autobiography of an Outcaste* disavows untouchable caste movements, what kind of historical reading would typically be produced? The Dalit text would once again be reduced to the revelatory ethnographic. This is, of course, complicated by the movement's own insistence on the genre of autobiography and its uncomplicated "truth-value." The temporary suspension of the historicist lens, however, would provide us with an alternative. I suggest here a conceptual framework for reading these texts anchored by three terms: unreading, eventfulness, and historical selflessness. Reading Dalit texts as an articulation of a posthistoricist (neither ahistorical nor apolitical) realism—a realism less indebted to a certain model of nineteenth-century historicism, a realism that isn't derived from the individual and his relation to the historical event—might allow us to do justice to texts that are otherwise too easily and too often read as identity-driven, ahistorical, or ethnographic material of limited theoretical import.[4] If, therefore, a Dalit text seems indifferent to Partition, and, more strikingly, to properly Dalit historical events, then this may not be simply a question for sociological and historical justification. This may also be a question of literary reading.

READING DALIT LITERATURE

Contemporary literary criticism is poorly equipped to read Dalit literature. If, as scholar Kancha Ilaiah calls it, Dalit historiography is "a history of white pages" (227), then Dalit literature is broadly read as a corrective to that history, a history of uppercaste elision and fabrication. Like other protest literatures, it has tasked itself with both a formalistic revolution that stretches the boundaries of what has been heretofore considered "literary" as well as a revisionist history that resurrects the Dalit from the abyss of anonymity. From its very conception, therefore, particularly as a "supplement" to uppercaste cultural monopoly, Dalit literature has been concerned with historical resurrection, representation, and revision, as well as with its own historicity, a fact apparent from the readings in the earlier part of this book. And yet the dominant theoretical frameworks for contemporary Indian fiction, those that have been produced largely by postcolonial literary studies (Nation, Other, Diaspora, Hybridity), have been fairly indifferent to the question of caste as an analytical category and the particular historical imperative this may engender. This is somewhat understandable, since the Anglophone material that has been the primary object of investigation has not produced the impetus to raise such questions. But even more subtly—and this is a problem unspecific to postcolonial literary analysis—such criticism understands historicity, and the historical event, as the central determinate fictional force within and around the text.[5] The irony is that such an analytical framework, one that has made only occasional mention of structures of caste as entirely separate and distinct from those of class, while being entirely sidestepped by Dalit literary criticism, is the one we are left with when reading Dalit literature abroad. *Joothan* thus provides us with a self-conscious example of an intricacy that has effectively structured our reading practices for decades. The notion of the "historical" has come to be a central evaluatory mechanism by which one reads the novel specifically, and fiction more generally.[6] This is of particular concern when the object of that analytical gaze falls on Dalit fiction, for which, it can very mildly be said, History means something entirely different.

Historical realism in the Dalit context conjures something quite different from that associated with the French bourgeois novelists of the mid-nineteenth century, as well as from that associated with the early Indian social realists like Premchand and Yashpal who predicated their work on a narrative objectivity, a wide-angled lens shadowed by the political concerns and imperatives of contemporary history.[7] These were realisms deeply indebted to the historical moment, the individual mired within it, and a progressive teleology, and consequently lent themselves to a historicist reading practice. But Dalit literature is a movement that claims to represent in its protagonists a collectivity, while insisting at the same time on their own radical individualism, as well as a movement that derives legitimacy from historical specificity while asserting a kind of posthistorical consciousness.[8] When Guru insists that "control over time and space becomes a background condition for deciding the quality of civilisational claims" (Dalit Vision 758), one realizes that this is as much a literary and narrative problem as a material one, a problem that generates a unique aesthetics of realism. But it is also a philosophical position taken by those who perceive themselves and are perceived to be outside history. Importantly, for Guru, time and space are premised equally, and Dalit literature treats both of these narrative questions with equal seriousness. All of this is to say that Dalit literature writes itself *in opposition* to a certain tradition, creating an antigenealogy of sorts, rather than as an outgrowth of an old model. The same should be said of its analytics.[9] This is the context in which the contributions to debates on realism that Dalit literature in Hindi offers must be understood. I argue here that reading "history" in Dalit literature would help us to identify a realism that has its origins in the humanism of a protest literature—i.e., in a totally different framework than that of the eighteenth- and nineteenth-century novel, bourgeois historicism, and European proto-nationalism.

Beyond underlining the very basic facts of Dalit stigmatized existence, social exclusion, atrocity, and poverty, criticism has pointed out how this might generate a distinctive relationship to questions of history.[10] As D. R. Nagaraj says, "The ideology of the Dalit movement derives its radical energy from the position that Indian history has been frozen in feudal time" (113). Dalit rage then—as Nagaraj describes it, a politics and an aesthetic—derives from the failures of history, which modern narrative forms attempt to rectify. Of course, it is not the simple failure of historical progression but also its very masquerade: historicism presumes a kind of movement that is unavailable to the Dalit. That stagnation, as Nagaraj points out, is the premise on which the Dalit text is based. Kancha Ilaiah reads Dalit history according to the well-known Hegelian model, but in his formulation, it is Dalit history that is originary and primary: the thesis. He underlines the labor-based knowledge of the "productive castes" as true knowledge, the knowledge of the proletariat transposed. The history of the uppercastes—History, in fact—should be read as an elaborate and cumulative response to Dalit self-assertion. "The relationship between these forces in the form of thesis and anti-thesis has resulted in producing a synthesis but it is a mutilated synthesis. It is unnatural for a section of human beings to acquire the role of anti-thesis and continue to play that role always" (113). Ilaiah's political hopes lie precisely in the unfinished and inevitable teleology that will eventually challenge a false and degraded synthesis.

Some Dalit textuality is clearly inspired by such a model of historicity and the starkest social realism allows it to conform to its demands and its vision of justice. Nagaraj, however, offers us a critique of origins. Concerned less with the question of historical origins per se, and more with "the moment of metaphorical birth," Nagaraj reads history less teleologically, across a wide range of culturalist practices. Rather than reading metaphor here as the refuge of the history-less, Nagaraj asserts the superiority of "metaphorical birth" over historical moments that can be demonstrated "in terms of factual data" (94). In his reading of the Gandhi-Ambedkar contestation over the question of separate electorates, and Gandhi's "fast unto death," Nagaraj excavates the story of the "untouchable youth." The youth, who was to bring an orange to break Gandhi's fast, claimed he was denied entry to Gandhi's camp. He later confessed that he had lied. Nagaraj writes, "By deliberately missing the appointment with Gandhi on that historical day, the unnamed youth had metaphorically begun the Dalit movement. The Gandhian project had no real role for untouchables. . . . The boy's lie was a truthful act to protect his self-respect, and thus began the strain-filled, necessary, imaginative search for the politics of Dalit identity" (102). Nagaraj's reading is unusual in many respects: it resurrects the buried actor, it rereads his intentionality, it makes of him a symptom of something as yet unnamed, that can only be read anachronistically.

The meditations of Nagaraj and Ilaiah offer certain suggestions that I will take up throughout this chapter. Firstly, Nagaraj's interpretation of the origins of Dalit protest offers us a precedent for a different type of reading, which is less reliant upon historical facticity and more upon metaphorical and metanarrative operation. Secondly, it is symptomatic of the Dalit critique more broadly; it is antinational, even nonnational, and thus refuses to structure any reading of historicity around the category of the nation. Thirdly, rereading historical primacy in the productive labor of the Dalit as Ilaiah does performs an interesting intellectual maneuver; it shifts the temporal map by creating not another myriad of actors but the Dalit (or *dalitbahujan*) as the world historical figure(s). Ilaiah suggests that the causal derivations of the Historical and the National must be sought elsewhere, in the location of the Dalit. This is a subalternist position that is distinct from the subalternist one that sought to resurrect the contributions of the marginalized into the mainstream of History.

What I attempt to do here is read such a historical disinvestment in the national and, counterintuitively, even in the local or Dalit, in terms of its aesthetic outcomes. In other words, what is realism without History? What I suggest is that it is particularly the Dalitization of narrative time—productive of a chronology that is nonnational, nonhistorical, event-driven, and most importantly, *nonhistoricist*—that complicates our ability to justly read such texts, dominated as our readings are by questions generated for an entirely different discourse. For these texts, in which the very desirability of a *savarna* historical consciousness, particularly in the slender form of eventfulness, is called into question, a new reading is required.

UNREADING

In her introduction to the anthology *Dusari duniya ka yatharth (The Realities of Another World)*,[11] an anthology of Dalit literature, Ramanika Gupta writes: "A great people has been made unaware and lifeless, not only towards life's most basic needs, but towards life itself. For centuries they have thought only of previous lives and future lives, this life they consider as atonement. Their pain and suffering, the barbarous atrocities that have been inflicted upon them, towards all of this they have for centuries remained inert, considering it their fate. They have been made into Premchand's Ghisu and Madhav" (ii).[12] This inaugural moment is an attempt to contextualize the collected stories for a non-Dalit reader, but I read Gupta's introduction as a prescription for reading the Dalit text more generally, as well as a deft dissection of a literary archetype. The subjects in this passage do not understand their condition within the discrete confines of present, biological life; the chronology referred to here is much older, much longer. The aforementioned atrocities are not nameable, datable events; rather, they have been compiled across time in the form of "transgenerational haunting." But this passage does not lead us into a debate about the qualitative differences between Western and vernacular conceptions of time, or for that matter, upper- and lower-caste conceptions. Gupta is an activist and though her comments may seem patronizing—degrading even, particularly because of the use of the intransitive verb construction, which seems to deny any form of agency to the subject—what she refers to is a social condition that is entirely historically determined. The timeless inertia she cites has been produced by a litany of miseries and must be read as such, not as immanent, or constitutive. The passive constructions throughout the passage insist that the reader unlearn his instinct: If they appear inert, they are not; if they appear lifeless, they are not; they have been produced as such. Gupta's comment seems to enter the Dalit into the cycle of the timeless, but rather, it makes an argument for a suspension of the "when?" of the *savarna*, rationalist, historical reading.

Gupta also reads the "great people," the Dalits, as masses of "Ghisu-Madhavs," Premchand's infamous father-son pair from the 1936 story *Kafan (The Shroud)*, using the "timeless" literary figures to characterize the material reality of a people. This is a strange rhetorical move given the controversial status we know now the father of Hindi letters holds in Dalit literature, critiqued for his sententious, pitiful representation of the Dalit. The characters of Ghisu and Madhav are unique, however, because of their unusually exploitative interpretation of the "timelessness" of their social condition. When faced with the death of his wife, Madhav and his father Ghisu, lowercaste laborers, go begging for money from higher caste villagers to provide for the proper burial shroud. Upon receiving it, the two men spend the money on food and drink, knowing that they will again be able to exploit the community's sense of propriety and social norms. The pair turn to such an option, it seems, because they sense the immutability of their condition, as well as the immutability of cultural practice (no doubt, the two are intimately related). In the story, the men laugh and eat roasted potatoes as the woman lies inside. Ghisu and Madhav are the most salient examples of what Dalit critics read as Premchand's irrevocable Kayastha uppercaste perspective; despite his attempts at a benevolent social realism that would incorporate into the literary sphere the world of the peasant, his uppercaste status could only see the Dalit as an object of pity and disdain. Gupta suggests a kind of alternative. If Dalit characters are easily read as Ghisus and Madhavs, then this is a reflection as much of a reading practice as of certain material conditions of oppression, both of which require an undoing. Ghisu and Madhav, in other words, are not realistic representations of Dalits; rather, literary Dalits are most easily *read* as Ghisu and Madhav.

The kind of rhetorical inversion that I am deriving from Gupta's comments is demonstrated in the very controversial reading of the same Premchand short story by Hindi Dalit critic Dr. Dharamvir. In 2005, in a public lecture, Dharamvir asserted that the reason that Ghisu and Madhav show such a disdainful indifference to the dying woman is because she was raped and was carrying the landlord's child. The wife of Madhav makes only the briefest appearance in Premchand's story, but her untimely death launches the entire plot. I won't advocate Dharamvir's reading here: there doesn't seem to be any evidence for rape in the story, and the gender politics it implies, including the "rape script"—the subject of much discussion in Dalit literary circles[13]—is indeed problematic. Nonetheless, this assertion raises, I think, two important strategies for an "unreading." When a woman lies dying in a novel peopled by uppercaste, upperclass characters in uppercaste, upperclass spaces, what does she suffer from? In contrast, what does a Dalit woman die of? Rape and childbirth. Dharamvir's assertion implies that asking a different question reframes Ghisu and Madhav entirely. While this seems like a liberal fictionality, it is also a kind of assertion of Dalit positionality. What is valuable about Dharamvir's critique is that it advocates a *reworking* of readerly assumption, not only its most basic acknowledgement. Secondly, Dharamvir's conclusion raises, I think, a different historical timeline that shifts from the "event" to its prehistory. Although it is the disturbing fact of rape that would give Ghisu and Madhav an ethical capital within the context of the story, it is also an essential reframing of narrative chronology that provides this ethical license and freedom. The story presents a narrative enigma—that of a young woman's untimely death—thereby raising the question of narrative "evidence." A typical reading of "Kafan" would never make much of the lack of explicit causality as it is not seen to be contextually necessary for a reading of Ghisu and Madhav's character; the enigma, if addressed at all, is answered via typicality, thereby burying the question of the cause of the woman's death. But to use the evidence of typicality raises the question of the allusive structure of reading, via which narrative gaps are often filled. "Progressive" literatures, texts, and literary movements are shaped by a certain ideological halo; they do not need to ask, for example, how a Dalit woman died. They are required, however, to demand a hegemonic structure of ethical accountability from all their subjects. A Dalit reading challenges the entire structure of narrative typicality, and of the ensuing allusive chain on which uppercaste reading is premised. And in this case, it also shifts the weight of the story such that the event is no longer Ghisu and Madhav's transgression but the nonnarrative rape. This is one example of what an "unreading" might do: unwork the assumptions underwriting the Dalit character as he has been produced by the literary canon, and expand the temporal and chronological map provided by the narrative fictional framework in a paratactic way such that the putative event is deconstructed.

In the following two sections of this chapter, I illustrate this rhetorical problem by offering a different type of reading of two Dalit texts. Both of these texts articulate a historical vision explicitly different from both Westernized and *savarna* historicity, thereby producing conceptual challenges for the non-Dalit reading practice. If certain forms of reading overprivilege historical determination, "unreading" acknowledges other forms of political—even metaphorical—causality.

HISTORICAL SELFLESSNESS

Mohandas Naimishraya's fictionalized autobiography *Apne-apne pinjare* (*Cages of Our Own*) was published in 1995; Naimishraya has since become very well known and is often anthologized. I should mention that this characterization, "fictionalized autobiography," is entirely my own. Both the author of the text and the author of the introduction to the text call it an *atmacharitra* (self analysis or portrait) or *atmavrat* (narrative or account of the self, autobiography), ostensibly alongside Omprakash Valmiki's *Joothan*, Sharankumar Limbale's *The Outcaste*, and many others. In fact, the insistence on experience, truth-telling, and accurate representation makes this a heated issue. The question of fictionality is central here as it changes the kind of analytical limitations associated with the reading of autobiography. H. S. Shivaprakash writes of the new generation of Dalit writers in Kannada, "Most of the younger Dalit writers bring in a lot of historically and sociologically manufactured material into their writings that have the rough-hewn authenticity and astuteness of the autobiographical" (124). For my part, the adjective "fictionalized" allows me (1) to blur the generic distinction between fiction and nonfiction, which I feel is unhelpful in literary analysis of Dalit texts, almost all of which proceed from the premise of illuminating the subject and the subjective, and (2) to characterize several moments, rhetorical strategies, and narrative patterns that seem to fall outside the traditional understanding of autobiography. Indeed, as I shall argue, the very underpinnings of autobiography, essentially the narrative reconstruction of the self as a result of social and historical forces, is undermined by Dalit texts.

The genre of Dalit autobiography offers us a particularly salient opportunity to dissect the problem of historicity. Undoubtedly one of the most important genres of the modern canon of this literature of protest, autobiography is in fact inaugural; it marks the start of Dalit literary movement. In Hindi, several major writers have contributed their life-writings, including Omprakash Valmiki, Surajpal Chauhan, and Sheoraj Singh Bechain. The critical reception of autobiography has been fairly nonvariegated, however. Typically read as the revelation of both one individual life and the community that created him, it is a genre—"documented Dalit history"—that seems to obviate the need for literary analysis.[14] One recent counterpoint would be Raj Kumar's *Dalit Personal Narratives*, which traces a different origin of, but still acknowledges, the ethnographic readings of these texts.[15] Debjani Ganguly reads Dalit life-writing as being at the intersection of the individual and communitarian, creating a complex articulation of "Dalit personhood," one that overlaps with the testimonio, political participation, and the demand for human rights. The suggestions of Ganguly and others would allow us to complicate Frederic Jameson's reading of autobiography as a symptom of postmodern crisis, as "one more private language among others: reduced to the telling of the truth of a private situation alone, that no longer engages the fate of a nation, but merely a single locality" (*Ideologies* 131). Autobiography, as a genre, as a form, as a mode of narrative engagement or as a subtext, is symptomatic for Jameson of social fragmentation and the crisis of modern collectivity. What I want to argue here is that, in contrast to both "private language" and "documented history," the genre of autobiography or life-writing concerns a reinvestigation of historical causality, the relations among things, and relationality more broadly; this is where its intervention lies.

In "Apna gav" ("Our Village"), discussed in chapter 3, Naimishraya takes the figure of the journalist to task for her foreignness, her intrusion, and her crass attempt to turn a tragedy into an event worthy of newspaper reportage. *Apne-apne pinjare* suggests a similar but metanarrative critique. The 1947 Partition of India, which as a historical object of study as well as a literary theme has dominated contemporary research, is treated uniquely in this text—evaded, even. The text does provide us with some contextual markers to situate the historical and political moment: key dates, the casual mention of the Poona Pact, hints of violence in the cities, newspaper headlines, occasional appearances by important local politicians. These signposts, however, signal only the distance, both spatial and metaphorical, from the real preoccupations of the text: the collapse of the family home in the rainy season, the protagonist's maltreatment by teachers, the lure of urban life. When Partition does become an object of the protagonist's focus and interpretation, it appears as an eight-page sequence sandwiched between an exposition on the perils of hot weather and a rather anthropological account of an important local festival. This is how the discussion of Partition begins: "From the beginning, my city has remained a battleground. That battle has been fought in the name of religion, in the name of clan, even over scraps of land. To settle one city, another would be destroyed. In this city, even after independence, the battle continued." I don't believe it is enough to say that Partition is someone else's history. Rather, Partition is not even *Partition*. In fact, as an event of profound historical consequence, it is dismissed, contextualized amid a host of other inconsequential battles: those that take place over seemingly unimportant bits of land, those that are fought in the name of minor political causes, those shortsighted rampages of destruction and creation. The tone of the passage suggests none of the reverence or even fear with which this topic is typically addressed, rather a distance in inflection that recalls the voice of an indifferent observer. The otherness of this history allows it to be read within a larger pattern of battles and wars, denying it any historical singularity.

With that comment, we enter the narrator's rendition of Partition, characterized most vividly in terms of the curfew. The curfew is imposed for days on end, and is characterized by constant police and army patrols, a rationing that stretches limited resources to the extreme, and a fear of Muslim attack. Despite this, the narrator's initial attitude of indifference is confirmed, for his sentiment is echoed by the narrator's aunt and her neighbor as they finally peek out of their windows after several days of locking themselves in their homes out of fear. "'Hey, mother of Mohan, what does this curfew have to do with us? We are simply neighbors. Let god destroy those responsible for the rioting.' . . . Let them order a curfew, they were neighbors and there was no wall strong enough to stand between neighbors. Toppling the wall was the very reason that the conversation began. That night we were all a little less fearful" (45). A small act of resistance perhaps, but a reflection of the notion that the curfew and its imposition are exterior things, announced from above, but largely irrelevant. This is localism, yes, or everyday life, but there is no investment in *reading* Partition as an event of structural consequence.

Still, these stories bear few hints of naiveté; if curfew and, by extension, Partition, is a problem of another world, it is clear that the lowercaste inhabitants of Meerut's slums are at the mercy of that very world. Sumit Sarkar attempts to finesse the subtlety of that relationship (between home and the world, between lowercaste communities and hegemonic politics, history and historiography); he writes that while he shares the critique of caste, which privileges a structural harmony and consensus, he finds the "assumption of a sharp and total disjunction between the domains of high-caste power and subordinate autonomy equally unhelpful" (42).[16] In this text, Partition isn't completely elided but is read—not just primarily, but solely—in terms of its exacerbation of the problems of hunger and clean water. Undoubtedly, more attention is devoted to the shrinking levels of flour in the canisters, the dried-up canal, the worsening quality of meals, than to the threat of communal conflict, the hints of violence in nearby streets, the ceaseless mobs yelling frightening slogans. If Partition is someone else's construction, it clearly has traumatic repercussions for all who fall within its scope. And yet, those repercussions are established in terms entirely different from those that have come to be representative: national, uppercaste, urban. There is no discussion, as there is in other texts that deal with Partition, of the potential loss of homes and fortunes, the dropping rates of currency, the ubiquitous threat of mob violence, and so forth.[17] Rather, Partition is measured by the amount of lentils left in the jars, the trickle of water in the canal, and the rising interest rates of moneylenders. Immediately after the curfew is lifted, the very next sentence of the text mentions the filling of the empty flour canisters. This is "real" life.[18]

This is clearly a reflection of a class positionality that experiences historical exigencies in differential ways. This is also a question of caste positionality that is not only antinational, but is additionally dismissive of the very eventfulness of Partition. The mild irony surrounding Partition in *Apne-apne pinjare* is only detectable by the contextual gaze, not by a close reading of tone. Yashpal's 1958–60 *Jhoot sach* makes of Naimishraya's eight pages a two-volume novel; Bisham Sahni's 1974 Partition novel *Tamas* is some three hundred pages. More to the point, in *Tamas*, Partition produces subjectivity: it is the means by which the characters demonstrate who they are. In *Tamas*, Nathu the Chamar takes upon himself the blame for the eruption of riots! Naimishraya's rendition is in direct contrast to those novels or Bapsi Sidhwa's *Cracking India* or Kushwant Singh's *Train to Pakistan*. In *Cracking India*, for example, the telescopic vision of the text is focused entirely on the events of Partition and the few years prior as they are read by a young Parsi girl in Lahore. While the novel does offer us the occasional incursion into the mind of the peasant, the villager, or the lowercaste laborer, this is deliberately secondary and singular compared to the real action of the text—the impending burning and destruction of the protagonist Lennie's Lahore. More importantly, the philosophical premise of *Cracking India*, its narrative drive, is towards a recovery of self—the implicit understanding being that the telling of Partition is the creation of Lennie, our narrator; it is the event that propels her into adult subjectivity. Similarly, at the end of the Mulk Raj Anand novel *Untouchable*, we return to Gandhi and the Indian National Congress from which we might have said to have been detoured. In a sense, the whole novel reads as a coming to consciousness not only of caste identity but of Gandhian politics as well. Each moment of abuse in the narrative, each interaction that Anand's Dalit character has, prepares him, directs him, and enables him in the end to be both receptive to and critical of Gandhi and this World (the world of nationalist history and historiography). This is as true of Anand as it is of Hindi writers such as Premchand and Agyeya, whose work featured caste questions often in an ideologically challenging way, albeit without explicitly focusing on them. In *Cages of Our Own* and *The Autobiography of an Indian Outcaste* (as we shall see shortly), however, the World is an interruption, largely sidelined for the day-to-day struggles, the day-to-day histories of one boy, one family, one community, one caste. The narrative eye is exclusively focused on, and in fact born from, the aforementioned peripheral space.

This is not to say at all that the official narrative of Partition does not encroach upon the psychosocial spaces inhabited in *Apne-apne pinjare*. Indeed, our narrator speaks of the metaphorical transformations under curfew when men of flesh and bone became ghosts, homes became graves, and the entire street a cemetery. However, the way in which that encroachment occurs is atypical. The night before the curfew is lifted, the sound of sobbing spreads through the street. The narrator's family learns that their Muslim neighbor's son has been killed, the body arriving home wrapped in a white sheet. Slowly, from across the roof, the grieving family turns their hateful stares onto their Chamar[19] neighbors. When the narrator asks his father why the Hindus are killing Muslims, his father replies, "Because they are Hindu." "And what are we?" replies the narrator. "We are Chamar." "But aren't Chamars Hindu?" His father replies, "Chamars are Chamars. Neither Hindu nor Muslim" (51). In the end, Partition does not serve to cultivate nationalist sentiment but rather to confirm caste marginality. In fact, the event serves as a vehicle for the construction and confirmation of an identity, an identity that until this moment in the text is suggested to have been somewhat fluid: "Questions began to rise up inside me, but I didn't ask anything further, so as not to anger Ba. We were neither Hindu nor Muslim. Why was that? We are Chamar, why is that? Who are Chamars? At that time I didn't know anything, I wanted to understand. But who to ask? Ba never had any free time from cutting, beating, and pounding skins. He seemed to have developed a strange relationship with these dead carcasses" (51). In an atmosphere polarized by Hindu-Muslim conflict, there seems to be no space for the construction of other identities. Even if this were true, on what basis is Chamarness constructed? Our answer comes ironically with the deferral of the child's question: his father unknowingly suggests that the answer lies in the labor of leather, in the relationship to a certain work. The death and destruction of Partition is supplanted by the mundane relationship to death experienced on a daily basis by the Chamar.

Partition therefore emerges less as a national tragedy than as a vehicle for the analysis of identity politics in the case of a young boy. The questions of legislative power, the redrawing of the maps, and the pervasive violence and slaughter so familiar to us from other Partition fiction do not appear at all. Most importantly, beyond the few pages dedicated to this subject, Partition is absent. Unlike in much contemporary writing from India, it does not hover over the text; it is not the inevitable locus of trauma nor is it the preeminent historical moment, that which divides literary chronology. How do we read a text that dehistoricizes the central historical event of modern Indian history? The genre of autobiography provides an easy critical exit. But in a communitarian literary movement read as an expression of Ambedkarism, social protest, and, crucially, the raising of Dalit consciousness, this reliance on genre is a trap. The very form of Dalit autobiography possesses a political valence absent from the term's more general usage since it claims the autobiographical as always historical. Denying Partition the primacy it might receive, for example, in novels of the Hindi middle class, or in Indian Anglophone texts, is in part a reflection of a certain caste logic that refers to such national events as someone else's history, a fact that has long been asserted by critics and intellectuals.[20] Gayatri Spivak's by now well-known readings of Mahasweta Devi's tribal communities recall precisely that fact. But I will argue something slightly different here: this is not necessarily a rereading of Partition from the local, nor a rendition of history as it "complicates" the life and direction of the protagonist; such a mode of reading would privilege, once again, the *ethnographic* disclosure a Dalit text seems to offer. I would say it is instead a reading that questions the category of historical knowledge and its role in the construction of identity, thereby domesticating Partition to the realm of the everyday. What I mean to stress here is that *Apne-apne pinjare* avoids not only a narrative chronology structured around a nationalist historiography but also an evolutionary logic that assumes the subject to be developmentally produced by such, or any such, historiography. The most significant departure is that these texts articulate a historical consciousness that does not propose to aid in the recovery of self typically proposed by the genre.

EVENTFULNESS

Apne-apne pinjare deprivileges the event such that the reader is forced to unread it: an attempt to anchor the text via Partition would fail, or more pointedly, would read the Dalit text as a failure. But as I have suggested, this deconstruction of the event is in the service of a larger point: the question of the narrative production of self. I read the following text as performing that very delinking between eventfulness and the subject. Considering the date of the text, 1951, and its seminal nature within the comparatively short history of Dalit assertion and literary production in the North, we might think of it as establishing a kind of literary precedent of selflessness. A very early example of Dalit literature from the Hindi/Urdu-speaking regions of India, Hazari's *I Was an Outcaste: The Autobiography of an Untouchable in India*, is a fictionalized autobiographical narrative of a Dalit boy that follows the author from birth until adulthood. One of the primary features of this text, and many other Dalit texts, is a skepticism towards textuality and all that it represents. Although the text uses a fairly linear format, it consistently throws historical chronology into question. Consider the following comment:

> The most memorable thing after leaving Simla and enjoying the train ride was the station where we alighted for our village. I cannot say whether this was my first, second or third coming home, but I remember we reached our home in the late afternoon....
>
> I cannot remember the exact dates of these early happenings as my people calculated dates by some important world event, or by some happening in the community or town which affected them personally, such as a big fire or an earthquake, a marriage or a death. Even then one is none the wiser as to a precise date or year, for no written records were kept of births, deaths and marriages.
>
> By the time I was seven or eight, I must have been to Simla several times and returned to our village for the winter months. (26)

How do we read the narrative construction of self, on which "autobiography" is premised, when the genealogy that has produced that self is so hazy? The fact of nonreliance upon written record is by no means unusual; a similar phenomenon is mentioned in many Dalit texts. However, the implications of such a comment early in the text are crucial. The lack of record-keeping and the consequent haziness of both official history as well as community history provide the subtext for a critique of written language—reliant upon and therefore subject to the same fallibilities in its attempt at reconstruction as individual memory. Hazari's text, which serves equally as a construction and a reconstruction of an individual life, is an example of the aforementioned "happenings" for which there is no documentary evidence. Both of the narrative musings that surround the comments on memory and history highlight the unknowability of the past, thereby providing an ideological framework for the narrative analysis of historical event that follows.

This initial comment sets the stage for a narrative that moves circularly through a series of spaces: from Simla to the village and back, from the village to Bombay and back, from the village to Delhi and back, again and again and again. Chapter titles such as "Delhi," "Northwest Frontier," "Snows of Simla" and "Kashmir" remind us that in this story of untouchability, location is a driving force and the passing of time is processed spatially; movement or passage is not only diachronic but also geographic. Most Dalit texts, in one way or another, address the politics of location. Caste marginality is clearly represented as not only a problem of birth and religious decree but of segregation in space. This is why in Hazari's *Outcaste*, in Valmiki's *Joothan*, and in Naimishraya's *Apne-apne pinjare*, there is a careful attention to village geography, the delineation of space and its relation to power, the price of transgression, and so forth. For the same reason, there is an underlying fixation on movement in the texts' literal, figurative, and metatextual registers. Such fixation appears in the very structuring of these narratives, in which intellectual and social freedom is coded through geographic change, in the image of trains and transportation, and even in the choice of certain verbs, which codes a desire for movement in the most confining of situations.

If we were to force a linear understanding of time on this text, we might say that it is moving towards an escape from the village, suggesting a type of social independence rather than a political statist one. But the escape from the village occurs in the text repeatedly, for each attempt is a failed one. The travels to the city bring neither financial nor emotional fulfillment to our narrator—the final displacement thus equaling zero. The very emplotment of the text, therefore—while not exactly cyclical—is premised on repetition, defying a teleological reading. The liberation of the Dalit, or at least of our narrator, which may be the only legitimate endpoint towards which the narrative could be said to be moving, never occurs—nor are we given the sense that this is a real possibility. This text is structured quite differently from Naimishraya's, yet it, too, refuses to become amenable to a linear, historical reading, not least because of a subtly detached gaze that produces the faintest sense of irony—a sense that circulates through the text and prefigures the analysis to follow.

What I refer to as a spatialized consciousness throws the historical event into a kind of metanarrative relief, demanding that it be read, appearing, as it does, like a rhetorical beacon for the non-Dalit reader. It is only after ninety pages of the narrative that we have the first reference to any moment that might appear on a national timeline: the narrator mentions "the new movement against British rule and for the acquisition of Home Rule." The language itself shows the narrator's unfamiliarity with these happenings as does the fact that this knowledge comes to him quite late. Furthermore, he learns of the events indirectly by overhearing a discussion about their newspaper coverage, since he himself is not able to read. This is noteworthy in and of itself since our narrator makes no comment on the presence of British troops in Simla and the agitation against them (which we as readers can glean from the narrative). This is what he writes of the Jallianwalla Bagh massacre:[21]

> What did stab my mind and feelings with great force was the mass shooting of men, women, and children at Jallianwalla Bagh, in 1919, by order of General Dyer. I felt the slaughter of innocent women and children could not be justified; but this did not make me wear the Gandhi cap, which many people were wearing at that time. My most pleasant hours were still spent in the solitude of nature. I enjoyed the snow and the clear skies. I could gaze upon the distant peaks and watch the little, colorful snow birds, hopping from one branch to another. I reveled in long walks during the snowfalls, and these things mean more to me than all the promises of a free India. (93)

Although Hazari mentions just prior to this passage, "The movement for the opening of Brahmin temples to untouchables meant nothing to me," he does say, "If I wore a Gandhi cap, no one would ask who I was" (61). But this moment passes and the sense of alienation he feels from the dominant political concerns surrounding him remains tangible. The narrator's position of liberal sympathy for the victims (and not the male ones, incidentally) is precisely that of Premchand for his peasants! The text therefore demonstrates an abstract humanism that takes as its object the slaughter of innocents as well as solitude and snow. All the clichés of Romantic poetry are present (and specifically British Romantic poetry, I should add, not the Indian literary movement called Chhayavaad, which is often translated as romanticism). We move from the language of allegiance and alliance to affect. The narrator's negotiation of the massacre most certainly seems provocative; his decided tone ensures that Gandhi will have to do better rhetorically than "Harijans" and "innocents" to persuade him to join his cause. And yet what might be perceived as a revolutionary turn away from a mainstream politics—a politics that has repeatedly failed the Dalit—and a turn towards Ambedkar instead—seems to be compromised by the narrator's interest in snowfall, skies, snowbirds, solitude, and his total repudiation of the Dalit movement. It may be convenient to read Hazari as the typical Anglophile as he longs to dress in a certain way and finds life as a servant with a British family much preferable to life as an untouchable in the village; after all, his only object of affection in the story is predictably a British mistress of household. But what we perceive as Anglophilia here is largely a construction that comes to us from the historical and literary evidence of the middle classes. In a similar vein, the landscape scenes—easily read as the inverse of historical actualities—would then be categorized as "personal reflections" or evocations of the "pastoral." But Hazari's "independence," his "freedom" to move through certain unmarked spaces can *only be* political, his disinterest in temple entry movements notwithstanding. This is a subjectivity deeply indebted not to Amritsar or the Dalit movement but to a series of putatively nonhistorical moments that culminate in the birds "hopping from one branch to another." As in Naimishraya's text, the historical event occupies a very different place; it is only a vehicle for the crystallization of a certain process of identification, and ultimately for a kind of separatist logic signaled by the shibboleths of "We are Chamar" and "I enjoy solitude" rather than the locus of the construction of the self. Hazari's narrative "I" is not produced through the slow accretion of eventfulness, that of the *savarna* or "his own." In fact, if we "unread" here, the narrative reconstruction of self circumvents the event entirely; Solitude, here, is the Time and Space, the event, that replaces Amritsar.

DALIT REALISMS REVISITED

Many critics and writers have elaborated the complex forms of Dalit belonging and the very varied relationships the "outcasted" may have to the national project, famed reformer Jyotirao Phule and Ambedkar not least among them. The Dalit literary text, I would say, has a kind of privileged ability to unravel that web, situated as it is among the realist, the pedagogical, and the potential. One thing that those texts demonstrate is that such affiliations are rarely monovalent and singular, and that they vary over time. This could, of course, be why Hazari says, "the movements of temple entry had no interest for me." Nor the Poona Pact, the various phases of Mahar assertion, the Chavdar Tank movement, the burning of the Manusmriti, or Ambedkar's 1956 public conversion—along with several hundred thousand others—to Buddhism. In Meerut alone, the proprietary city of *Apne-apne pinjare*, both the Scheduled Caste Federation and Ambedkar's Republican Party of India were very active in the 1940s and 1950s but receive no attention in Naimishraya's narrative.[22]

The work of the Subaltern Studies Group might seem to complicate such an analysis. Justifiably groundbreaking, the seductive simplicity of this project of recovery helped to build a revolutionary historical consciousness.[23] The argument that I make in this essay should not be misunderstood as a denial of the making of that history on behalf of Dalit actors, whether their own or that of the nation to which they may or may not belong—contributions that are now being beautifully catalogued in several languages. But there is also a vast range of creative materials that invent, ironize, and fictionalize caste histories—histories that bear only tenuous relation to what modern narrative forms might categorize as historical.[24] My argument thus offers a literary explanation of the underpinnings of such a recovery project, an explanation of an ostensible "lack," precisely the kind of lack that certain historicist readers of literature would seek to recuperate, but that may not be a lack at all. This *narrative* hole should be read not as a hole but as an active disinvestment in the transformative power of the filler, especially insofar as it contributes to the creation of the subject.[25] Reading Naimishraya or Hazari, one sees that place emerges as a critical category of utmost importance in texts that consider not only historical ways of knowing, but spatial ones as well. What these texts tell us is that the focus on historical eventfulness, even on its putative recovery, is only one way of reading world experience and the emergence and transformation of the self; it is neither definitive nor necessary. Diminishing the power of the historical process, at least narratively, divesting it of its centrality in literary production, helps to dismantle the hegemony of a mainstream historical discourse even if it does not suggest an alternative. Reading Dalit literature thus challenges a tradition that has worked itself into the fibers of literary praxis.[26]

If these Dalit texts seem indifferent to the properly historical, the nationalist, as well as to a project of subaltern recovery, what can we say about their narratological demonstration of a historical understanding?

In the previous two texts, the Amritsar massacre and Partition are present but refashioned. The texts also do not organize themselves around moments of subaltern "eventfulness." The issue, I think is less *what* the event means in Dalit texts but more that it simply does not *mean*—i.e., possess meaning—in the same way at all. What they signify, like Flaubert's barometer, is an investment in the category of the real. This is what makes the Dalit text challenging to read; according to the critical paradigm of modern literary praxis available to us, the narrative eye appears weightless, unanchored by the force of the historical.

These texts question the logic of causality, they render the notion of historical making and unmaking suspect. While the crisis of history may be responsible for, or at the origins of, the subject's plight—and indeed subalternity itself—this crisis demonstrates only one ideological strain in the complex web that is the formation of character; the texts actually discourage a historicist reading. This is to say that the narrative method of reading character is not necessarily informed by a traditional conception of history, by political and social events, or by state intervention, but by individual and social genealogies, by the collective practices of day-to-day life. The larger structural forces (the smaller ones, too, in fact) that have played a role in the present conditions—Amritsar, the Poona Pact, Partition—are not ignored, they are simply not privileged. If the historical process as a mode of interpretation is discredited, this is not to say that history as an entity is absent from the text, but that it might be perceived as a compromised analytic, a failed hermeneutics, and that the notion of historical perspective may not be as horizontally appropriate as it might seem.

Franco Moretti mentions in his study of the genre of the bildungsroman that historical consciousness in Europe, or the understanding of meaning as constructed through historical perspective, is largely a product of the nineteenth century. Modern fiction generally, and modern Indian fiction particularly, has, of course, privileged this reading for a host of historical reasons specific to a South Asian context too complicated to address here. But Dalit texts oblige us to unlearn this form of "rationality." The focus on a series of synchronic stories whose determinacy is constantly thrown into question and the fixation with the geographic as a conceptual category are neither ahistorical nor subaltern but constitute a rejection of the overwhelming weight of the historical in our systems of interpretation. "Unreading" doesn't make Hazari into a patriot, but a partisan certainly. Analyses of the national as well as the alienation from the national will unfortunately be unable to help us determine of what, however. A text such as Hazari's is thus challenging to accommodate not because it lacks an understanding of history, but because it moves away from a deliberately diachronic reading of identity, character, and meaning; it exhibits a posthistoricist vision. The two Dalit texts present a radical delinking of historical determination and the production of character, suggesting a concept of time and history within the literary text that simply cannot be accommodated by prevailing critical paradigms. In other words, they assume a form of "Dalit realism."

What does a Dalit realism look like? As I've attempted to demonstrate in the preceding chapters, this is a realism that rewrites the notion of the sympathetic character, the logic of the type, the universalizing gesture, the ethnographic gaze, and binary logic. Additionally, the two autobiographies just discussed would suggest a critique of the developmentalist subject. They refuse, in other words, to stage the process of "becoming" that forms a central arc in other fictions, even those seemingly indifferent to the historical event. To read Dalit realism, then, as a new geographic and cultural transposition of an older form is problematic. This is particularly the case when it comes to historical and political questions, answers for which critics often favor ethnographic and revelatory literature written by Dalits. The overreliance within the critical canon on a model of narrativizing history derived largely from the nineteenth-century European novel, and specifically the bildungsroman, produces a model of reading that generates not the wrong answers, but the wrong questions. Instead of asking: "How does one read the historical consciousness of the Dalit?" I would ask: "Why privilege the role of that historical consciousness in the reading of a Dalit text?" Protest literatures clearly embody their own historicist notions, but should historicism be the determining category of their elaboration? In the case of Hazari and Naimishraya, Dalit realism suggests a different sort of inscription in time as well as a kind of scalar shift—a re-placing that moves *away* from national, and sometimes caste, politics *to* nature, a *distancing* literally and metaphorically from the violence of Partition. To read this as a retreat into solipsism or the comforts of the personal reifies the category of the historical once again.

To return to the provocative question raised earlier: what *is* a realism without history? Throughout this chapter, I have relied on terms such as "quotidian," "daily," "mundane" and "everyday." I want to suggest that the everyday becomes a central category for the understanding of a Dalit realism. D. R. Nagaraj puts it beautifully: "The obsession with the historical hardly respects the existential and the quotidian" (x). Dilip Menon suggests in "An Inner Violence" that communalism—in the form of the periodic—has subsumed casteism, which manifests itself in the quotidian. Modern fiction, particularly in the context of the texts discussed in this book, has been less invested in the quotidian, being instead largely driven by the engine of History. The failure of translating the day-to-day practices of casteism into the register and idiom of the Historical demonstrates the origins of one Dalit critique. But Dalit writing isn't simply invested in the reproduction of the quotidian; it is also invested in the demonstration of everyday life as spectacularly eventful. In "Apna gav," the Naimishraya story discussed in chapter 3, there is a haunting moment of existential meditation as the father-in-law, who has just seen his son's wife stripped naked and surrounded by armed men, stares upwards. "He peeked at the sky with sunken eyes. The sky was still there, just like that, exactly the same. He thought that it might have fallen. That the earth would crack open. But the sky hadn't fallen and the earth hadn't cracked" (97). A powerful indication of the collation of chronological register: the time of atrocity and the time of the quotidian are inextricably linked. The material world does not, cannot, register Dalit atrocity, which barely disturbs the everyday of others. There is no consonance between the vision of the Dalit character and the world outside. This is a privilege retained by certain narrative forms in which individual histories cause the world to bend towards them. In Dalit realism, the tracks of the Historical rarely veer towards the subject. This is perhaps why Gopal Guru argues that the disciplinary apparatus of archaeology or philosophy may be the appropriate mode to conjure the experience of untouchability.[27] Making of the Historical a kind of reality effect gives Dalit texts the ethical capital that realism offers while also allowing them other freedoms—to dabble in the utopian, the grotesque, the visionary.

Underlying an aesthetic of Dalit realism is a humanism that is hostile to the kind of deep historical structures that certain analytical protocols assume. If caste, as the Dalit text might argue, is that "deep structure" in which we swim, it is decidedly an exceptional one, and cannot be read in terms of the event as it has been understood in terms of repression, resistance, rebellion. Still, comprised of avowedly liberationist texts, this literature exhibits an intensive humanist perspective that is embraced by Dalit studies generally. As Priyamvada Gopal says, "The privileged texts and reading protocols of postcolonial studies tend to be antihumanist and hostile to systemic analysis. . . . Even when an unambiguously liberationist and realist author such as Mahasweta Devi is brought to metropolitan academic attention by a distinguished theorist such as Gayatri Spivak, she must first be made fit for refined theoretical company. Her text must be '[reconstellated] to draw out its use,' a process that entails undoing the distinction between history and fiction" (9). While Devi's work may not be so simply classified as realist, Gopal's point seems particularly valid. The frankly liberationist and human-centered rhetoric of Dalit texts seems dated according to a contemporary literary reading practice, if not naively universalist yet partisan at the same time. This perception is related to the imposition of a model of reading narrative time and history that has been directly imported from an older European model of realism, thereby doing an injustice to the Dalit text, which, though realist, has no interest in following the historical diagram of realism nor its temporal orientation. In light of Ramanika Gupta's comments, to do the Dalit text literary justice requires as much an "unreading" as it does a "rereading" of both the fictional text and the tropes of realism.

MIMESIS: THE REPRESENTATION OF REALITY IN OTHER LITERATURES

Literary critics must now acknowledge that the entire range of interrelated concepts that includes mimesis, veracity, referentiality, authenticity—the problem of literary truth, in effect—is impossibly casteized, or, in other words, dependent upon the social origin of the text, the context, the author, the habitus. The realist burden expresses itself not impartially but unequally—the lower that one is located within any hegemonic cultural hierarchy, the greater the ethnographic burden one has to bear. The realist is thus an aesthetics that emerges from a combination of political project, ideological commitment, and aesthetic undertaking, as well as readerly imposition. The central irony to remember, however, as Roberto Schwarz points out, is the extent to which "our desire for authenticity had to express itself in an alien language" (27). The cultural problem par excellence, bequeathed by the legacy of colonialism, is transposed in the context of Dalit literature where the very act of literary production involves a complex hermeneutics of renunciation that is derived from the segregation from uppercaste cultural forms (including modern novelistic narrative) as well as the abandonment of older Dalit cultural practices. To participate in anything realist must thus be read as an oscillation between a delicate yield to its cultural and political capital and a resistance to the concessions it demands, which would include a transitive intelligibility across castes. "Cry in the language of the modern poor—to this we respond. Shout in the language of the socially humiliated—this we understand," writes Nagaraj (203). As Nagaraj says, the language and metalanguage of the Dalit text must be readable by others, even when that requires the abandonment of other "languages." The textuality of any protest literature is thus inevitably handcuffed by its need to be *recognized*; recognition actually requires a certain level of repudiation, hence the "bonsaization" to which the epigraph refers. What I will suggest is that despite the carefully casteized construction of worlds in Dalit texts, at the level of discourse, imagery, and ideology, "language"—in the previous theorizations of Schwarz and Nagaraj—must include "form" and "genre." One way of addressing this issue is to acknowledge that it is in the modern genres of autobiography, personal narrative, and short fiction that Dalit literature has found form, rather than in "indigenous" cultural practices. In this sense, its realist impulse is partially preempted; a certain level of generic and aesthetic conformity offers the Dalit text the ability to make more radical humanist claims precisely because genre speaks "in a language we [both] understand." Autobiography can thus say, "This is a subject" long before its "content" is revealed. Genres perform their own modes of textual foreshadowing.[28] And yet that structural imperative offers certain freedoms and many more difficulties. To rely on the intellectual work that certain formal features perform means that subtleties of recuperation, revision, and rebellion become much more difficult to read. How, for example, might the Dalit text revise Schwarz's argument that, "to adopt the novel was to accept the way in which it dealt with ideologies" (*Misplaced Ideas* 41)? Dalit autobiography, as I have suggested, denies at some level the reconstruction of the self on which the genre has historically been premised.

Beyond genre, "language as form" would comprise the entire range of aesthetic practices that determine cultural production, from the length of the line to literary trope. These are stylistic protocols constructed in large indifference, if not opposition, to "lower caste cosmologies" (Nagaraj 224). To assume a realist mantle, then, would seem to acknowledge and indeed privilege one epistemology. Furthermore—and here we can return to the Jameson citation in the introduction to this project—it would mean to be committed "to the density and solidity of what is": that of uppercaste culture. If realism is a construct largely indebted to a certain casteized hermeneutic, then a protest literature will be required to instrumentalize realism's features in order to construct something else. It is in this light that one must read the fierce "artlessness" of the Dalit text. The important analytical project would thus be to derive the political origins of the putatively realist and referential, rather than to dismiss the nakedly "nonliterary." Dalit literature clearly labors under another literary genealogy, and the job of the critic is to discern its ideological parameters.

I will offer one brief suggestion here. Much has been said about the ways in which Dalit texts introduce a new vocabulary: literally, in the form of dialects, of caste-bound speech, and of nonstandardized, nonhegemonic Hindi—a bent it shares with the regionalists; figuratively, in the form of a new language of resistance, atrocity, and violence heretofore unknown within the space of the literary. It also presents us with certain metacritiques that can be read in various symptomatic and nonsymptomatic ways. Text after text, for example, delineates the trickery, chicanery, manipulations, and deceits of uppercastes against Dalit. One Dalit story illustrates this paradigm beautifully. In Pardeshiram Varma's "Phaansi" ("Noose"), a young lowercaste man, at his father's urging, becomes the village cooperative's night watchman, the *chowkidar*.[29] One day, spying on someone running off with a sack of grain, he attempts to catch the thief who escapes leaving the grain in the pitiable watchman's hands. Brought to the station, his protestations are ineffectual; the police superintendent is in cahoots with the cooperative's manager, the real thief, who has been emptying sacks upon their arrival. As the story mockingly hints from the outset, the manager—an important man in the village—was searching for a watchman who would understand the corrupt "functioning" of the cooperative, unlike the previous ones who were rudely dismissed. But this watchman, in his innocence, is genuinely perplexed, misunderstanding the words of the manager and the police superintendent as they insist that only he could be the thief. Finally, after he threatens to hang himself (this is, after all, a question of honor), the superintendent and the manager agree that if the watchman himself can catch the thief, he will be permitted to go free. In the end, our protagonist is faced with the impossible condition of either *apprehending the thief* or *being the thief*. Curiously, the village community, despite knowing intuitively the falsity of the charges, is harshly unsympathetic; for those who choose to engage with the uppercastes, and are subsequently punished by their laws, this is only to be expected. The *phaansi*, the noose, is not only that which the watchman threatens to rope around his neck, but the condition of his caste, particularly when faced with the all-too-legal machinations of others. For the *chowkidar*, the *phaansi* was strung upon him from day one.

There is little narrative detail here, broad swathes of character, indifferent description. But there is both region-specific and caste-specific speech, which functions to indicate difference and distinction. This polyglossia of both individual texts and the entire field of Dalit literature is one of its most remarkable aesthetic innovations, one that speaks beyond the ethnographic. What Dalit texts do is to *de-standardize* language, effectively provincializing its uppercaste national status. Yet this occurs on several levels beyond the linguistic, in the space of casteized worlds. The deconstruction of deceit introduces a correspondent vocabulary into the space of the literary: *apratyaksh* (hidden), *dhamki* (threat), *dhoka* (trickery). The landscape of these stories is quite literally littered with the subtle vocabularies of manipulation, coercion, and menace. This is a language of guile.

There is no doubt that a language of guile is determined by the thematic demands made by a protest literature in order to demonstrate an archive of subterfuge. But a critique of guile should underline, I would suggest, how the rational, and hence the realist, came to be asserted as a value in the Dalit text. Much of Dalit literature expends its investigative energy on the deconstruction of plots, conspiracies, and manipulations, the revelation of which serves as one means of drawing narrative to a close. In their attempt to de-hegemonize an uppercaste logic, it would follow that Dalit texts would espouse the values of clarity, transparency, and secular rationalism. Realism, which has historically indicated a supposed artlessness in terms of language, is here put in the service of a thematic and discursive demystification by which it converts mystery and chicanery into transparent discourse. This is just one genealogy for what I am describing as Dalit realism.

Realisms that are less invested in the characterological type as constructed by class habitus, in Historical Eventfulness, or in holism, seem to have little intersection with the classical Lukácsian understanding of the term. And yet the Lukácsian designation of realist is remarkably prescient and remains relevant across all historical anachronism even for the Dalit text. Frederic Jameson clarifies Lukács: "The kinds of works which Lukács called realistic were essentially those which carried their own interpretation built into them, which were at one and the same time fact and commentary on the fact" (*Marxism* 416). In the world of modernity, this kind of text, says Jameson, is no longer produced. "The two are once again sundered from each other" (416). The crucial difference here is that the Dalit text is realist not out of organic historical circumstance but despite it. The problem of metacommentary is a political one. Dalit texts are required, in fact, to "carry their own interpretation," or to have explanatory guides "built into them" in order to be counterhegemonic. Faced with a literary analytics that cannot decipher other caste-worlds, it does the work of reading in the act of fiction.

Just as the aesthetic "fate" of European colonial/anticolonial modernism was "sealed by the logic of its moment in history" (Jameson, *Marxism* 198), so too the aesthetic fate of Dalit literature is demanded by a certain moment. This is the moment after the rise of the Dalit and OBC political parties as well as of Dalit leadership in Uttar Pradesh and Bihar, after the emergence of a readable Dalit symbolism, but also alongside the stunning persistence and regularity of anti-Dalit atrocity. Dalit realism is a product of its strange historical moment, whereby it must be revolutionary and pedagogical at one and the same time. That it might therefore be responsible for experimentalism, aesthetic revisionism, and formalistic revolution has hardly been considered. Because it is understood and indeed promoted by readers, practitioners, and critics alike as a movement by and for Dalits, its contribution towards a revisionist critique of the canon and its inauguration of new representational strategies are often viewed as unlikely aspects or simply pass unnoticed. The crisis, as Nagaraj puts it, is that "the deepest tragic experiences of a society have to be worked out in a language understood by both the parties" (203). There is little doubt as to whose "language" this is. If caste critique and, more broadly, caste analysis have become almost exclusively the province of Dalit literature, and if realism—motivated by principles of liberal reformism—has demonstrated its various shortcomings, then Dalit realism still must work within hegemonic knowledge structures in order to be understood. The realist must now be reconceived beyond its originary novelistic elaboration and the ensuing critique of complicity with bourgeois ideologies, as well as beyond its later socialist realist incarnation and the ensuing critique of imprisoning didacticism. This is the only means by which the new aesthetic innovations of that "language" may be read and entered into the ledgers of history.

Epilogue
Aesthetics and Their Afterlives

Identarian literary movements draw their strength from past ideological failures while being deeply indebted to the cultural politics, and even the forms, of the movements they leave behind. This is in both the Adornian sense of the cultural scars that remain, marring the newness of any artistic project, as well as in the more capacious sense of the literary genealogy. Michael Denning writes that the "aspirations and aesthetics of the novelists' international remain the forgotten repressed history behind the contemporary globalization of the novel" (72). Yet this repressed history of progressive literary and cultural solidarities, inspired largely by the Communist International, lies not only behind the globalization of the novel, but also behind its localism, vernacularization, and indigeneity. The desires and the often-utopian visions that girded those movements are lost, erased, and reformed so as to return in the new literary and cultural modes that shape contemporary history. The "aspirations and aesthetics" of the Progressive Writers Association return not only in the shadow of the cosmopolitanism of the Anglophone novel (which is only one side of South Asian literary modernity), but also in the negativity of subaltern literatures of protest. One aim of this book was to provide a "thick description" of the rise of identity-driven cultural movements that are often read within a naked presentism. Literary movements do not simply emerge but demand a certain genealogical tree.

This is true even for the claims made about Dalit textuality, sprung Athena-like from Dalit consciousness, written by Dalits, for Dalits, in a Dalit public sphere. In its complex web of the negation of History,

Literature, Culture, and Caste, Dalit literature, despite itself, dialogues with other worlds. Poet Nirav Patel writes,

> Literary academies
> Like prostitutes in red light areas
> Painted paths with fresh blood and
> For ages, (beautiful) language
> Stared at impotents (10)

There is no doubt that Dalit literature is infused with a radical newness and is quite literally unlike anything lettered before. However, it is this newness in conjunction with a certain formal inheritance that allows for its metanarrative critique. Progressive literary movements—religious, socialist, communist, black nationalist, Naxalite, and Buddhist—have all contributed to the Dalit literary movement and even to its radical critique.

And yet those movements, whether realist or modernist, regionalist or internationalist, have not served the Dalit well. Thus, the second aim of this project was to trace the origins of the demand for a new aesthetic. The case of Vikram Seth's 1993 *A Suitable Boy* provides a salient example of the problematic nature of this genealogy. Recently appearing in Hindi, the translation of Seth's English modern realist novel was greeted with accolades, as well as claims that it was even more authentic than the original. But the translation differs on one major score: it excises a section on the Chamars.[1] In the novel, one of the potentially suitable boys for the marriageable Lata is Harish Trivedi, a shoe and leather salesman emblematic of the rising middle class, sprung from little and determined to succeed via meritocratic endeavor. In the English original, Trivedi visits Chamar leatherworkers in their homes. The novel produces a graphic description of this slum, a Dalit home, and the surrounding locale in all its filthy detail. Indicating Trivedi's desire for financial success as well as his tenuous class position, which requires him to occasionally visit the segregated locations of poverty, the character's interactions with the Chamars provide a foil for his consummate modernity. Pruning them from the text reifies the bourgeois sites of the novel in such a way as to cement their rarified status. The excision of the Chamar in this version of the novel might be read as the most legible of realism's deficiencies, most of which are too subtle to properly catalogue. I have attempted to trace some of those literary reflexes here.

It is unsurprising, then, that in *The Flaming Feet*, the late Kannada critic D. R. Nagaraj expressed doubt that realism as a style, form, or genre could properly incorporate "lower caste cosmologies" (224). Derived from rationalism and empiricism, realism, writes Nagaraj, is best confined to the verifiable and the historical. It is unable to incorporate the nonmimetic, mystical traditions of others; it cannot conjure the multilayered realities of other caste-ness. "The restrictions placed on the writer do not merely reflect aesthetic rules of the game. They are basically restrictions of philosophy and ideology. Even if these realms of experiences and world-views barred by realism seek entry into the fictional world, they are permitted only after making sure that they do not wreck the narrative which acts as a prosecutor who summons the witnesses" (229). What kind of subaltern worlds present themselves in the literary universe? And what kind of universe makes its home in modern narrative forms?

This critique of realism enters us into a larger debate on the role of culture in caste politics, one that draws on questions that have been raised by culturalist protest movements worldwide. For negritude, for the American Indian Movement, and of course, for Gandhi's Harijan uplift campaign, the question of stigmatized cultural practice and other life-worlds—whether reified, glorified, or abandoned—was a central issue. The secularist position charted by B. R. Ambedkar required a range of cultural repudiations: intermarriage would end caste endogamy, education would eradicate casteized forms of labor. The Ambedkarite "Social Rage School," as Nagaraj calls it, "believed passionately in the total rejection of the traditional Dalit self which was steeped by and large in the Hindu ethos" (221). The slow eradication of casteized cultural forms was the necessary corollary of any modern anticaste project; the entire cultural legacy of Hinduism was deemed irreconcilable not only with a new caste politics, but also individualism and a democratic sensibility. When the Dalit Panthers emerge in Maharashtra two decades after the death of Ambedkar, they draw on a global culturalist logic: The Black Panthers, Paris in 1968, Castro's Cuba. This is the modernist warehouse of symbolism. The vast realm of folk and vernacular cultural practices often anchored in caste specificity were not to be reread and/or revalorized, but violently excised. It is in this sense that the relentless modernism of the Ambedkarite project required the culling of certain stigmatized social practices, but also, crucially, productive cultural forms. The cultural traditions of the lowest castes was thus excised and "the man who creates"—i.e., the Shudra, the artisan, the laboring caste—became almost exclusively "the man who suffers" (221).

The reinsertion of Dalit cultural traditions into the spirit of the protest movement might not have produced the modern novel and the contemporary short story, but the folk narrative. Realist narrative, realism, in effect, is a legacy of the paring, the violent bonsaization of the spiritual and cultural identity of the lowercaste (Nagaraj 222). The attempt at radicalization of the realist is also a tragic concession to the modern, premised to some degree on the truncation of the Dalit self as well as the regional, the vernacular, the indigenous, and the casteized.

This is a sobering suggestion for protest literatures, which have often staked their transgressive claims on radical forms of realism that perform a poetic justice. In fact, it is a damning indictment of an aesthetic whose radical origins, however long forgotten, were seminal in the basic democratization of the literary sphere. In light of the alleged inability of realist writing to properly narrativize Dalit life-worlds, one must ask: Why is it that Dalit fiction turns again and again to the basic tropes of realism? Clearly, Ambedkarite rationalism plays a central role in the embrace of modern Western narrative forms that offer a platform for the articulation of suffering and its verifiable, indeed juridical—and therefore punishable—truth. There is an obvious consonance among realism, the testimonio, the autobiography, and the evidentiary logic and typescript of something such as the Truth and Reconciliation Commission.

But the tragic origins of aesthetic causalities are not only those that are most legible. The first incarnation of this type of subaltern protest culture must be recognized as that very realm of the spiritual and the folk—i.e., explicitly casteized cultural forms: vernacular song, poetry, parody, street theater. These forms were antihegemonic on principle as they privileged a singular worldview (that of lowercaste cosmologies) and, it should be said, a spirit of revolt (Dalit *chetna*). Neil Lazarus reminds us of the way in which modernism became *the* literature of modernity, and in doing so displaced other forms of coexistent cultural production as "premodern, or relics, anachronisms" (429). Contemporary subaltern literary forms like Dalit literature have been so effectively delinked from the realm of the folk, the vernacular, and the oral that, even in realist fiction, only traces of these older, and sometimes contemporaneous, forms remain. It is these cultural scars that produce its ideology of form. Dalit writing may thus read as belated and anachronistic, revivalist even, in its return to high referential values, but as a realism produced by the fractured lens of caste, its form, its tone, and its ideology is a critique of the hegemony of often-casteless "progressive" narrative forms. The casteization, or particularization, of the literary sphere must eventually give way to new aesthetic paradigms.

Perhaps the afterlives of aesthetic turns also lie elsewhere: in the failure of "lowercaste cosmologies" to become true sites of revolutionary potential, as they had for centuries before. Will folk narrative be tenable, and transgressive, in the context of the drive towards social mobility and new forms of capital? Will magical realism, replete with talking cots and the dictatorial world of gods, challenge the very conventional—and very readable—nature by which traditional realism articulates itself? These other realisms may challenge basic philosophical premises about the representation of reality, mimesis, and veracity, while arguing on behalf of subaltern mythologies/histories that typically neither follow nor are recuperable by materialist epistemologies. Dalit aesthetics will have to seek a new source of radicalism, somewhere and sometime else. The question we may ask instead: Are other forms of realism possible?

In the meantime, Dalit realism, as I have suggested, charts its own course. What *can* Dalit realism do? It can retrain the sympathetic gaze by rewriting the pitiable figure, forcing it to do something other than invoke pity. Dalit realism can deconstruct the old quasi universalisms, and demonstrate particularism and localized knowledge, to offer new models for the rendering of the real. It can shift the unfolding of narrative action so that its chronology moves away from the gradual development of political or psychological consciousness, and rather towards a vision of the utopian. Dalit realism can theorize the problem of metonymy and the notion of contingency, both aesthetic and ideological. It can reconceive the protagonist, splintering narrative power into several characterological channels. It can offer us a different reading of ethnographic knowledge and the native informant, and shed light on intertextuality. Dalit realism can function as a silent critic of Anglophone modernism, and reveal its structural reliance on the categories of nation and novel. It can trouble the basic notions of community and collective that have been constructed by a class politics in the absence of caste. Finally and most crucially, it can complicate the basic assumptions regarding realism and historicity, realism's debt to history, and its stranglehold on narrative time.

The most narratively obvious and yet subtly evocative of these is the symbolic reinsertion of the casteized figure, Dalit realism's narrative and metanarrative goal: the Chamar pushed to the margins by Premchand and excised by Seth. A story like Ajay Navariya's "Patkatha" (collected in *Patkatha aur anya kahaniyam*) goes out of its way, literally and metaphorically, to mention the Chamar, to throw him in narrative relief. "Patkatha," as mentioned in Chapter 5, concerns three generations of Khatik characters who, over the course of time, transition from village to city. This is a familiar narrative arc, but the story presents two unusual and singular details. Early in the story our narrator reminds us that, "In the village, most of the residents were Chamar, and it was they who bore the brunt of the violence" (121). Later in the narrative, as Kalyaram, the protagonist of the first episode, moves towards his disastrous encounter with the *thakur*, the narrator says, "Kalyaram turned, passed by the Chamar quarter, and taking a long roundabout route, arrived at the *thakur*'s doorstep" (122). There are many sociological and ethnographic explanations for the insignificant detail of the Chamar, but what might the narrative ones be? The inclusion of the Chamars certainly draws the distinction between the Khatiks and others; by the book's third section, the Khatik identity has become a Dalit one, a significant political gain in the context of the story, and "they" refers only to uppercastes. But the figure of the Chamar is its own literary icon, since at least the time of Premchand. As the metonymic name for caste and its degradations in the literary sphere, the Chamar occupies a particularly important place; it conjures the depraved, the backward, the antimodern. In the discourse of the liberal reformer, the Chamar indicates a certain representational politics: that of another India. What happens in a Dalit realism? There is an irony here, in that the Chamar is not a literary prototype but rather completely unremarkable. Mentioning the Chamar quarter outside the village functions as a kind of reality effect; one is now in the realm of Dalit space. This is an "effect" that uppercaste realism has been hard-pressed to produce. The reality effect, the insignificant detail, the nonsymbolic realm, or the contraindication of the symptom, indicates Dalit normativity more powerfully than any model of reformist inclusion could.

Within this sentence, "Kalyaram turned, passed by the Chamar quarter, and taking a long roundabout route, arrived at the *thakur*'s doorstep," is an entire world, one that sketches out a certain model of relationality. This appears in the interjection of Sudip's father in the classroom, in the lodging of revolutionary consciousness in Nathu's wife, in the centrality of love to that political awakening in the work of Ajay Navariya. Relationality would be crucial to the utopian vision articulated in the village exodus and the intercaste affair. If realism appears different, facile, compromised, or belated in the hands of its Dalit practitioners, it is perhaps because of the relentless apparition of caste-as-family, which refuses to cede space. Caste relationality—the assumption on which caste movements rely (i.e., that of a shared, blood-stained imperative irrespective of the concrete experience of occupation)—produces a literary relationality explicitly distinct from the narrative individualism demanded by modern narrative forms.

Dalit texts might thus be said to articulate a "peripheral realism" that can only be referred to as a Dalit realism, in that it inculcates a naked partiality and a strategic essentialism, the development of which can be read against a genealogy of "progressive" literature in India. Dalit realism in Hindi has moved away from the abstract categories of Labor, Nation, and the Universal, and towards a language of specification, distinction, nontransferability, and exceptionalism. There is an implicit threat in such radical specialization, in the revision of that putative Universalism that could never accommodate the angle of the subaltern. The rejection of broader social types, of a well-rehearsed model of political awakening, of a Marxist understanding, clearly seem to limit certain potentialities, while reveling in the atomized difference so characteristic of the contemporary period. In the context of a rapacious modernity, this can only be read as identarian default. Indeed, one question that surrounds the Dalit literary movement is precisely this identarian rigidity. Why, for example, in a historical period that has demonstrated the rise of a range of political formations dominated by lower castes, does this body of work remained wedded to the symbolics of upper-caste power? Why is the Brahmin, the *thakur*, the Rajput, still the lone figure of oppression in Dalit fiction when, in postliberalization India, the backward castes are those who have monopolized violence against Dalits? The Hegelian model that remains the engine of Dalit narrative only partially reflects the nature of contemporary caste conflicts, which pit those at the bottom against each other for the promise of education or economic opportunity previously unattainable for both. This is, in part, another argument for the rereading of the complexities of the realist framework, which must be considered in its most recent, and most strident, configurations. In one recent controversy, the republication of a 1949 cartoon featuring

Ambedkar riding a snail about to be whipped by Jawharlal Nehru has been roundly criticized. The cartoon, satirizing the delays in the preparation of the Indian constitution, was to appear in the Class XI political science textbook prepared by the National Council of Education, Research, and Training (NCERT). The critique takes several forms, one of which uses the language of humiliation and insult, another of which reinserts the detailed historical facticity of the period and the hyperbolic nature of the graphic. Still others remind us of the heavily casteized experience of education, in which languages, texts, and images of denigration have a long and complicated genealogy, to which this book attests. But Dalit philosopher Gopal Guru reminds us that the assumption of a politics of representational insult also carries within it its own insult to the Dalit. Accordingly, "with its Brahmanical backbone it suggests that the dalit community is pathologically condemned to being emotional. They are denied the privilege of being equal partners in any deliberative process. They cannot be considered capable of rational debate. They seem to only have emotions and sentiments. These sentiments can be hurt or assuaged. But they must remain sentiments and emotions, and never be allowed to turn into critical rational questions. The current cartoon controversy thus was an insult to a long tradition of deliberative processes, a tradition that has remained an integral part of the dalit public sphere" ("Foregrounding Insult"). Guru cites here the problem of the "thick emotionalism" that is then imposed on the Dalit public sphere, counter to decades of Ambedkarite rationalism, dialogue, and incisive debate. The critique of "thick emotionalism" is in fact implicit in the various shades of left and progressive responses to the incident, which decry the tragic devolution of a radical anticaste movement now forced to fight for the proper, yet petty, allocation and adulteration of images.

The subaltern critique may seem to be a fossilized position derived from the failures of history that endlessly reappear in new incarnations. But the identarianism of Dalit literature is, I would argue, a necessary stage that accompanies the earliest articulations in the literary field, especially when it emerges in deliberate contradistinction, even segregation, from the range of other folk, performance, and casteized narrative forms. As the occasional stirrings of utopianism indicate, however, this body of text is moving somewhere else. Peripheral realisms, subaltern realisms—in short, Dalit realisms—are the comeuppance of the progressive ideologies that have dominated narrative forms, from the contingencies of genre to the plausibility of metaphor. In their commitment to local forms of knowledge, to a discourse of legibility and an artful artlessness, these new realisms are committed to the expansion of the aesthetic terrain, as it has been thus far imagined.

NOTES

THREE BURNINGS: AN INTRODUCTION

1. Dalit, which might be translated as "oppressed," from the Sanskrit root *dal* for "broken down, crushed," is the term that has come to replace the British designation of Scheduled Caste and Gandhi's appellation Harijan for the untouchable castes. I use the term Dalit here in reference to the contemporary literature in question, which is explicitly a literature of protest. I reserve "untouchable caste" for those situations in which it would be anachronistic to do otherwise—for example, the pre-Ambedkarite historical period.

2. This includes the states of Bihar, Haryana, Himachal Pradesh, Uttar Pradesh, Madhya Pradesh, and Rajasthan. The center of the Hindi Dalit literary sphere, says critic Laura Brueck, is Delhi, the home of several important organizations, publishers, and writers.

3. See Sharankumar Limbale's *Towards an Aesthetic of Dalit Literature* and Omprakash Valmiki's *Dalita sahitya ka saundaryashastra*.

4. In the context of Marathi, see Eleanor Zelliot's entire oeuvre, including *From Untouchable to Dalit*, and *An Anthology of Dalit Literature*, as well as Gail Omvedt's *Dalit Visions*.

5. The rare focus on aesthetic aspects of modern Dalit texts functions alongside a keen attention to genre; many critics demonstrate the caste-specific generic production of which contemporary Dalit texts are an heir. See, for example, Gail Omvedt's "Social Protest and Revolt in Western India."

6. Amrit Rai, Premchand's biographer, points out that in his position as district head of schools, Premchand was required to travel extensively across the state, to various cities, district towns, and villages (Premchand, *Duniya* 9); it was these travels that put him in contact with the people and communities that would become the central material for his writings.

7. The Mandal Commission was established in 1979 in order to reevaluate "reservations," the system by which caste discrimination was redressed through the reservation of seats for "backward castes" in government and educational institutions. The commission confirmed the 22.5% reservations for Scheduled Castes and recommended an additional reservation of 27% for Other Backward Castes in government institutions. Its potential implementation in 1989 led to widespread resistance. See Anupama Rao's

"Caste Radicalism and the Making of New Political Subject" in *The Caste Question*.

8. The Akademi's critique was defended through the citation of the Prevention of Atrocities Act, passed in 1989. The use of the slur "Chamar," it was argued, could potentially incite discriminatory behavior and violence towards Dalits.

9. The text of Rangbhumi used in in the school curriculum was indeed eventually changed; "Chamar" was replaced by "Dalit."

10. Omprakash Valmiki's autobiography *Joothan* begins with just such a scene: a teacher tears out the pages on Ambedkar from a school primer and instructs his students to do the same.

11. *Varna* refers to the traditional idealized four-fold division of caste hierarchy cited in Vedic texts and the *Manusmriti*. The *varna* system, or *chaturvarna* (the four varnas) is comprised of Brahmins (priests, scholars), Ksatriyas (warriors), Vaishyas (merchants) and Shudras (laborers, artisans). The "untouchable" theoretically falls outside the *varna* order. The ideology of *varna*, literally "color," gained a renewed importance in the nationalist period when it was revindicated by Gandhi as an idealized division of labor.

12. For an analysis of the nationalist critique particular to North India, as it is related to the failures of the Congress Party, see Christopher Jaffrelot's *India's Silent Revolution*.

13. The Progressive Writers Association (PWA) was founded in England by Sajjad Zaheer, Mulk Raj Anand, and others and officially established in 1936 in Lucknow with the First Progressive Writers Conference. Drawing together writers and intellectuals under a platform of anti-imperialism, antifascism, and intellectual commitment, the PWA also offered a powerful critique of social life and cultural tradition. I discuss this in more detail in chapter 2.

14. This is particularly the case in Hindi/Urdu, where reform movements were triangulated through religious discourse, as Mukherjee points out (*Early Novels* xviii). Dilip Menon argues that caste was a central category of analysis in the nineteenth-century novel in Malayalam, a much more salient axis than "the national." See his essay "No, Not the Nation: Lower Caste Malayalam Novels of the Nineteenth Century."

15. In fact, the most "realistic" portion of the story comes towards the end when the hero happens upon the battlefield full of corpses, located in "Hindustan." The mix of realist and fantastic, historical and magical, is characteristic of early novelistic writing in India (Mukherjee, *Realism* 38).

16. For a brilliant analysis of this relativization, see Schwarz's "The Importing of the Novel to Brazil" in *Misplaced Ideas*. "This explains the modern preference for this narrative style, in which the Absolute values, which still today drain us of our energy and morale, are relativized, because they are linked to the shifting, human—illusory, it is worth repeating—basis of interpersonal relations" (59).

17. This was a position Lukács honed throughout his career. For crucial moments of the Lukácsian defense of realism, see "Franz Kafka or Thomas Mann" and "The Ideology of Modernism" in *The Meaning*

of *Contemporary Realism*, "To Narrate or to Describe" and "Art and Objective Truth" in *The Writer and the Critic*, and *Studies in European Realism*.

18. The canon of debates from African American literary criticism is clearly echoed here, from the late nineteenth century onwards. More recently Kenneth Warren's work on racism and realism, Stacey Morgan's reconsideration of social realism as an art from, and Gene Jarrett's *Deans and Truants* all consider the question of a strategic essentialism in relation to the politics of art.

19. See "New Directions in Dalit Politics" in Anupama Rao's *The Caste Question* for a detailed discussion of the conflagrations among such factions in the Maharashtra of the 1970s, as well as the political structure of the Panthers.

20. "The latter [Ad-Dharmi movement] developed as a vehicle to assert the rights and demands of the untouchables and to challenge the disabilities and exclusions they faced in the towns on account of their low ritual status" (Gooptu 153). See "Untouchable Assertion" in her book, *The Politics of the Urban Poor*.

21. For a more detailed discussion of the question of "experience," see Sundar Sarukkai's "Dalit Experience and Theory" and his consideration of the work of Gopal Guru. Sarukkai argues that the deconstruction of the "outsider" be based on the notion of lived reality, "experience" as specifically "freedom from choice."

22. See Misra and Narayan's introduction to *Multiple Marginalities*.

23. See Gail Omvedt's *Dalits and the Democratic Revolution*, S. M. Gaikwad, "Ambedkar and Indian Nationalism," and Eleanor Zelliot's *From Untouchable to Dalit*.

24. For elaborate documentation and analysis of this process, see Vasudha Dalmia's *The Nationalization of Hindu Traditions: Bharatendu Harischandra and Nineteenth-Century Banaras*, Alok Rai's *Hindi Nationalism*, and Christopher King's *One Language, Two Scripts*.

25. See Mukherjee's *Realism and Reality* for the broad development of this argument.

26. See Hira Dom's "Acchut ki shikayat" and Ramchandra Shukla's "Acchut ki aah" in the "Acchut ank" of Mahavir Prasad Dwivedi's literary journal *Saraswati*, 1916.

1. THE DALIT LIMIT POINT: REALISM, REPRESENTATION, AND CRISIS IN PREMCHAND

1. The development of Hindi prose literature prior to Premchand has received significant attention that complicates the brief summary given here. See the work of Francesca Orsini, including *The Hindi Public Sphere* and "Detective Novels: A Commercial Genre in Nineteenth-Century North India"; Vasudha Dalmia's *The Nationalization of Hindu Traditions* (1999); Christopher King's *One Language, Two Scripts* (1994); Harish Trivedi's "The Progress of Hindi"; and the collection edited by Blackburn and Dalmia, *India's Literary History* (2004).

2. Premchand began writing in Urdu; his first five novels and eighty short stories were written in Urdu. Even after making a decisive switch to fictional production in Hindi in 1915, he continued to write essays and stories in Urdu. Throughout his life, he translated and supervised translations between the two languages.

3. See Francesca Orsini's "Peasants as Subjects" in *The Hindi Public Sphere* for a rich discussion of the evolution of this trope in public discourse.

4. See also Ramchanda Shukla's poem "Acchut ki aah," published in *Saraswati* in 1916.

5. An appeal launched in 2008 makes the use of the word "Chamar," viewed as derogatory and insulting, a punishable offense under the Schedule Caste/Scheduled Tribe Prevention of Atrocities Act (1989). The judges cited in the appeal mention the importance of the "popular" usage of the term rather than the "etymological." Of course, the literary-historical use of the term occupies another terrain, deliberately conjoined here. See, for example, the poet Nirala's 1935 *Chaturi chamar*.

6. This phrase recalls Laura Brueck's paper "The Problem with Premchand."

7. See Mukherjee's *Realism and Reality* as well as *Early Novels in India*.

8. For a discussion of the particular intermingling of generic tendencies during this period, see Barbara Lotz's "Romantic Allegory and Progressive Criticism" and Francesca Orsini's "Reading a Social Romance" in Dalmia and Damsteegt's *Narrative Strategies*.

9. See, for example, the essays "Kahani kala" ("The Art of the Story") and "Upanyas" ("Novel") in *Premchand rachna-sanchayan*, in which Premchand begins to theorize the problem of the ideal versus the real, the question of characterization and truth, and the dialectic between art and the material conditions of society.

10. The Progressive Writers Association was a forum for leftist writers and thinkers across India, founded in the early 1930s in the spirit of anticolonialism, societal transformation, and aesthetic intervention in the field of literature, part of a broad politics of cultural and political radicalism across the subcontinent from 1936–54. See Shabana Mahmud's "Angare" as well as Zeno's "Professor Ahmed Ali" and most recently, Priyamvada Gopal's *Literary Radicalism*.

11. "What I say is that if I had enough strength, I would devote my whole life to freeing the Hindu community from the priests, the parasites who feed off religion. . . . Who does not know that caste distinctions and nationhood are opposed to each other like poison and nectar?" See "Kya ham vastav me rashtrivadi hain?" ("Are We Nationalists?") in Premchand's *Vividh prasang* (2:71). See also note 14 in this chapter.

12. As Harish Trivedi points out, European theories of novelistic production that tie the development of the genre to the rise of nationalism and the stirrings of the middle class are challenged by the Indian context, where the novel "sought to narrate not the nation but its own particular linguistically constituted (or imagined) regional continuity" (1001). Dilip Menon states that the crucial category in the nineteenth-century Malayalam novel

was caste rather than nation ("No, Not the Nation"). Early twentieth-century Hindi, however, as Trivedi does underline, is in an unusual position, having already established itself as a potential "national language" according to Gandhi and others, such that Premchand's novels' foregrounding of "nation" rather than other categories of belonging such as caste is unsurprising.

13. The classic example would be Premchand's "Thakur ka kuan." Sudhir Chandra suggests a kind of division of labor between Premchand's novelistic and short-story writing: the short story becomes the repository of idealism and patriotic zeal whereas the novel presents a critique of nationalism. See also "Poos ki raat," "Dhoodh ka daam," "Sadgati," and "Mandir" (collected in *Premchand rachna-sanchayan*)—stories that attempt to address untouchability as a social problem.

14. Cited in Alok Rai's "Poetic and Social Justice."

15. Alok Rai cautions against this in his reading of the novel *Nirmala*: "Yesterday's radicalism starts ossifying into tomorrow's vilified orthodoxy even before it is fully articulated" (198).

16. See Sahi's *Dalit sahitya ki avdharana aur Premchand*. Dharamvir's *Premchand: Saamant ka munshi* and Singh's *Aaj ka dalita sahitya* as well as Alok Rai's essay in R. Bhargave's *Justice*.

17. I adapt here the basic premise asserted by Roberto Schwarz: the adoption of the realist novel (in Brazil) implied the adoption of its liberalist ideologies, thereby producing a social, and consequently formal, dislocation in a society reliant upon slavery (41). The case of India, and Hindi, is clearly radically different from that of Brazil; I mean only to suggest that the assumption of liberal individualism presents a similar dislocation when the social sphere is informed by caste.

18. Himansu Mohapatra argues that Premchand's *Godaan* cannot fully articulate its social critique precisely because it is enmeshed in a reductive realism, mired in the logic of "interpersonal space" (64). Basing his analysis on Satya Mohanty's conception of a postpositivist realism, the realism of *Godaan*, Mohapatra argues, despite its faithfulness to one kind of referent, to a model of mimesis, is challenged in its ability to produce proper "causal explanations . . . of the micro-structures of the social world" (62).

19. Lukács is one of the most astute critics on the nineteenth-century novel and one of the few who insist on realism's radical potential (a mantle Dalit writers will take up), which makes his work useful to us here. Beyond this, however, there is a clear critical resonance between Lukács and writers like Premchand—for both of them, the category of the "real" was valid, meaningful, inspired, and yet to be dismantled. That is to say, for Lukács, a Marxist reading practice wasn't simply the only one that was intellectually available to him but also the one that was the most persuasive, the most plausible, the most "real." In commenting, in the preface to *Studies in European Realism*, on the contemporary historical circumstances that demand such a reading, he writes, "For it is no easy matter to look stark reality in the face and no one succeeds in achieving this at the first attempt. . . . Only later

does it grow clear how much more genuine humanity—and hence genuine poetry—attaches to the acceptance of truth with all its inexorable reality and to acting in accordance with it" (1). This may be overstating the case, but the insistence on the reality of the materialism on which Marxism relies is central if not dominating, in the late work of Premchand, particularly *Godaan* with its relentless underlining of the debt economy, as well as the Karmic one, to which Hori is bound. This is also the novel that demonstrates, as Alok Rai points out, Premchand at his most radical, his disillusionment with Gandhi, and his embrace of a less sentimental, less melodramatic realism. The desire to see things "as they are" was one he shared with Lukács. Lukács's analytical categories, derived from readings of Balzac, Tolstoy and Mann, were also built for Premchand.

20. See Lukács's introduction to *Studies in European Realism*, as well as his writings on Balzac and Tolstoy in the same volume. See also "Marx and Engels on Aesthetics" in *Writer and Critic*.

21. See Lukács, *The Theory of the Novel*. This is for Lukács the "ideology" of realism, its pretense, its mask. The novel trades in a sense of totality that mimics being, rather than is, organic, "a conceptual [totality] which is abolished again and again" (76).

22. I focus on the novel here as an actual (in the case of *Rangbhumi*) and potential (in the case of *Godaan*) site of Dalit critique and because the short stories, such as "Kafan," "Thakur ka kuan," and "Sadgati" (in in *Premchand rachna-sanchayan*) have received thorough treatment already. Most importantly, though, the novel is the genre in which the features of realist narrative are most perfectly realized.

23. See, for example, Moretti's *The Way of the World*.

24. See Benedict Anderson's chapter "Cultural Roots" in *Imagined Communities*.

25. Just as he did for the female victim in *Nirmala, Gaban*, and *Sevasadan*, Premchand devotes himself to the construction and elucidation of the peasant victim in *Godaan*, working with a narrative tone both deft and clever. In the initial pages of the novel, that narrator does not speak to inform, but rather to confirm what the reader already knows. The narrator becomes responsible here for the literary creation of a "peasant mentality" but his tone bears traces of that which has already been confirmed. This is accomplished partially through figural narration, but also through a knowing voice that makes use of the now familiar paradigm of the "native informant" theorized by Gayatri Spivak. However, in this case, the informant is speaking across class rather than cultural lines.

26. I should stress that I do not mean to imply that these factors, and caste hierarchy, are mutually exclusive, but rather are mutually constitutive. The question in Premchand, then, would be of how caste occupies causal space.

27. Various critics have theorized the narrative modality of sympathy, via an omniscient narrator, and free indirect discourse, as well as its ideological basis, and its particular role in relation to other possible affective forms—empathy, for example. See Audrey Jaffe's *Scenes of Sympathy* and Amit Rai's *Rule of Sympathy*.

28. See, for example, the work of Rae Greiner, Suzanne Keen, and Wayne Booth.

29. See Alok Rai's forward to *Nirmala* in *The Oxford India Premchand*.

30. How exactly does this model work on a narrative level? Take one example from Premchand's novel *Nirmala*. In a winding conversation between two characters, we are informed of what Pandit thinks of Balchandra though Balchandra himself doesn't know and wonders (32). The reader is thus offered a privileged positioning and a certain monopoly over knowledge. His or her pity, condescension, or sympathy can be accorded on the basis of such elective knowledge: an essentially melodramatic mode. Nirmala muses, "One who is sentenced to life imprisonment cannot afford to go on crying. And even if she should, who will heed her? Who will waste their pity on her?" (53). The answer to this question is clear. One argument is that this melodramatic mode remained with Premchand even when he moved towards a more politically voracious social realism, particularly in the realm of the Dalit characters.

31. I am drawing here from M. S. S. Pandian's recent work that asserts that caste appears as "always something else." See, for example, "One Step outside Modernity." In this essay, Pandian is largely concerned with upper-casteness, which masks as generalized social attributes in modern writing, particularly the autobiography. However, the notion of caste in the public sphere requiring a mask of discursive difference might clearly be traced to a much earlier time.

32. This is also the subplot of a programmatic short story by Rana Pratap in which the protagonist, Ganesi, a Chamar man, has a daughter who is propositioned by her Brahmin teacher. The Chamar community, outraged, forces the teacher to propose and undergo a conversion ceremony whereby he becomes outcaste; they pour dirty water over his head. Dirty water thus does the work of poetic justice: it is defiling, and thus "converting," thereby giving the Brahmin teacher his due. The ceremony of conversion parodies the Sanskritizing aspirations of *shuddhi* and water here becomes the vehicle for a different kind of caste consciousness. I discuss this piece in chapter 4.

33. I owe this insight to Dr. Rajeswari Sunder Rajan.

34. *Shuddhi* (purification) refers to the ritual of conversion propagated by the Arya Samaj, the Hindu reform movement, in the early part of the twentieth century. *Shuddhi* aimed to symbolically purify untouchables, thereby reintroducing them to the Hindu fold and deterring conversion to Christianity and Islam. See R. K. Ghai's *Shuddhi Movement in India* and Kenneth W. Jones's *Arya Dharm: Hindu Consciousness in Nineteenth-Century Punjab*.

35. Let me stress again that this is less a problem of the "representation of reality" than of the importation of realism, one basic demand of which was the close observation of the other.

36. In this sense, Amit Rai's comment in *Rule of Sympathy* is particularly useful: "My sense is that as practices, as discourses, as forms of sociality, sympathy and solidarity have a shared history" (xiii). The latter haunts the former.

37. Mohandas Naimishraya is an important contemporary Dalit writer in Hindi; his autobiography *Apne-apne pinjare*, alongside Omprakash Valmiki's *Joothan*, are central to this new body of work.

38. This story appeared in the collection edited by Ramanika Gupta, *Dusari duniya ka yatharth* (1997), and Valmiki's collection of short stories *Salaam* (2).

39. All translations of this story, and the other Hindi Dalit texts discussed in this work, are mine. Dalit literature has been mired in language and translation politics from its very inception. In 1972 when the Marathi poet Namdeo Dhasal published his collection of poems *Golpitha*, it was introduced by the preeminent contemporary Marathi playwright Vijay Tendulkar who claimed to have found in it twenty-seven words he did not know (Zelliot 451). Translation is therefore an issue across castes, registers and languages. The translation of these texts has posed all the usual problems expected for a conscientious and concerned translator. In an attempt to reproduce the speed and brevity of dialogue, for example, I have often been required to gloss over the complexity and variances of a nonstandardized, often highly caste-specific speech. I chose, however, to do my own translations of these texts (an English translation of *Joothan* is available), as it seemed irresponsible to do otherwise. The readings of the texts presented in this argument have thus been produced by that very act of translation; I have paid only secondary attention to the perfection of that translation for an English audience.

The following comment, by eminent modern Kannada playwright and poet H. S. Shivaprakash, has been very valuable. "In present-day India, translation is a most crucial and responsible activity. Crucial, because it has to negotiate between a bewildering heterogeneity of cultural and subcultural expressions of an exceedingly plural society. Responsible, because it should respect the culture's (or subculture's) right to self—expression, which cannot happen if one's objective is reduced to producing an eminently readable (therefore saleable) translation. Literary texts, particularly those emphasizing culture or group specificity, are inscribed with specific worldviews and attitudes to things. Theses should not be too smoothly made to fit into the worldviews and attitudes built indiscernibly into the target language" (126).

40. In 1980, the government-appointed Mandal Commission confirmed the continuing need for "reservations," by which a certain percentage of seats are reserved for Scheduled Castes and Scheduled Tribes in public universities and government employment. The Commission report, having increased the quotas dramatically, met with widespread opposition.

41. This debate is discussed, and the use of such language defended, by Ramanika Gupta in the introduction to *Dusari duniya ka yatharth* (*The Reality of the Other World*). Gupta makes the argument that not only is the use of certain forms of language to be defended in the name of realism as a representation of lowercaste speech patterns (which had been largely sanitized by earlier writers who did depict such characters, in particular Premchand), but also because such language has long been used in a derogatory fashion to "name" lowercastes and as forms of address.

42. The narrative presentation of the father's deception might be contrasted with the earlier example from *Nirmala* (see note 31 in this chapter). The summary explanation of that episode never puts the reader in a position of privilege, and Sudip's unraveling in front of the teacher occurs only after his establishment as a legitimate subject.

43. This story is distinct, however, from others in which education is the process that erases the Dalit from casteized, often village, life. That is also clearly a trope within the body of Dalit textuality.

44. It should be mentioned that the word *daya* itself has a long history in the discourse of social reform, as Chakrabarty has pointed out with the writings of Vidyasagar and Roy (122). The narrative power to create a subject worthy of *daya* is a significant thing; here it is accorded to a Dalit subject.

45. As Omprakash Valmiki has stated in an interview with Alok Mukherjee (see Valmiki, Ghusapaithiye.), many of his stories are autobiographical, many others are inspired by "real" events.

46. See, for example, H. S. Shivaprakash's "Translating the Tehsildar."

47. All translations of *Joothan* are mine.

48. I will return to this discussion of autobiography in chapter 5.

2. MODERNISM, MARXISM, METAPHOR: THE ORIGINS OF A LITERARY POLITICS OF PARTICULARISM

1. See also Anand's *Two Leaves and a Bud*, a novel that depicts the social and economic crisis of the Punjabi peasant.

2. The important reference here would be the work of Swami Acchutanand, who wrote one historical tract and the drama *Ramrajya*, the ideal polity represented by the mythological rule of Rama. These are crucial texts in the history of Dalit writing in North India, as their inclusion in Misra and Narayan's recent anthology, *Multiple Marginalities*, demonstrates. Contemporary Dalit writing, however, decidedly follows the model of short prose fiction that originated in the West and has a long and illustrious history in South Asia. It is for this reason that I focus on Anand, whose shift in narrative focalization clearly signals one trajectory for contemporary Dalit literature.

3. Symbolic evidence may be the very fact of the publication in 1935 of the experimentalist *Untouchable*, and in 1936 of Premchand's starkly social realist *Godaan*, discussed in the previous chapter.

4. The critical reception of this novel forms a corpus of its own. On the question of aesthetics in particular, see Anand's own writings in *Conversations in Bloomsbury* and *Author to Critic*, as well as Saros Cowasjee's *So Many Freedoms* and more recently, Benjamin Baer's "Shit Writing" and Jessica Berman's "Towards a Regional Cosmopolitanism."

5. Mulk Raj Anand's *Untouchable* is an unusual text, even within the cultural sphere of progressive writing in English; it would be difficult to construe his work as "representative" or as originary. Benjamin Baer describes it as a "strange and errant intervention, through an experiment with modernism" (586). While this is an apt categorization of the uniqueness of Anand's project, *Untouchable* also participated in a certain zeitgeist that sought to

harness literary potential in the service of caste. The problem of caste had, in any case, long been in circulation in vernacular fiction. In the history of English-language fiction, however, and the intellectual equation of caste and labor, Anand plays a crucial role. His interest in producing an untouchable subjectivity is also unprecedented, particularly because of the generic choice of the novel. Poetry would trace a different kind of trajectory.

6. This may be the origin of the postcolonial interest in the Chamar specifically, as in Rohinton Mistry's *A Fine Balance*, or Vikram Seth's *A Suitable Boy*.

7. The kind of analysis I perform here necessarily leaves much unsaid; I am throwing metaphor into relief in order to make certain claims regarding modernist aesthetics and this particular text's thematic implications. *Untouchable* is obviously a rich semantic, semiotic, and political text on which much has been written (beyond its metaphorical shortcomings). See note 4 in this chapter.

8. *Untouchable* was written in England, specifically for a British audience, and later revised after being shown to Gandhi.

9. The important essays for this highly influential theory would be "Metaphoric and Metonymic Poles," "On Realism in Art" and "The Twofold Character of Language."

10. Colonial mimicry has been theorized by Homi Bhabha, who derives its textual imperative from Thomas Macaulay's famed "Minute on Indian Education" (1835), and recuperates its transgressive potential and threat. The class of colonized interpreters, Anglicized but not English, are potentially destabilizing precisely because they have similar class status to their colonial counterparts. "The effect of mimicry on the authority of colonial discourse is profound and disturbing. For in 'normalizing' the colonial state or subject, the dream of post-Enlightenment civility alienates its own language of liberty and produces another knowledge of its norms" (86). See "Of Mimicry and Man" in *The Location of Culture*.

11. The important text in this regard would be Bhabani Bhattacarya's *He Who Rides a Tiger* (1954), which addresses mimicry and Sanskritization. In this novel, Kalo is a lowercaste villager who "becomes" a Brahmin.

12. This would be fetishism in the sense in which Michael Taussig describes it, i.e., the older interpretation of "fetish" that comes to us from the discourse of anthropology. My thanks to Elaine Freedgood for this point.

13. It is in this way that *Untouchable* is distinct from Anand's other novels—namely *Coolie*, which also features an impoverished youth as protagonist, in this case an orphan who becomes a railway worker. *Coolie*, however, is a more straightforward social realist text, less interested in caste as an analytic and more concerned with the rapaciousness and cruelty of a modernizing India.

14. "He often thought of his mother, the small, dark figure, swathed simply in tunic, . . . a bit too old-fashioned for his then already growing modern tastes, Indian to the core and sometimes uncomfortably so (as she did not like his affecting European clothes), but so loving, so good" (14).

15. Udaya Kumar, Translation, Migration and Modernity (lecture). See also Kumar's "Seeing and Reading."

16. See, for example, D. R. Nagaraj's *Flaming Feet* and Gyan Pandey's "Can There Be a Subaltern Middle Class?"

17. See Lukács's comparison of the description of the races in Zola and Tolstoy in "To Narrate or Describe?" from *Writer and Critic*.

18. This is a crisis reminiscent of that described by Roberto Schwarz in "The Poor Old Woman and Her Portraitist." Schwarz considers how the pitiable figure of Dona Placida in Machado's *The Posthumous Memoirs of Bras Cubas* betrays certain bourgeois notions of work and dignified labor by dying impoverished and morally uncompensated. Meanwhile, the brute facts of slavery hover in Brazilian society and the text, eviscerating any simple notion of work as virtuous. The irony, writes Schwarz, is that, "Looked at as a whole, it [Dona Placida's life] is a dizzyingly compressed reversal of the perspectives of providentialism, of the Englihtenment and of faith in science, all for the convenience of the Brazilian ruling class, which in this way universalizes its own incongruities" (98). See Schwarz's *Misplaced Ideas*, 94–100.

19. This point on metonymy derives from important analyses of the realist canon—the work of J. Hillis Miller on Dickens, for example. Miller writes that metonymy is the central device of Dickensian realism and evokes "a necessary similarity between a man, his environment and the life he is forced to lead within the environment" (95). Culler confirms this by suggesting that the symbolism of realist novels functions via metonymic contiguity (*Structuralist Poetics* 265). Both of these critiques derive essentially from the Jakobsonian position.

20. From Hazari's *I Was an Outcaste: The Autobiography of an Untouchable in India* (1951), discussed in chapter 5: "As regards the dead animals, we watched in the same way as the vulture watches; there is no difference between the vulture and the sweeper in this respect" (7).

21. Jonathan Culler traces the interlocking possibilities of metaphor and metonymy in "The Turns of Metaphor" in *The Pursuit of Signs*, deriving this question of interrelation from Stephen Ullmann and Gerard Genette, who refer to "essential" and "contingent" connections. Culler then walks us through Paul de Man's analysis of this interdependence, hierarchically tilted towards metaphor, in the work of Proust.

22. See also Surajpal Chauhan's "Parivartan ki baat." In this tightly woven story, Kisna, a Dalit, refuses to remove a dead cow from the village despite the *thakur*'s demands. In the name of social progress, he maintains that he is abandoning the work of his forefathers. In the end a deal is struck: Kisna agrees to remove the cow on the condition that upon the death of his mother she is treated with the same proprieties. The *shirth* or condition/wager that makes these gains for the Dalit communities is produced on the basis of a similar equation of corpse and carcass via a similar metonymic chain: cow=mother goddess=spiritual being=mother=corpse.

23. Chauhan has published an autobiography *Tiraskrit* (*Scorned*) in 2002, two collections of short stories including *Harry kab aayega* (*When*

Will Harry Come?) in 1999, and two collections of poetry. He is the editor of an important anthology, *Hindi ke dalit kathakaron ki pahli kahani*, 2004. *Tiraskrit* generated a certain amount of controversy for its depiction of conflict among Dalits, particularly Chamar and Valmiki communities.

24. All translations of "Sajish" are mine.

25. The epiphany of the modernist novel was made famous by James Joyce in *A Portrait of the Artist as a Young Man* (1916).

26. The question of the emergence of a political consciousness is cited by Aamir Mufti as central to realist writing in the colony more generally. See "Sadat Hasan Manto" in *Enlightenment and the Colony*.

27. For a brilliant discussion of this very problematic in the context of two South Indian literary texts and their elaboration of Gramscian theory, see Rajeswari Sunder Rajan's "Questioning Intellectuals: Reading Caste with Gramsci in Two Indian Literary Texts." Sunder Rajan effectively asks: What is the role of the political leadership in new political movements, and who will that leadership comprise? The withering of the vanguard, she suggests, now means that movements (i.e., constituents) lead themselves. Arun Mukherjee makes the point in "The Exclusion of Postcolonial Theory" that there is no possibility of a self-directed Dalit politics in Anand's novel, despite its clear historical possibility.

28. The location of social critique within the female subject, is in and of itself a kind of trope in Dalit fiction. See for example Omprakash Valmiki's "Yah ant nahin" ("This Is Not the End") in the collection Guspaithiye (*The Infiltrators*), or another story from Chauhan's *Harry kab aayega*, "Parivartan ki bat" ("Speaking of change"). "Parivartan" also once again takes up the vexed question of "traditional profession" or the abandonment of work considered religiously and socially polluting. There is also the varied work of writers such as Kusum Meghwal, Sushila Taakbhaure, and Rajat Rani Meenu.

29. See, for example, Woloch's discussion of the figure of the servant, who helps to create "majorness" both structurally and topically ("Minor Minor Characters: Representing Multiplicity" in *The One versus the Many*).

30. There were of course, many other literary possibilities; these are exemplified by Venkataramani's *Murugan the Tiller* or Rao's *Kanthapura*, which take other routes entirely. My reading of Anand's *Untouchable* attempts to read the establishment of one strain of a literary precedent that is later inherited by contemporary Anglophone writers. More recent Anglophone literature, however, works with a reading of caste-as-class, for different reasons, as I demonstrate in chapter 4.

3. A PERFECT WHOLE: KNOWLEDGE BY TRANSCRIPTION AND RURAL REGIONALISM

1. *Nayi kahani* or the New Story movement, in Hindi and in other regional languages, came to refer to the rapid proliferation and celebration of the genre of short fiction published in the 1950s and '60s, often in prominent literary journals like *Kahani* and *Dharmayug*. This fiction was largely categorizd as "modernist" in style and sensibility in contrast to an older social realist mode. The rubric of *nayi kahani* worked alongside the equally broad categorizations of *nayi katha* (new writing) and *nayi kavita* (new poetry) all of which shared a largely individualist, urbanist and self-conscious aesthetics. See Ramchandra Shukla's "Aadhunik gadhya sahitya parampara ka pravartan" in *Hindi sahitya ka itihas*, Preetha Mani's *Gender and Genre: Hindi and Tamil Short Story Writing and the Framing of the Postcolonial Indian Nation, 1950–1970* (unpublished manuscript) and the recent collection *Hindi Modernism*.

2. All citations of *Maila anchal*, along with the page numbers, refer to Indira Junghare's 1991 translation, *The Soiled Border*.

3. An abbreviated list of texts included within the canon of *anchalikta* (excluding the work of Renu, which I will discuss in some detail): Shiv Prasad Singh's *Alag alag vaitrani*, Rangeya Ragav's *Kab tak pukaru*, Rahi Masum Raza's *Aadha gav*, Ramdarash Mishra's *Jal tuttha hua*, and almost all the novels of Nagarjun, including *Balcanma*, *Varun ke bête*, and *Jamaniya ka baba*.

4. I would stress here that *anchalik sahitya* cannot really be read as distinct from *nayi katha* though it moved through different literary contexts. Many of Renu's famed short stories on folk culture in the village were indeed considered fine examples of *nayi kahani*, and the larger project of the *anchaliks*—to expand the scope, form, and contexts of literary Hindi—was generally consonant with *nayi katha*.

5. A major figure among the *anchalik* writers, Nagarjun (1911–98), born and raised in Bihar, was a poet and novelist renowned in both Maithili and Hindi. A Brahmin who became for some time a Buddhist monk, Nagarjun was educated in Benares and Calcutta. He was heavily influenced by Marxism-Leninism, and a follower of the Bihari peasant-leader Swami Sahajanand. He became a member of the Communist Party of India but eventually dissociated himself from it. Nagarjun was an active supporter of the 1967 Naxalbari revolt as well as J. P. Narayan's antigovernment agitation, and his fiction demonstrates an interest in practical revolution at the level of individual struggle while also elaborating Maithili rural and semiurban culture. Some important novels that have informed the discussion here: *Ratinath ki chachi* (1948), *Balcanma* (1952), *Varun ke bête* (1956), and *Baba Batesarnath* (1961), *Jamaniya ka baba* (1968). Nagarjun published several collections of poetry and essays; he also wrote articles in Bangla for newspapers and magazines.

6. Renu was born in 1922 to a landed, well-educated Kurmi family and was raised and schooled in Bihar. He became active in nationalist politics while a student at Benares Hindu University and was a member of the

socialist party but became quickly disillusioned. His intellectual formation was heavily influenced by Bisheshwar Prasad Koirala, the Nepali socialist, as well as J. P. Narayan and the Janata movement. Seminal texts include the novels *Maila anchal* (1954), *Parati parikatha* (1957), *Julus* (1961), *Dirghtapa* (1963), and the short story collections *Thumri* (1959), *Adim ratri ki mahak* (1967), and *Aginkhor* (1973).

7. See the anthology *Maila anchal ka mahatva* by Madhuresh for a range of critical responses to the novel.

8. Renu's work is described as a mix of Maithili, spoken Bangla, and spoken Hindi, particularly in his early period, and a more standardized Hindi from the 1960s onwards. There is an element of destabilization here, an attempt to challenge the hegemony of a newly standardized tongue that had been granted national-language status. But Katherine Hansen also adds that in addition to the realism seemingly provided by a mix of languages and registers, and the entry into the "oral universe" that this mix indicates, there is a sense of "play," crucial to Renu's oeuvre as a whole ("Renu's Regionalism" 282). At the same time, the use of a certain Sanskritized Hindi would indicate not only forms of orality but entry into a differential time-space from the urban.

9. "No wonder that Hindi critics complained that some of these novels do not present a single human character of the stature of Surdas of *Rangabhumi* and Hori of *Godaan* by Premchand" (Pandey, *Regionalism* 16).

10. Prakash describes this as a dialectic between "social reality and explanatory comment" (6). It should be noted here that Premchand's was the necessary labor demanded by a new literary subject, as we have seen in chapter 1, which could now be taken for granted by Renu and later postindependence writers.

11. See "Yatharthvaad aur *anchalik* upanyas" ("Realism and the *Anchalik* Novel") by Shivakumar Mishra. This important essay bridges the intellectual gap between the realism of the progressive writers and the "realism" or naturalism of novelists like Renu.

12. This is also why the Lukácsian and Jamesonian critiques are entirely relevant here. Lukács sees in the privileging of naturalist description the collapse of realism's historicity and the hypertrophy of symbolic detail. Jameson rightly reads Lukács's analysis of modernism and naturalism as a dialectic, two poles linked by the exaggeration of form. The entire problem of historicity is paramount in the *anchalik* reading of culture.

13. I use the word romanticism here somewhat lightly; I do not refer to the literary movement in Hindi referred to as Chhayavaad, often translated as romanticism. Romanticism here is linked with romantic love for an object, as Dr. Prashant is colored by his love for the village. I am concerned with the way in which the realist imperative singles out certain elements as romanticized. Kathryn Hansen, as mentioned, critiques the notion that these elements simply do the work of authenticating.

14. Minor gods of the Ahirs, a cow-herding tribe of North India.

15. A proper analysis of "folk" falls outside the scope of this argument. It should be mentioned however, that recent work has very thoroughly

interrogated the categories of "folk" and "folklore" for their romanticist notions and deconstructed the seminal distinction between "folk" and "classical." See, for example, Arjun Appadurai's afterword to *Gender, Genre, and Power in South Asian Expressive Traditions* as well as Stuart Blackburn's "The Burden of Authenticity" in *India's Literary History* and Kathryn Hansen's *Grounds for Play: Nautanki Theatre of North India*. "Folk" in this chapter is used to refer to oral cultural traditions associated with village social organization, and is seen, within the text, as distinct from "literary" and "classical" forms of culture—i.e., those creative practices that might be seen as worthy of ethnographic rescue.

16. For example, the following passage:

> The make-up of the women is particularly eye-catching. They might look untidy during the day, but as night falls they dress their best and meticulously comb their hair. They curl their hair and put bamboo combs into it. The number of combs a maiden may have is limitless. A comb is a memento from a young man to a young woman. The more the number of combs she possesses, the greater is the popularity the girl enjoys. It is also a tribute to her charms. Necklaces of beads and conch shells form an integral part of her ornaments. Some ornaments are carved out of bamboo and wood. Colored seeds collected from the jungle are also threaded together to form necklaces. The neck is fully covered with these multicoloured ornaments that are generally hung loose over the breasts. Breasts are seldom covered. And why should they cover them? Keeping the body uncovered is no sin for them, as love is no sin. (Awasthi, *Jangal* 9)

17. Kumkum Sangari has discussed the figure of the tribal as the "unconscious" of the nation, and potentially, of Hinduism. In terms of the culturalist argument I am making here, her observation on the tribal woman in two very different novels is quite helpful: "Rather, it is the preservation of what appears to be a kind of cultural capital or reified heritage wherein the woman and the tribal, separately as well as together, become the 'unconscious' of the nation, the essence of a collectivity" (80).

18. Fanon may seem like an odd choice in the context of a postindependence regionalist India but his discussion of the relations between culture and the political is evocative in many contexts, including the case of *anchalik sahitya*. Fanon is concerned with a theorization of the national as it is linked with the anticolonial struggle whereas the *anchalik*s attempt to elaborate a regional identity in contradistinction to the nation. But the intellectual operation performed by the intelligentsia in line with a project of recovery is beautifully captured by Fanon; it is this particular operation that is relevant in the case of the *anchalik*s in that it is primarily a movement of intellectuals that becomes hegemonic. The essay "On National Culture" was first presented at the Second Congress of Black Writers and Artists in 1959 in Rome (*Wretched of the Earth* 180).

19. The crucial example here would be the model of Dalitization advocated by Kancha Ilaiah. See *Why I Am Not a Hindu*. Vasant Moon's

autobiography *Growing Up Untouchable in India* describes the explicit renunciation of cultural (Hindu) practice in the spirit of Ambedkarite modernization.

20. This story first appears in the collection *Dusari duniya ka yatharth*, and is then reprinted in *Dalit kathakaaron ki pahli kahani*.

21. See also Naimishraya's *Avaaj* (1998), *Helo Kamrade* (2001), *Virangana Jhalkaribai* (2003), *Aaj bazaar band hai* (2004), *Kya mujhe kharidoge* (2005), and *Hamara javab* (2005).

22. See Ambedkar's "Castes in India" in *The Essential Writings of B. R. Ambedkar* (241–62), for his explanation of "girl marriage" and its role in the construction of uppercasteness.

23. The rape of Laxmi, the *dasin* of the Kabir temple in *Maila anchal*, receives poignant but limited attention.

24. My thanks to Rajeswari Sunder Rajan for this wonderful point.

25. In brief commentary on this story, Naimishraya recalls a conversation with the eminent contemporary Hindi author Rajendra Yadav, who describes "Apna gav" as an "experiment." Naimishraya: "I said, 'No, this is what should happen—.' He responded, 'The villages would become empty.' 'Let them empty,' I said. 'At least they will not become our graveyard.'" See Gupta, 54.

26. For a thorough analysis of the successive changes that the "ethnographic gaze" has undergone within the discipline of anthropology, see James Clifford's "On Ethnographic Authority" in *The Predicament of Culture*.

27. Kardam, based in Delhi, is one of the most prolific Hindi Dalit writers working today. He is the editor of the journal *Dalit Sahitya* and the author of *Talash*, a collection of short stories, as well as *Gunga nahin tha main* and *Tinaka tinaka age*, two collections of poetry. Kardam has also published several critical texts on Ambedkarism, on race and caste in India, and on the contemporary Dalit movement.

28. In fact, D. R. Nagaraj suggests precisely this in the service of establishing a new Indian poetics of culture: the abolishment of the distinction between folk and classical (190). It should be mentioned that in Dalit literature in other languages, Kannada for example, there is a deeper interest in the category of the folk that that which has been evinced in Hindi. Nagaraj discusses this question in the work of Siddalingaiah (see "Between Social Rage and Spiritual Quest: Notes on Dalit Writing in Kannada" and "Cosmologies of Castes, Realism, Dalit Sensibility, and the Kannada Novel" in *The Flaming Feet*.

29. This debate, between those who would modernize and abandon any notion of casteized culture in the model of Ambedkar and those who would attempt to recover and reread modern Dalit identity in terms of that very denigrated cultural sphere, is the central topic of D. R. Nagaraj's *The Flaming Feet*. See in particular "Social Change in Kannada Fiction."

30. In the novel, the *maila anchal* refers specifically to Kamli's virginity. Her mother tells her father that "her sari border has been stained" (Renu, *The Soiled Border* 272). In the original Hindi: "'Kuch nahin,' Ma fisafisakar

kahti hai, 'Kamli ne ... Kamli ne to aanchal mein dag lagva liya. ...' 'Aa yein? Aanchal mein?' Tahsildar sahab ko laga ki Kamli ke kapade mein aag lag gai hai. Kamli jal rahi hai. 'Ha, char mahina...!' Tahsildar sahab aur ma donon ek hi saath lambi sas chodate hain" (Renu, *Maila anchal* 290).

31. This would be demonstrated by several of Renu's short stories as well. See for example "The Messenger," in which a messenger contemplates his obsolescence in light of the new post office, or the famous "Panchlight," which demonstrates the effect of modern technology on traditional practices.

32. This analysis is clearly indebted to Spivak's theorization of the native informant, made most powerfully in *The Critique of Postcolonial Reason*. The native informant is a complex philosophical position, often feminized, often debased. That position of indigenous knowledge is tracked through the literature of the dominant, "a name for that mark of expulsion from the name of Man—a mark crossing out the impossibility of the ethical relation" (6). Spivak deconstructs the informant as a "blank," and "unlisted trace" who provides data that is then to be analyzed by others; "a site that can only be read" (49); a guide to "information retrieval," devoid of its own worlding (118). This understanding of the informant clearly undergirds the narrative practices of what I refer to as "knowledge by transcription" and "pure revelation."

33. See Mieke Bal's *Narratology* as well as her essay "Over-Writing as Un-Writing: Descriptions, World-Making, and Novelistic Time" for a narratological discussion of literary description and its defining features.

4. CASTELESS MODERNITIES: THE CONTEMPORARY ANGLOPHONE NOVEL AND ITS INVISIBLE INTERLOCUTORS

1. This autobiography is one of the few Dalit autobiographies published in English. The Dalit critic Sheoraj Singh Bechain suggests that this autobiography was originally published in fragments in Urdu, in a weekly newspaper, but I have been unable to find evidence confirming this. I discuss Hazari's text in more detail in chapter 5.

2. As I've mentioned elsewhere, there has been much work done on Dalit alienation from both Congress Party politics and nationalist concerns more generally. For a cursory discussion of this problem as it is relevant to the argument of this chapter, see Christopher Jaffrelot's *India's Silent Revolution* on the evolution of caste-based parties in North India; Gail Omvedt's "Ambedkar and Dalit Labor Radicalism" as well as her more elaborate *Dalits and the Democratic Revolution*, on the relations between Ambedkarite politics and mainstream elite nationalism; and Vijay Prashad's "Between Economism and Emancipation: Untouchables and Indian Nationalism," which takes issue with some of Omvedt's arguments while focusing on early labor politics and Dalit activism. See also the section of the Dalit Panthers Manifesto, reproduced in Joshi's *Untouchable!: Voices of the Dalit Liberation Movement*, entitled "What Have Other Parties Done for Dalits?"

3. Hindi Dalit critics level a similar criticism at Premchand (1880–1936), father of the modern Hindi novel, whose work portrayed with sympathy and compassion the plight of the peasant. Sohanpal Sumanakshar argues that the

image of Dalits in Premchand's work, despicable and deplorable as it is, was produced precisely to curry favor with the uppercaste literary establishment. See chapter 1.

4. There will clearly be exceptions to the trends I am sketching here; one question for critics of Anglophone fiction may concern the particular sociohistorical contexts that produce such outliers. However, as I am concerned here with the creation of a certain culture of literary acceptability, I am thinking of texts that broadly confirm the uppercaste—i.e., secularist worldview—while avoiding any systemic analysis of the role of caste in the problems they explore.

5. The argument made in this chapter for the mutually constitutive space of Anglophone and Dalit literature is possible particularly because the Dalit textuality under discussion is written in Hindi. In its strident claims for national language status, its emergence as a lingua franca in commercial and cultural transactions in the North, as well as its association with cosmopolitanism via Bollywood and other cultural forms, Hindi shares with English many spaces and ideological concerns in a way arguably distinct from Marathi, Telegu, or Kannada, other languages in which Dalit literatures have flourished. See Harish Trivedi's "The Progress of Hindi."

6. Valmiki's discussion of Marxism comes as a response to a debate with eminent Marxist critic Namvar Singh, who insists on Marxist evaluations of Dalit literature. Valmiki reads this request as tantamount to the erasure of caste (93). See Valmiki's "Kab tak in prashnon se bachega marxvad" in *Dalit sahitya ka saundaryashastra*.

7. This point is clearly indebted to Partha Chatterjee's crucial formulation in *The Nation and Its Fragments*, by which the "spiritual" became the location of a nationalism that countered the usurpation of the "material" sphere by British colonialism.

8. Let me state clearly that I am not suggesting that the analytical categories of caste and class are somehow easily discernible in the material realm. What I mean to stress is a lineage of rhetorical disentanglement by which class and caste are understood to be either mutually incompatible and hierarchizeable (as in the case of some Dalit writing and most Marxist rhetoric) or easily subsumable (as in the case of much nationalist discourse), as well as a range of possibilities in between.

9. I'm indebted here, to a certain extent, to Fredric Jameson's discussion in *The Political Unconscious* of the symptom and the reading practice this might engender. The psychoanalytic model of repression, however, may be insufficient to explain the literary logic of caste although this is the model on which critics like Dhareshwar and Menon rely. In the case of the Anglophone sphere, the narrative of repression is also accompanied by an active and overt discrediting of the structural power of caste as a social phenomenon.

10. See Susie Tharu's "The Impossible Subject: Caste and Desire in the Scene of the Family."

11. Paranjape concludes that most of the writers in his small sample survey are indeed Brahmins, if not of other uppercaste origin. Indeed, this evidence alone seems to superficially explain the disinterest in the caste question

in this body of work; most Indian English authors are urbanized, Western educated, and, if not permanently diasporic, then residents abroad for long periods. The caste privilege that may have structurally ensured these class privileges, including the privilege of the occupation of fiction writing, hasn't been a major preoccupation of the novels of this genre. As a result it might seem that caste, as a subject of fictional exploration, has gradually come to mean specifically lowercaste, and uppercasteness has been largely ignored. K. Satyanarayana points out, however, that to align the putative progressive values of these texts and authors with "debrahminised Brahminism" is problematic. See his "The Politics of (Self) Representation: Case of a Debrahminised Brahmin."

12. This is in contrast to the late nineteenth- and early twentieth-century novel in the vernacular languages (those written by Tagore, Bankim, Sharatchandra, and Premchand), which, in the social reform effort, often critiqued the openly casteist, orthodox, Brahminical position (Paranjape, *Caste* 58).

13. Paranjape has mentioned a few others, including Bhattacharya's *He Who Rides a Tiger* (1954).

14. Rashmi Sadana follows the debate around the excision of the Chamar sections of this novel in "A Suitable Text for a Vegetarian Audience." I will take up this issue again in my conclusion.

15. Naipaul's life's work has been thoroughly dissected. For his relationship to the diasporic in particular, see Edward Said's essay "Among the Believers" in the collection *Reflections on Exile*, as well as Bruce King's *V. S. Naipaul* and Fawzia Mustafa's *V. S. Naipaul*. On caste politics, on which very little has been written, in addition to Naipaul's several nonfiction collections on India, see Lilian Feder's *Naipaul's Truth: The Making of a Writer* and Naipaul's own work, *India: A Wounded Civilization*.

16. The following conciliatory gesture is abandoned by Rao's later novels, which are unabashedly Brahminical:

> "No, no, no, no," and he looks this side and that and thinks surely there is a carcass in the back yard, and it's surely being skinned, and he smells the stench of hide and the stench of pickled pigs, and the room seems to shake, and all the gods and all the manes of heaven seem to cry out against him, and his hands steal mechanically to the thread, and holding it, he feels he would like to say, "Hari-Om, Hari-Om." . . . and Moorthy with many a trembling prayer, touches the tumbler and brings it to his lips, and taking one sip, lays it aside. (Rao, *Kanthapura* 72).

17. The Dalit critique, crystallized by the Poona Pact of 1932 and the question of a separate electorate for "depressed classes," will cite Ambedkar as the radical path not taken by novelists like Rao and his contemporary Mulk Raj Anand.

18. "My decision was simple. It was to turn my back on our ancestry, the foolish, foreign-ruled starveling priests my grandfather had told me about, to turn my back on all my father's foolish hopes for me as someone high in the maharaja's service, all the foolish hopes of the college principle to have me

marry his daughter. My decision was to turn my back on all those ways of death, to trample on them, and to do the only noble thing that lay in my power, was to marry the lowest person I could find" (Naipaul, *Half a Life* 12).

19. The sole potential example might be Naipaul's 2002 novel *Magic Seeds*, the sequel to *Half a Life*, which features a shadowy guerilla movement that appears to be modeled after India's People's War Group. This Naxalite (Marxist-Leninist-Maoist) organization was founded in 1980 and joined Bihar's Maoist Communist Centre in 2006 to form Communist Party of India (Maoist), and has been influential among the lowercastes of Andhra and Bihar. In *Magic Seeds*, Willie falls in with the movement in a misguided desire to do something, prodded by his activist sister. But the guerillas are hired hands and psychopaths, and the political movements are motivated by anger, vanity and egotism. The novel cancels political agency, reading it as ultimately hollow. And once again, the lowercaste actors in *Magic Seeds* (presumably the only novel in English on the numerous and influential far leftist movements in India) only come to the surface via a movement, however discredited, that advocates class warfare.

20. Criticism on Roy's *The God of Small Things* is abundant and exhaustive so I have chosen to limit my comments here. The novel is surely to be commended for bringing the question of caste politics and the failure of the left into the public space of Anglophone writing. It does, however, present a highly romanticized, simplistic, bilateral vision of caste politics, buttressed by the narrative vision of a disenchanted, disgraced divorcee and her children rather than a Dalit character. An interesting reading of the novel sensitive to the question of enfranchisement is Nalini Natarajan's "Motherhood, Home and Property: Arundhati Roy's *God of Small Things*."

21. Paranjape points out the correlation between uppercaste origin and a professed secularism: Indian English writers are "de-brahminised Brahmins," "caste-less uppercastes ("Caste" 57). "What actually binds them together is not the incidental fact that they all belong to the same varna so much as their repudiation of several of those structures and values which are compulsory to their belonging to the varna" ("Caste" 55).

22. "Reservations" refers to the system of affirmative action for "backward" and untouchable castes that is mandated by the Indian constitution. Seats are reserved for these contingencies, according to population, in government institutions, the public sector, and educational institutions.

23. This is totally unlike, for example, the essay entitled "The Question of the Big and the Small People," published in a Hindi journal in 1938. The author Kashi Baba works with the same metaphor of big and small that motivates Adiga, but he qualifies this by tracing the nature of these terms to caste (cited in Gooptu 143–44).

24. I want to add here that this point also conforms to the aesthetic logic of the text, which, while not explicitly allegorical, moves comfortably and sardonically through a series of diametrically opposed images and concepts: darkness and light, big and small, and so forth.

25. The general disinterest in caste in this body of work, other than a few salient examples, might be read most easily in terms of the very literary

realism that it has largely espoused: as fiction often produced in and about urban centers, and often in and about diasporic communities, where caste no longer plays a salient role in the politics of social life. Of course, this is hardly true, as myriad examples would show. Caste violence in the village is often anchored ideologically or financially by people in the cities, while the urban is often a failed escape for victims of casteism. This elision is also easily read via biographical positionality, as Paranjape asserts. Urbanized, affluent, Anglophone writers can exhibit a kind of postcaste consciousness (which remains casteist, I would add) precisely because of the salient class, caste, and geographic network out of which they are produced.

26. Halwais are categorized as OBCs in other states of India (Rajasthan, Haryana) but not in Bihar.

27. Instead, Balram might be read as a descendant of certain literary figures; he conjures, in a vague way, the pathology of Albert Camus's stranger, although the very clear political motivation of his murder might be said to mock the latter's excuse for his murder of the Arab.

28. See the work of Kusum Meghwal, Rajat Rani Minu, and the collection *Dalit mahilaon ka carcit kahaniyaan* for an introduction.

29. In a strange conflation of both Franz Fanon's *Wretched of the Earth* and Dostoevsky's *Crime and Punishment*, Balram rages against class injustice but creates a methodology accessible to only the very few who are determined to become New Men. For Fanon in *The Wretched of the Earth*, the native Last would be First after the process of decolonization. In this analysis of the apartheid and imminent doom of the colonial state, the "damned" (in the original French) became agents through the overthrow of the state. Their revolutionary power is derived from their collective ethical consciousness and violence. But as Raskolnikov says in *Crime and Punishment*, in his proto-Nietzschean way, only a few can act. Raskolnikov's determination to murder the wretched pawnbroker is produced as much by his own monomania, his "superman complex," as it is by his sense of injustice. While the exploitative pawnbroker is a worthy target, Raskolnikov, the impoverished student, imagines himself as a Napoleon. Balram's ideology strikes me as drawn very heavily from these texts. Richard Wright's *Native Son* (1940), the story of Bigger Thomas's murder of a white woman, has also been cited by Adiga himself as influential.

30. The "servant novel" was a standard of nineteenth-century British fiction, suggesting once again the continuing invisible interlocutor that Indian Anglophone fiction finds in British literature rather than in the tradition of writing in the vernacular languages.

31. This Maoist movement has become increasingly attractive to Dalits and tribals in certain states, like Bihar, since its inception in 1967, and has coerced and intimidated lowercaste communities into complicity in others, gradually replacing the students and middle-class intellectuals that once formed an important contingent of the movement. Operating in the northeast and central regions of India, the movement, drawn from several and varied political organizations with different regional and economic concerns, proclaims an anti-imperial, antifeudal, and anticaste ideology that has helped

to garner popular support, a support that is sometimes violently demanded. The Naxalites kill landlords, burn debt papers, torch homes, reappropriate land, and organize jailbreaks on behalf of, and with the help of, the poorest communities they seek to represent: Dalits and tribals. Retaliatory movements, governmental and paramilitary, have cropped up; in Bihar, the Ranvir Sena that represents the interests of the Bhumihar and other uppercaste landlords is well known for its ferocity. Laxmangarh, Balram's village, actually recalls the village Laxmanpur-Bathe, famous for a Ranvir Sena massacre of sixty-one Dalits in 1997 (see Smita Narula's *Broken People*, the 1999 Human Rights Watch Report). On the Naxalites, see Rabindra Ray's *The Naxalites and Their Ideology*, Sumanta Bannerjee's *India's Simmering Revolution*, and Anand Chakravarti's *Red Sun*.

32. See, for example, Vijay Tendulkar's Marathi drama *Kanyadaan*, U. R. Anantha Murthy's Kannada novel *Samskara*, Kota Shivarama Karanth's Kannada novel *Chomana dudi*, and Thakuzi Pillai's novels *Thottiyue Makan* and *Randidanghazi*, both written in Malayalam.

33. When discussing the Khairlanji atrocity, S. Anand makes an illuminating point. In a case of caste atrocity, the judge pronounces the death penalty sentence, but not on the basis of the Prevention of Atrocities Act. As a result, an instance of caste massacre (as well as rape) can now be read as "abstract human rage." I won't suggest that something similar can be traced here. But there is a persistent problem by which analytical abstraction has become psychically desirable or palatable rather than the grit of a caste analysis that varies regionally, linguistically, and historically. Class analysis is not an abstraction per se, but it often performs the role of abstracting caste conflict.

34. Dilip Menon's *Blindness of Insight* takes on this very question: that of the relationship between communalism, or otherism, and caste violence. He argues that the quotidian violence of caste is often usurped by the more spectacular forms of communalism.

35. Dhareshwar writes that "one often notices a certain slippage that equates caste exclusively with lower-caste. The slippage is systematic rather than accidental" (121).

36. See, for example, Narendra Jadhav's *Untouchables: My Family's Triumphant Escape from India's Caste System*. For a more detailed discussion of the politics of translation of Dalit literature, see S. Anand's *Touchable Tales*.

37. See Navariya's story collection *Patkatha aur anya kahaniyam*, which I will discuss here, as well as the novel *Udhar ke log*, which follows the romantic and political life of an urbanized, middle-class Dalit.

38. As Sadana insightfully points out, "These spheres [Indo-English and vernacular] have distinct sets of authenticity markers that continually intersect" (312).

39. This has the unique side effect of also challenging the uppercaste literary monopoly on love and affective questions more generally. Navariya has publicly discussed his desire for Dalit literature to take more seriously questions of aesthetics, and also to assert a right to beauty in all its forms.

Dalitness, therefore, can also be about romance. See "The Lover and the Other."

40. This was Pratap's stated goal. "I have made an effort to capture the conflict between Dalit consciousness and class consciousness in this story. The protagonist's tug-of-war must be understood in this context" (Gupta 195).

41. See Valmiki's "25 x 4 = 150," discussed in chapter 1.

5. SOME TIME BETWEEN REVISIONIST AND REVOLUTIONARY . . . : READING HISTORY IN DALIT TEXTUALITY

1. This may be translated as "leavings," "remnants of food," "an object previously used by another" (and so made impure and unfit for use). (*Oxford Hindi-English Dictionary*).

2. The exception would be written versions of the traditionally oral *jati-puranas*, the origin tales that often trace the heroic exploits and tragic downfall of a certain caste.

3. This is the critical truism asserted by critics and writers alike: Dalit literature is the uncomplicated expression of a monolithic Dalit identity. This is in fact the underlying assumption of the critics Sharankumar Limbale and Omprakash Valmiki, as well as scholars like Eleanor Zelliot and Gail Omvedt who examine Dalit literature in the context of broader social movement. Such assertions must of course be contextualized as a response to a certain sociohistorical condition; to be Dalit was to be, definitionally, deprived of access to cultural productions that required literacy (see Tej Singh's *Aaj ka dalita sahitya*). However, they have also allowed Dalit writing to fit smoothly into the narrow grid of identity politics.

4. I will elaborate further on this term "posthistoricist realism" in the final section of this chapter, "Dalit Realisms Revisited."

5. Critic Rita Kothari asks, for example, "If protest literature is 'grounded in history,' why is the treatment of an oppressor and oppressed in Dalit short stories ahistorical?" (4310).

6. Franco Moretti's premise in *The Way of the World* is that that which we have traditionally considered properly historical has largely been excised from the novel, in particular the nineteenth-century bildungsroman, which has gifted to us realism in its most memorable form. "In the classical bildungsroman, the significance of history does not lie in the 'future of the species,' but must be revealed within the more narrow confines of a circumscribed and relatively common individual life" (35). History is the force with which the protagonist must reckon. I've mentioned Moretti here not because the bildungsroman is necessarily part of the genealogy of Dalit literature but because this issue of the absence or presence of history is one with which postcolonial literature, in its broadest configuration, is quite taken. Even the most cursory glance at the genre shows this to be true: Salman Rushdie's rewriting of the moments before and after independence in *Midnight's Children*, Rohinton Mistry's unraveling of Indira Gandhi's Emergency, Amitav Ghosh's generic interest in the historical novel. Postcolonial literature has taken seriously the notion of "writing

back" to the historiography of empire, thereby confirming, rather than dislodging, the historicist fixation. Indeed, the "old" question of historical representation and the historical event, and the more current one of historical time and determination, have become central to contemporary reading of literary texts, particularly for those categorized as postcolonial.

7. Like the Gandhian Premchand (1880–1936), the staunchly Marxist Yashpal (1903–76) wrote large novels as well as short stories in Hindi, works that demonstrated the vast interconnections among characters of different strata. Both writers were heavily influenced by the French and Russian nineteenth-century novelists.

8. "This anguish of Dalits is the progenitor of Dalit literature. It is not the pain of any one person, nor is it of just one day—it is the anguish of many thousands of people, experienced over thousands of years" (Limbale 31).

9. In fact, one of the definitions of Dalit *chetna*—that elusive quality required for the production of Dalit literature—is an opposition to Ramchandra Shukla's definition of great poetry. See Valmiki's *Dalita sahitya ka saundaryashastra*.

10. See Partha Chatterjee's *Nation and Its Fragments* and Gayatri Spivak's discussions of Mahasweta Devi (*Imaginary Maps*; *Critique of Postcolonial Reason*) for such deconstructions of nationalist historiography. The work of scholars such as Rajeswari Sunder Rajan, Flavia Agnes, and Nivedita Menon has addressed this failure of nationalism via a feminist practice. The Subaltern Studies Group parsed the nature of this critique specifically for the Dalit, most recently in issue 12, *Dalits, Muslims, and the Fabrications of History*. In more recent work on Dalit nationalism, Gail Omvedt's *Dalit Visions*, for example, or Kancha Ilaiah's *Buffalo Nationalism*, this is implicit.

11. I've drawn on Gupta's anthology throughout this book. It is a broad-ranging and fine collection that showcases presciently the work of several soon-to-become-heralded writers as well as those who never made fiction writing a professional occupation but have briskly, in one story, contributed to the new delineations of the Hindi Dalit field as such. The anthology also demonstrates the typical trajectory of Dalit literary movements. Gupta is an uppercaste activist, writer, and poet, and former member of the Bihar legislative assembly who has been very involved in the struggle for tribal rights in Jharkand and Bihar. She is the editor of *Yuddharat Aam Aadmi*, an influential journal that has been central in the recognition of Dalit literature. Gupta has been instrumental in the creation of a Dalit public and literary sphere, her own home often serving as the central location for political and cultural exchange. Gupta's involvement thus demonstrates the overlap between progressive and Dalit spheres.

12. From *Dusari duniya ka yatharth*. Translation mine.

13. See Laura Brueck's paper, "Rewriting the Rape-Script in Dalit Women's Literature" as well as Dharamvir's elaboration of this argument in his *Premchand: Saamant ka munshi*.

14. See Alok Mukherjee's introduction to the English translation of Omprakash Valmiki's *Joothan*.

Notes

15. See also Beth, "Dalit Autobiographies," Kothari, "The Short Story in Gujarati Dalit Literature," and Rege, "Dalit Women Talk Differently," and Guru and Geetha, "The New Phase of Dalit-Bahujan Intellectual Activity."

16. Said makes a similar point: "No matter how one tried to extricate subaltern from elite histories, they are different but overlapping and curiously interdependent territories. This, I believe, is a crucial point" (quoted in Guha, "Introduction," *Selected Subaltern Studies*, vii).

17. Ismat Chugtai's *Garam Hawa*, for example.

18. In contrast, see the work of Mulk Raj Anand, considered the father of the Anglophone literature movement in India. Anand depicts with detailed compassion the problems of lowercaste life, yet despite the narrative dominance of lowercaste characters, one always has the sense that the world is elsewhere, that "real life" is made outside the peripheral lives among which we as readers are presently situated. In fact, the use of third-person narration in *Untouchable* or *Coolie*, for example, continuously reminds us that although the narrative eye is with Bakha and the cleaning of the latrines, its selection is just that, a mere selection.

19. Chamar, as mentioned earlier, is from the word *chamda* (leather), and refers to the Dalit caste traditionally responsible for the removal of carcasses, the skinning of animals, and leatherwork.

20. Dalit journalist Chandra Bhan Prasad stated in a 2001 column in the newspaper *The Pioneer*, "History shows that imperialism has been fairer to Dalits than the native rulers have ever been" (132).

21. The 1919 massacre of between five hundred and a thousand Indian civilians by British soldiers during an unarmed protest is also referred to as the Amritsar massacre. Salman Rushdie's *Midnight's Children* launches the construction of the character Aadam Aziz as a political subject with this event.

22. See Sudha Pai's "New Social and Political Movements of Dalits: A Study of Meerut."

23. And, of course, influential. Sarah Beth, for example, argues that Valmiki's *Joothan*, and Dalit literature more generally, "details events in the political history of the Dalit movement" (10). This is the most common understanding of Dalit writing.

24. See, for example, Badri Narayan's "Inventing Caste History."

25. Partha Chatterjee, explicating such a methodology says, "The task will be to extract from the immediate reality . . . the implicit element which stands in opposition to the dominant form" ("Caste" 172). The premise here is that Dalit texts create a chronotope of their own. This second reading reads the presumed gap as a historical consciousness submerged, one that follows a different paradigm, presumably, but one that is still wedded to the basic premise of historical thinking. This is, in part, Gayatri Spivak's critique of the work of subaltern studies. "To investigate, discover, and establish a subaltern or peasant consciousness seems at first to be a positivistic project—a project which assumes that, if properly prosecuted, it will lead to firm ground, to some *thing* that can be disclosed" (quoted in Ranajit Guha 10).

26. Omprakash Valmiki's discussion of Marxist literary criticism would be an appropriate place to begin a discussion of how work in subaltern studies might be accommodated in Hindi Dalit writing. His analysis comes as a response to a debate with eminent Marxist critic Namvar Singh, who insists on Marxist evaluations of Dalit literature. Valmiki reads this request as tantamount to the erasure of caste (93). See "Kab tak in prashnon se bachega marxvad" in *Dalit sahitya ka saundaryashastra*.

27. See Gopal Guru's "Archaeology of Untouchability."

28. I draw here from Jameson's notion of genre as "mediatory" and "contractual." See "Magical Narratives: On the Dialectical Use of Genre Criticism" in *The Political Unconscious*.

29. Anthologized in Ramanika Gupta's *Dusari duniya ka yatharth*.

EPILOGUE: AESTHETICS AND THEIR AFTERLIVES

1. See Rashmi Sadana's "A Suitable Text for a Vegetarian Audience: Questions of Authenticity and the Politics of Translation."

WORKS CITED

Abbas, Khwaja Ahmad. "Social Realism and Change." In *Aspects of Indian Literature: The Changing Pattern*, edited by Suresh Kohli, 145–54. Delhi: Vikas, 1975. Print.
Achebe, Chinua. *Hopes and Impediments*. New York: Doubleday, 1988. Print.
Adiga, Aravind. *The White Tiger*. Noida: Harper Collins Publishers India. 2008. Print.
Adorno, Theodor. "Commitment." *New Left Review* 87–88 (1974): 75–89. Print.
Agnes, Flavia. *Law and Gender Inequality in India*. New Delhi: Oxford University Press, 2000. Print.
Ahmad, Aijaz. *In Theory: Classes, Nations, Literatures*. Delhi: Oxford University Press, 1992. Print.
———. "Reading Arundhati Roy Politically." In *Arundhati Roy's "The God of Small Things": A Routledge Study Guide*, edited by Alex Tickell, 110–19. London: Routledge, 2007. Print.
Ambedkar, B. R. "The Annihilation of Caste." *Columbia CNMTL*. <http://www.columbia.edu/ccnmtl/projects/mmt/ambedkar/web/index.html>. Web.
———. *What Congress and Gandhi Have Done to the Untouchables*. Bombay: Thacker, 1946. Print.
———. *The Essential Writings of B. R. Ambedkar*. Edited by Valerian Rodrigues. New Delhi: Oxford University Press, 2002. Print.
Anand, Mulk Raj. *Author to Critic*. Calcutta: Writers Workshop, 1973. Print.
———. *Conversations in Bloomsbury*. London: Wildwood House, 1981. Print.
———. *Coolie*. New York: Penguin, 1994. Print.
———. *Two Leaves and a Bud*. New York: Liberty Press, 1954. Print.

———. *Untouchable*. New York: Penguin, 1990. Print.
Anand, S. *Touchable Tales: Publishing and Reading Dalit Literature*. Pondicherry: Navayana, 2003. Print.
———. "Understanding the Khairlanji Verdict." *The Hindu*, 5 Oct. 2008, Magazine section, n. p. Print.
Anderson, Benedict. *Imagined Communities: Reflections on the Origin and Spread of Nationalism*. 2nd ed. London: Verso Books, 1991. Print.
Appadurai, Arjun. Afterword to *Gender, Genre, and Power in South Asian Expressive Traditions*, edited by Arjun Appadurai, Frank Korom, and Margaret Ann Mills, 467–76. Print.
———, ed. *The Social Life of Things: Commodities in Cultural Perspective*. Cambridge: Cambridge University Press, 1986. Print.
Appadurai, Arjun, Frank Korom, and Margaret Ann Mills, eds. *Gender, Genre, and Power in South Asian Expressive Traditions*. Philadelphia: University of Pennsylvania Press, 1991. Page Numbers. Print.
Awasthi, Rajendra. *Jangal ke phool*. Dilli: Rajapala, 1976. Print.
———. Introduction to *Selected Hindi Short Stories*, edited by Rajendra Awasthy, 7–14. New Delhi: Diamond Pocket Books, 2006. Print.
———. "Like a Pigeon." In *Selected Hindi Short Stories*, edited by Rajendra Awasthy, 109–19. New Delhi: Diamond Pocket Books, 2006. Print.
———. *The Red Soil*. Translated by Shrawan Kumar. New Delhi: Vikas Publishing House, 1982. Print.
Baer, Benjamin. "Shit Writing: Mulk Raj Anand's *Untouchable*, the Image of Gandhi, and the Progressive Writers Association." *Modernism/Modernity* 16, no. 3 (2009): 575–95. Print.
Bal, Mieke. *Narratology: Introduction to the Theory of Narrative*. Toronto: University of Toronto Press, 1985. Print.
———. "Over-Writing as Un-Writing: Descriptions, World-Making, and Novelistic Time." In *The Novel*, edited by Franco Moretti, 571–610. Vol. 2. Princeton: Princeton University Press, 2008. Print.
Bannerjee, Sumanta. *India's Simmering Revolution: The Naxalite Uprising*. London: Zed Books, 1984. Print.
Berman, Jessica. "Towards a Regional Cosmopolitanism: The Case of Mulk Raj Anand." *Modern Fiction Studies* 55, no. 1 (2009): 142–262. Print.
Beth, Sarah. "Dalit Autobiographies in Hindi: Transformation of Pain into Resistance." Swedish South Asian Studies Network, 9 July 2007. <http://www.sasnet.lu.se/ EASASpapers/4SarahBeth.pdf>. Web.
Bhabha, Homi. "Of Mimicry and Man: The Ambivalence of Colonial Discourse." In *The Location of Culture*, 85–92. New York: Routledge, 1994. Print.

Bhattacharya, Bhabani. *He Who Rides a Tiger.* New York: Crown Publishers, 1954. Print.

Bhattacharya, Soumya. "The White Tiger, by Aravind Adiga: Tales from the Shadowy Side of Booming India." Review of *The White Tiger*, by Aravind Adiga. *The Independent*, 11 Apr. 2008. n.p. Print.

Blackburn, Stuart. "The Burden of Authenticity: Printed Oral Tales in Tamil Literary History." In *India's Literary History*, edited by Blackburn and Dalmia, 119–45. Print.

Blackburn, Stuart, and Vasudha Dalmia, ed. *India's Literary History*. Delhi: Permanent Black, 2004. Print.

Bloch, Ernst. *Aesthetics and Politics.* London: NLB, 1977. Print.

Booth, Wayne. *The Rhetoric of Fiction.* 2nd ed. Chicago: University of Chicago Press, 1983. Print.

Brueck, Laura. "Dalit Chetna in Dalit Literary Criticism." *Seminar Web Edition* 558 (2006): n.p. <http://www.india-seminar.com/2006/558/558%20laura%20r.%20obrueck.htm>. Web.

———. "The Emerging Complexity of Dalit Consciousness." *Himal Southasian* (2010): n.p. <http://www.himalmag.com/The-emerging-complexity-of-Dalit-consciousness_nw3952.html> . Web.

———. "The Problem with Premchand: Historigraphic Trends in Hindi Dalit Literary Criticism." AAS Annual Meeting. Marriot, San Francisco. 6–9 Apr. 2006. Lecture.

———. "Rewriting the Rape-Script in Dalit Women's Literature." *South Asian Feminisms: Gender, Culture and Politics.* University of Pennsylvania, Philadelphia. 29 Mar. 2008. Lecture.

Chakrabarty, Dipesh. *Provincializing Europe: Postcolonial Thought and Historical Difference.* Princeton: Princeton University Press, 2000. Print.

Chakravarti, Anand. "Caste and Agrarian Class: A View from Bihar." *Economic and Political Weekly* 36, no. 17 (2001): 1449–62. Print.

Chakravarti, Sudeep. *Red Sun: Travels in Naxalite Country.* New Delhi: Penguin, 2008. Print.

Chandra, Sudhir. "Premchand and Indian Nationalism." *Modern Asian Studies* 16, no. 4 (1982): 601–21. Print.

Chatman, Seymour. *Coming to Terms: The Rhetoric of Narrative in Fiction and Film.* Ithaca: Cornell University Press, 1990. Print.

Chatterjee, Partha. "Caste and Subaltern Consciousness." In *Writings on South Asian History and Society*, edited by Ranajit Guha, 169–209. Subaltern Studies 6. Delhi: Oxford University Press, 1989. Print.

———. *The Nation and Its Fragments: Colonial and Postcolonial Histories.* Princeton: Princeton University Press, 1993. Print.

Chauhan, Surajpal. *Harry kab aayega*. Gaziabad: Anubhav Prakashan, 1999. Print.

———. *Hindi ke dalit kathakaron ki pahli kahani*. Delhi: Anubhav Prakashan, 2004. Print.

———. "Parivartan ki baat." In *Harry kab aayega*. Print.

———. "Sajish." In *Dusari duniya ka yatharth*, edited by Gupta, 84–90. Print.

———. *Tiraskrit*. Ghaziabad: Anubhav Prakashan, 2005. Print.

Clifford, James. *The Predicament of Culture: Twentieth-Century Ethnography, Literature, and Art*. Cambridge: Harvard University Press, 1988. Print.

Cowasjee, Saros. *So Many Freedoms: A Study of the Major Fiction of Mulk Raj Anand*. Delhi: Oxford University Press, 1977. Print.

Culler, Jonathan. *Literary Theory*. Toronto: Sterling Publishers, 2009. Print.

———. *The Pursuit of Signs: Semiotics, Literature, Deconstruction*. Ithaca: Cornell University Press, 1981. Print.

———. *Structuralist Poetics: Structuralism, Linguistics and the Study of Literature*. Ithaca: Cornell University Press, 1975. Print.

Dalmia, Vasudha. "Generic Questions: Bharatendu Harishchandra and Women's Issues." In *India's Literary History*, edited by Blackburn and Dalmia, 402–32. Print.

———. "Introduction: Hindi, Nation and Community." In *Nationalism in the Vernacular: Hindi, Urdu, and the Literature of Indian Freedom*, edited by Shobna Nijhawan, 33–64. Ranikhet: Permanent Black, 2010. Print.

———. *Narrative Strategies: Essays on South Asian Literature and Film*. Leiden: CNWS Publications, 1998. Print.

———. *The Nationalization of Hindu Traditions: Bharatendu Harischandra and Nineteenth-Century Banaras*. Delhi: Oxford University Press, 1999. Print.

———. "A Novel Moment in Hindi: Pariksha Guru." In *Narrative Strategies: Essays on South Asian Literature and Film*, edited by Vasudha Dalmia and Theo Damsteegt, 169–84. Delhi: Oxford University Press, 1998. Print.

Dangle, Arjun. *Poisoned Bread: Translations from Modern Marathi Dalit Literature*. Bombay: Orient Longman, 1992. Print.

Denning, Michael. *Culture in the Age of Three Worlds*. New York: Verso Books, 2004. Print.

Deo, Veena. "Dalit Literature in Marathi." In *Handbook of Twentieth-Century Literatures in India*, edited by Nalini Natarajan and Emmanuel S. Nelson, 363–81. Westport, CT: Greenwood Press, 1996. Print.

Dharamvir, Dr. *Premchand: Saamant ka munshi*. Delhi: Muhim Prakashan, 2005. Print.

Dhareshwar, Vivek. "Caste and the Secular Self." *Journal of Arts and Ideas* 25–26 (1992): 115–26. Print.

Dickens, Charles. *Hard Times*. Oxford: Oxford University Press, 1991. Print.

Dom, Hira. "Acchut ki shikayat." *Saraswati* (1914): 512–13. Print.

Fanon, Franz. *The Wretched of the Earth*. Translated by Richard Philcox. New York: Grove/Atlantic, 1961. Print.

Feder, Lilian. *Naipaul's Truth: The Making of a Writer*. Lanham: Rowman and Littlefield, 2001. Print.

Freedgood, Elaine. *The Idea in Things: Fugitive Meaning in the Victorian Novel*. Chicago: University of Chicago Press, 2006. Print.

Gaikwad, S. M. "Ambedkar and Indian Nationalism." *Economic and Political Weekly* 33, no. 10 (1998): 515–18. Print.

Gandhi, M.K. *Hindi Swaraj*. Cambridge: Cambridge University Press, 2001. Print.

———. *India of My Dreams*. Delhi: Rajpal and Sons, 2009. Print.

Ganguly, Debjani. *Caste, Colonialism and Counter-Modernity: Notes on a Postcolonial Hermeneutics*. New York: Routledge, 2005. Print.

Ghai, R. K. *Shuddhi Movement in India: A Study of Its Socio-Political Dimensions*. New Delhi: Commonwealth Publishers, 1990. Print.

Ghosh, Amitav. *The Glass Palace*. New York: Random House, 2002. Print.

Gikandi, Simon. *Maps of Englishness: Writing Identity in the Culture of Colonialism*. New York: Columbia University Press, 1996. Print.

———. "Modernism in the World." *Modernism/Modernity* 13, no. 3 (2006): 419–24. Print.

———. *Writing in Limbo: Modernism and Caribbean Literature*. Ithaca: Cornell University Press, 1992. Print.

Gooptu, Nandini. *The Politics of the Urban Poor in Early Twentieth-Century India*. Cambridge: Cambridge University Press, 2001. Print.

Gopal, Priyamvada. *Literary Radicalism in India: Gender, Nation and the Transition to Independence*. New York: Routledge, 2005. Print.

Greiner, Rae. "Sympathy Time: Adam Smith, George Eliot, and the Realist Novel." *Narrative* 17, no. 3 (2009): 291–311. Print.

Guha, Ramchandra. *India after Gandhi: The History of the World's Largest Democracy*. London: Macmillan, 2007. Print.

Guha, Ranajit. "The Prose of Counter-Insurgency." In *Selected Subaltern Studies*, edited by Guha and Spivak. 45–88. Print.

Guha, Ranajit, and Gayatri Chakravorty Spivak, ed. *Selected Subaltern Studies*. Delhi: Oxford University Press, 1988. Print.

Gupta, Ramanika, ed. *Dusari duniya ka yatharth*. Hazaribag: Navalekhana Prakashan, 1997. Print.

Guru, Gopal. *Dalit Cultural Movement & Dialectics of Dalit Politics in Maharashtra*. Mumbai: Vikas Adhyayan Kendra, 1997. Print.

———. "Archaeology of Untouchability." *Economic and Political Weekly* 44, no. 37, (2009): 49–56. Print.

———. "Dalit Vision of India: From Bahishkrut to Inclusive Bharat." *Futures* 36, no. 6–7 (2004): 757–63. Print.

———. "Foregrounding Insult." *Kafila*. June 2, 2012. Web.

———. *Humiliation: Claims and Context*. Delhi: Oxford University Press, 2009. Print.

———. "The Language of Dalit-Bahujan Political Discourse." In *Class, Caste, Gender*, edited by Mohanty, 256–70. Print.

Guru, Gopal and V. Geetha. "The New Phase of Dalit-Bahujan Intellectual Activity." *Economic and Political Weekly* 35, no. 3 (2000): 130–34. Print.

Habib, Irfan. *Essays in Indian History: Towards a Marxist Perception*. New Delhi: Tulika, 1995. 161–79. Print.

Hai, Ambreen. "Border Work, Border Trouble: Postcolonial Feminism and the Ayah in Bapsi Sidhwa's *Cracking India*." *Modern Fiction Studies* 46, no. 2 (2): 379–426. Print.

Hansen, Kathryn. *Grounds for Play: The Nautanki Theatre of North India*. Berkeley: University of California Press, 1992. Print.

———. "Renu's Regionalism: Language and Form." *Journal of Asian Studies* 40, no. 2 (1981): 273–94. Print.

Hardt, Michael, and Frederic Jameson. *The Jameson Reader*. Oxford: Blackwell, 2000. Print.

Hazari, Itwari. *I Was an Outcaste: The Autobiography of an Untouchable in India*. New Delhi: Hindustan Times, 1957. Print.

Ilaiah, Kancha. *Buffalo Nationalism*. Kolkata: Samya Press, 2004. Print.

———. "Caste or Class or Caste-Class: A Study in Dalit-Bahujan Consciousness and Struggles in Andhra Pradesh in 1980s." In *Class, Caste, Gender*, edited by Mohanty, 227–54. Print.

———. "Productive Labour, Consciousness and History." In *Writing on South Asian History and Society*, edited by Shahid Amin and Dipesh Chakrabarty, 165–200. Delhi: Oxford University Press, 1996. Subaltern Studies Series 9. Print.

———. *Why I Am Not a Hindu: A Sudra Critique of Hindutva Philosophy, Culture and Political Economy*. Calcutta: Samya, 2007. Print.

Jaaware, Aniket. "Eating, and Eating with, the Dalit: A Re-consideration Touching upon Marathi Poetry." In *Indian Poetry: Modernism and*

After: A Seminar, edited by K. Satchidanandan, 262–93. New Delhi: Sahitya Akademi, 2001. Print.

Jadhav, Narendra. *Untouchables: My Family's Triumphant Escape from India's Caste System*. Berkeley: University of California Press, 2006. Print.

Jaffe, Audrey. *Scenes of Sympathy: Identity and Representation in Victorian Fiction*. Ithaca: Cornell University Press, 2000. Print.

Jaffrelot, Christopher. *India's Silent Revolution*. Delhi: Permanent Black, 2003. Print.

Jakobson, Roman. "Metaphoric and Metonymic Poles." In *Modern Criticism and Theory*, edited by David Lodge, 56–60. New York: Longman, 2008. Print.

———. "On Realism in Art." In *Language in Literature*, edited by Roman Jakobson, Krystyna Pomorska, and Stephen Rudy, 19–27. Cambridge, MA: Belknap Press, 1987. Print.

———. "The Twofold Character of Language." In *Fundamentals of Language*, 72–76. Berlin: Mouton de Gruyter, 2002. Print

Jameson, Frederic. "The Experiments of Time: Providence and Realism." In *The Novel*, edited by Franco Moretti, 95–131. Vol. 2. Princeton: Princeton University Press, 2006. Print.

———. *The Ideologies of Theory*. Minneapolis: University of Minnesota Press, 1988. Print.

———. *Marxism and Form: Twentieth-Century Dialectical Theories of Literature*. Princeton: Princeton University Press, 1971. Print.

———. *The Political Unconscious: Narrative as a Socially Symbolic Act*. Ithaca: Cornell University Press, 1981. Print.

———. "Progress versus Utopia: Or, Can We Imagine the Future?" *Science Fiction Studies* 9, no. 2 (1982): 147–58. Print.

Jones, Kenneth W. *Arya Dharm: Hindu Consciousness in Nineteenth-Century Punjab*. Berkeley: University of California Press, 1976. Print.

Joseph, Manu. *Serious Men*. New York: W. W. Norton, 2010. Print.

Joshi, Barbara R. *Untouchable!: Voices of the Dalit Liberation Movement*. London: Minority Rights Group, 1986. Print.

Kanaganayakam, Chelvanayakam. *Counterrealism and Indo-Anglian Fiction*. Waterloo, ON: Wilfrid Laurier University Press, 2002. Print.

Karanth, Kota Shivarama. *Chomana dudi*. Translated by U. R. Kalkur. Delhi: Hind Pocket Books, 1978. Print.

Kardam, Jai Prakash. *Chappar*. Delhi: Sangita Prakashan, 1994. Print.

Keen, Suzanne. *Empathy and the Novel*. New York: Oxford University Press, 2007. Print.

Keer, Dhananjay. *Dr. Ambedkar: Life and Mission.* 3rd ed. Bombay: Popular Prakashan, 1990. Print.

King, Bruce. *V. S. Naipaul.* New York: St. Martin's Press, 1993. Print.

King, Christopher. *One Language, Two Scripts: The Hindi Movement in the Nineteenth-Century North India.* Bombay: Oxford University Press, 1994. Print.

Kothari, Rita. "The Short Story in Gujarati Dalit Literature." *Economic and Political Weekly* 36, no. 45 (2001): 4308–11. Print.

Kumar, Amitava. "On Adiga's *The White Tiger*." *The Hindu*, 2 Nov. 2008. Print.

Kumar, Raj. *Dalit Personal Narratives.* Delhi: Orient Blackswan, 2010. Print.

Kumar, Udaya. "Seeing and Reading: The Early Malayalam Novel and Some Questions of Visibility." In *Early Novels in India*, edited by Meenakshi Mukherjee, 161–211. New Delhi: Sahitya Akademi, 2002. Print.

———. Translation, Migration and Modernity: South Asia and Beyond Workshop, Newcastle University, Newcastle upon Tyne (UK), 27 May 2010. Lecture.

Lazarus, Neil. "The Politics of Postcolonial Modernism." In *Postcolonial Studies and Beyond*, edited by Ania Loomba et al, 423–38. Durham, NC: Duke University Press, 2005. Print.

Limbale, Sharankumar. *Towards an Aesthetic of Dalit Literature: History, Controversies, and Considerations.* Translated by Alok Mukherjee. Hyderabad: Orient Longman, 2004. Print.

———. *The Outcaste.* Translated by Santosh Bhoomkar. London: Oxford University Press, 2003. Print.

Lodge, David. *The Modes of Modern Writing: Metaphor, Metonymy, and the Typology of Modern Literature.* Ithaca: Cornell University Press, 1977. Print.

Ludden, David. *An Agrarian History of South Asia.* The New Cambridge History of India 4. Cambridge: Cambridge University Press, 1999. Print.

Lukács, György. *The Meaning of Contemporary Realism.* London: Merlin Press, 1962. Print.

———. *Studies in European Realism.* New York: Howard Fertig, 2002. Print.

———. *The Theory of the Novel: A Historico-Philosophical Essay on the Forms of Great Epic Literature.* Translated by Anna Bostock. Cambridge: MIT Press, 1971. Print.

———. *Writer and Critic: And Other Essays.* Translated by Arthur Kahn. London: Merlin Press, 1978. Print.

Madhuresh, ed. *Maila anchal ka mahatva*. Allahabad: Sumit Prakashan, 2000. Print.

Mahmud, Shabana. "Angare and the Founding of the Progressive Writers' Association." *Modern Asian Studies* 30 (2): 39–43.

Marx, Karl. *Capital: A Critique of Political Economy, Volume 1*. Translated by D. Fernbach and Ben Fowkes. London: Penguin Books, 1976. Print.

McGregor, R. S., ed. *The Oxford Hindi-English Dictionary*. Oxford: Oxford University Press, 1997. Print.

Menon, Dilip. *The Blindness of Insight: Essays on Caste in Modern India*. Pondicherry: Navayana, 2006. Print.

——. "An Inner Violence: Why Communalism in India Is About Caste." In *The Future of Secularism*, edited by T. N. Srinivasan, 60–82. New York: Oxford University Press, 2007. Print

——. "No, Not the Nation: Lower Caste Malayalam Novels of the Nineteenth Century." In *Early Novels in India*, edited by Meenakshi Mukherjee, 41–72. New Delhi: Sahitya Akademi, 2002. Print.

Menon, Nivedita. *Gender and Politics in India*. New York: Oxford University Press, 2004. Print.

Merotra, Arvind. *A History of Indian Literature in English*. New York: Columbia University Press, 2003. Print.

Miller, J. H. "The Fiction of Realism: Sketches by Boz, *Oliver Twist*, and Cruikshanks's Illustrations." In *Dickens Centennial Essays*, edited by Blake Nevius and Ada Nisbet, 85–154. Berkeley: University of California Press, 1971. Print.

Mishra, Pankaj. "Hindi or Hinglish." *London Review of Books*. 20 November, 2008. Print.

Mishra, Shivakumar. "Yatharthvaad aur *anchalik* upanyas." In *Maila anchal ka mahatva*, edited by Madhuresh, 11–20. Print.

Misra, A. R. and Badri Narayan, eds. *Multiple Marginalities: An Anthology of Identified Dalit Writings*. New Delhi: Manohar, 2004. Print.

Mistry, Rohinton. *A Fine Balance*. New York: Vintage, 1997. Print.

Mohanty, Manoranjan, ed. *Class, Caste, Gender*. Thousand Oaks, CA: Sage, 2004. Print.

Mohanty, Satya. *Literary Theory and the Claims of History: Postmodernism, Objectivity, Multicultural Politics*. Ithaca: Cornell University Press, 1997. Print.

Mohapatra, Himansu. "Two Classic Tales of Village India." *Economic and Political Weekly* 43, no. 1 (2008): 62–69. Print.

Moon, Vasant. *Growing Up Untouchable in India: A Dalit Autobiography*. Oxford: Rowman & Littlefield, 2001. Print.

Moretti, Franco. "Conjectures on World Literature." *New Left Review* 1 (2000): 54–68. Print.

———. *Signs Taken for Wonders: Essays in the Sociology of Literary Forms*. Rev. ed. London: Verso, 1988. Print.

———. *The Way of the World: The Bildungsroman in European Culture*. Rev. ed. New York: Verso, 2000. Print.

Mufti, Aamir. *Enlightenment in the Colony: The Jewish Question and the Crisis of Postcolonial Culture*. Princeton: Princeton University Press, 2007. Print.

Mukherjee, Arun. "The Exclusion of Postcolonial Theory and Mulk Raj Anand's *Untouchable*: A Case Study." *Ariel* 22, no. 3 (1991): 27–48. Print.

———. Introduction to *Joothan*, by Omprakash Valmiki. Print.

———. Introduction to *Towards an Aesthetic of Dalit Literature: History, Controversies, and Considerations*, by Sharankumar Limbale. Print.

Mukherjee, Meenakshi, ed. *Early Novels in India*. New Delhi: Sahitya Akademi, 2002. Print.

———. *Realism and Reality: The Novel and Society in India*. Delhi: Oxford University Press, 1985. Print.

Murthy, U. R. Anantha. *Samskara*. Delhi: Oxford University Press, 1978. Print.

Mustafa, Fawzia. *V. S. Naipaul*. Cambridge: Cambridge University Press, 1995. Print.

Nagaraj, D. R. *The Flaming Feet: A Study of the Dalit Movement in India*. Bangalore: South Forum Press, 1993. Print.

Nagarjun. *Balcanma*. Delhi: Raj Kamal Prakashan, 2007. Print.

———. *Ugratara*. Delhi: Raj Kamal Prakashan, 2007. Print.

———. *Varun ke bête*. Delhi: Raj Kamal Prakashan, 2006. Print.

Naimishraya, Mohandas. "Apna gav." In *Dusari duniya ka yatharth*, edited by Gupta. 54–83. Print.

———. *Apne-apne pinjare*. New Delhi: Vani Prakashan, 1995. Print.

Naipaul, V. S. *Guerillas*. New York: Picador, 2002. Print.

———. *Half a Life*. New York: Vintage, 2002. Print.

———. *A House for Mr. Biswas*. New York: McGraw-Hill, 1961. Print.

———. *India: A Wounded Civilization*. New York: Knopf, 1977. Print.

———. *Magic Seeds*. New York, Vintage, 2005. Print.

Nandy, Ashis. *The Secret Politics of Our Desires: Innocence, Culpability and Indian Popular Cinema*. Delhi: Zed Press, 1999. Print.

Narayan, Badri. "Inventing Caste History: Dalit Mobilisation and Nationalist

Past." *Contributions to Indian Sociology* 38, no. 1–2 (2004): 193–220. Print.

———. *Jamaniya ka baba*. Nayi Dilli: Vani Prakashan, 1989. Print.

———. *Multiple Marginalities: An Anthology of Identified Dalit Writings.* Delhi: Manohar Press, 2004. Print.

Narula, Smita. *Broken People: Caste Violence against India's "Untouchables."* Human Rights Watch Publications. Human Rights Watch. 11 Aug. 2008. Web.

Natarajan, Nalini. "Motherhood, Home and Property: Arundhati Roy's *God of Small Things*." In *Women and Indian Modernity*. New Orleans: University Press of the South, 2003.

Navariya, Ajay. "The Lover and the Other." *Tehelka Magazine* 6, no. 24 (2009): n.p. <http://www.tehelka.com/story_main42.asp?filename=hub 200609the_lover.asp>. Web.

———. *Patkatha aur anya kahaniyam*. New Delhi: Vani Prakashan, 2006. Print.

———. *Udhar ke log*. New Delhi: Vani Prakashan, 2008. Print.

———. "Usar mein kasht ki." In *Hindi ke dalit kathakaron ki pahli kahani*, edited by Surajpal Chauhan. Dilli: Anubhav Prakashan, 2004. Print.

Nirala, Suryakant Tripathi. *Caturi chamar*. Nayi Dilli: Rajkamal Prakashana, 2. Print.

Nochlin, Linda. *Realism: Style and Civilization*. New York: Penguin, 1972. Print.

Omvedt, Gail. "Ambekdar and Dalit Labor Radicalism: Maharastra 1936–1942." *South Asia Bulletin* 10 (1990). 12–22. Print.

———. *Dalits and the Democratic Revolution: Dr. Ambedkar and the Dalit Movement in Colonial India*. New Delhi: Sage Publications, 1994. Print.

———. *Dalit Visions: The Anti-Caste Movement and the Construction of an Indian Identity*. New Delhi: Orient Longman, 1995. Print.

———. "Social Protest and Revolt in Western India." *South Asia Bulletin* 7 (1987). 78–85. Print.

Orsini, Francesca. "Detective Novels: A Commercial Genre in Nineteenth-Century North India." In *India's Literary History*, edited by Blackburn and Dalmia, 435–82. Print.

———. *The Hindi Public Sphere 1920–1940: Language and Literature in the Age of Nationalism*. New Delhi: Oxford University Press, 2002. Print.

———. Introduction to *The Oxford India Premchand*, by Premchand, vii–xxvi. New Delhi: Oxford University Press, 2004. Print.

Pai, Sudha. "New Social and Political Movements of Dalits: A Study of Meerut." *Contributions to Indian Sociology* 34, no. 2 (2000): 189–219. Print.

Pandey, Geetanjali. "How Equal? Women in Premchand's Writings." *Economic and Political Weekly* 21, no. 50 (1986): 2183–87. Print.

———. "Premchand and the Peasantry: Constrained Radicalism." *Economic and Political Weekly* 18, no. 26 (1983): 1149–55. Print.

Pandey, Gyan. "Can There Be a Subaltern Middle Class? Notes on African American and *Dalit* History." *Public Culture* 21, no. 2 (2009): 321–42. Print.

———. "In Defense of the Fragment: Writing about Hindu-Muslim Riots in India Today." *A Subaltern Studies Reader: 1986–1995*, edited by Ranajit Guha, 1–33. Minneapolis: University of Minnesota Press, 1997. Print.

Pandey, Indu Prakash. *Regionalism in Hindi Novels*. Wiesbaden: Franz Steiner Verlag, 1974. Beiträge zur Südasienforschung 3. Print.

Pandian, M. S. S. "One Step outside Modernity: Caste, Identity Politics and Public Sphere." *Economic and Political Weekly* 37, no. 18 (2002): 1735–41. Print.

Paranjape, Makarand. "The Caste of the Indian English Novel." In *Towards a Poetics of the Indian English Novel*, 51–59. Print.

———. *Towards a Poetics of the Indian English Novel*. Shimla: Indian Institute of Advanced Study Press, 2000. Print.

Prakash, Anand. Introduction to *Carcit kahaniyam*, by Phaniswarnath Renu. New Delhi: Vani Prakashan, 2009. Print.

———. *Kalankmukti*. Trans. Satti Khanna. New York: Oxford University Press, 2006. Print

Prasad, Chandra Bhan. *Dalit Diary: 1999–2003: Reflections on Apartheid in India*. Pondicherry: Navayana, 2004. Print.

Pratap, Rana. "Antata." In *Dusari duniya ka yatharth*, edited by Gupta. Print.

Prashad, Vijay. "Between Economism and Emancipation: Untouchables and Indian Nationalism, 1920–1950." *Left History* 3, no. 1 (1995): 5–30. Print.

Premchand. "The Aim of Literature." In *The Oxford India Premchand*, unnumbered appendix. Print.

———. *Duniya ka subse anmol rattan*. Delhi: Hind Pocket Books, 1999. Print.

———. *The Gift of a Cow*. Translated by Gordon C. Roadarmel. Bloomington: Indiana University Press, 2002. Print.

———. *Godaan*. In *Premchand rachna-sanchayan*, 259–630. Print.

———. "Kafan." In *Premchand rachna-sanchayan*, 214–21. Print.

———. "Mahajani sabhyata." In *Mangal sutra evam anya rachnae*, 163–69. Print.

———. *Mangal sutra evam anya rachnae*. Delhi: Bharati Bhasha Prakashan, 1991. Print.

———. *The Oxford India Premchand*. Translated by David Rubin, Alok Rai, and Christopher R. King. New Delhi: Oxford University Press, 2004. Print.

———. *Premchand rachna-sanchayan*. Edited by Nirmal Verma. Delhi: Sahitya Akademi, 2002. Print.

———. *Rangbhumi*. Delhi: Star Publications, 2002. Print.

———. "Sahitya ka udeshya." In *Mangal sutra evam anya rachnae*, 148–58. Print.

———. "Thakur ka kuan." In *Premchand rachna-sanchayan*, 222–25. Print.

———. *Vividh prasang*. 3 vols. Allahabad: Hans Prakashan, 1962. Print.

Raghav, Rangeya. *Kab tak pukarun*. Dilli: Rajpal, 1993. Print.

Rai, Alok. Foreword to *Nirmala*. In *The Oxford India Premchand*, by Premchand, 197–211. Print.

———. *Hindi Nationalism*. New Delhi: Orient Longman, 2002. Print.

———. "A Kind of Crisis: *Godaan* and the Last Writings of Munshi Premchand." *Journal of the School of Languages* 2, no. 1 (1974): 1–13. Print.

———. "Past Recovery: Postcolonialism, the View from India." Postcolonial and the Hit of the Real Conference. New York University, NY. 6–8 Mar. 2008. Lecture.

———. "Poetic and Social Justice: Some Reflections on the Premchand-Dalit Controversy." In *Justice: Political, Social, Juridical*, edited by Rajesev Bhargave, Michael Dusche, and Helmut Reifeld. New Delhi: Sage, 2008. 151–68. Print.

Rai, Amit. *Rule of Sympathy: Sentiment, Race and Power 1750–1850*. New York: Palgrave, 2002. Print.

Rajyadhaksha, Ashish. *Indian Cinema in the Time of Celluloid: From Bollywood to the Emergency*. New Delhi: Tulika Books, 2009. Print.

Rakesh, Mohan. "Hindi kathasahitya: navin pravrittiyam." In *Sahitya aur Samskirti*. 30–36. Delhi: Radhakrishna Prakashan, 1975. Print.

Rao, Anupama. *The Caste Question: Dalits and the Politics of Modern India*. Berkeley: University of California Press, 2009. Print.

———. "Representing Dalit Selfhood." *Seminar Web Edition* 558 (2006): n.p. <http://www.india-seminar.com/2006/558/558%20anupama%20rao.htm>. Web.

Rao, Raja. *Kanthapura*. Bombay: Oxford University Press, 1963. Print.

Ray, Rabindra. *The Naxalites and Their Ideology*. Delhi: Oxford University Press, 1988. Print.

Raza, Rahi Masum. *Adha gav.* Dilli: Rajkamal Prakashan, 1975. Print.

Rege, Sharmila. "Dalit Women Talk Differently: A Critique of 'Difference' and towards a Dalit Feminist Standpoint Position." *Economic and Political Weekly* 33, no. 44 (Oct. 31—Nov. 6, 1998), WS39–WS46/. Print.

Renu, Phaniswarnath. *Carcit kahaniyam.* New Delhi: Vani Prakashan, 2009. Print.

———. *Kalankmukti.* Trans. Satti Khanna. New York: Oxford University Press, 2006. Print.

———. *Maila anchal.* New Delhi: Rajkamal Paperbacks, 2010. Print.

———. *Parati parikatha.* Dilli: Rajakamala Prakasana, 1957. Print.

———. *Racnavali.* Edited by Bharat Yayawar. Dilli: Rajakamala Prakasana, 2007. Print.

———. *The Soiled Border.* Translated by Indira Junghare. Delhi: Chanakya Publications, 1991. Print.

———. *The Third Vow & Other Stories*, translated by Katherine Hansen. Delhi: Chanakya Publications, 1986. Print.

Roy, Arundhati. *The God of Small Things.* New York: Random House, 1997. Print.

Rushby, Kevin. Review of *The White Tiger*, by Aravind Adiga. *The Guardian*, 15 Oct. 2008. Print.

Rushdie, Salman. Interview by Christopher Hitchens. *The Progressive* 61, no. 10 (1997): 34–37. Print.

———. *Midnight's Children.* New York: Penguin Books, 1980. Print.

———. Introduction to *The Vintage Book of Indian Writing*, ix–xxiii. New York: Vintage, 1997. Print.

Sadana, Rashmi. "A Suitable Text for a Vegetarian Audience: Questions of Authenticity and the Politics of Translation." *Public Culture* 19, no. 2 (2007). 307–28. Print.

Sahi, Sadanand. *Dalit sahitya ki avdharana aur Premchand.* Gorakhpur: Premchand Sahitya Prakashan, 2000. Print.

Said, Edward. "Among the Believers." *Reflections on Exile.* Cambridge, Mass: Harvard University Press, 2000. Print.

———. "Intellectuals in the Postcolonial World." *Salmagundi* 70 (1986): 44–64. Print.

Sangari, Kumkum. *Politics of the Possible: Essays on Gender, History, Narratives, Colonial English.* London: Anthem, 2002. Print.

Sankaran, Lavanya. *The Red Carpet: Bangalore Stories.* New York: Dial Press, 2005. Print.

Sarkar, Sumit. *Beyond Nationalist Frames: Relocating Postmodernism, Hindutva, History.* New Delhi: Permanent Black, 2002. Print.

Sarukkai, Sundar. "Dalit Experience and Theory." *Economic and Political Weekly* 42, no. 40 (2007): 4043–48. Print.

Satyanarayana, K. "The Politics of Self-Representation: Case of a De-Brahminised Brahmin." *Economic and Political Weekly* (1991). Print.

Schwarz, Roberto. "A Brazilian Breakthrough." *New Left Review* 36 (2005): 91–107. Print.

———. *Misplaced Ideas: Essays on Brazilian Culture*. Edited by John Gledson. New York: Verso, 1992. Print.

Seth, Vikram. *A Suitable Boy*. New York: Harper Perennial, 1993. Print.

Sharma, Pradeep. *Dalit Politics and Literature*. Delhi: Shipra, 2006. Print.

Sharma, Ram Nath and Rajendra Kumar Sharma. *History of Education in India*. New Delhi: Atlantic Publishers & Dist, 1996.

Shirshir, Kurmendu. "Daangar." In *Dusari duniya ka yatharth*, edited by Gupta, 270–86. Print.

Shivaprakash, H. S. "Translating the Tehsildar." In *Translating Caste*, edited by Tapan Basu and Arupa Patamgiya Kalita, 122–30. Studies in Culture and Translation 2. Delhi: Katha Press, 2002. Print.

Shukla, Ramchandra. "Acchut ki aah." *Saraswati* (1916): 222+. Print.

Sidhwa, Bapsi. *Cracking India*. Minneapolis, MN: Milkweed, 1991. Print.

Singh, K. P. "Liberation Movements in Comparative Perspective." In *Dalits in Modern India: Vision and Values*, edited by S. M. Michael, 162–80. Delhi: Sage Publications, 2007. Print.

———. "Premchand's Ideology." *Social Scientist* 5, no. 51 (1976): 69–76. Print.

Singh, Khuswant. *Train to Pakistan*. London: Penguin India, 2009. Print.

Singh, Shiv Prasad. *Alag alag vaitrani*. Ilahabad: Lokbharati Prakashan, 1977. Print.

Singh, Tej. *Aaj ka dalita sahitya*. Delhi: Atish Prakashan, 2000. Print.

Spivak, Gayatri. *A Critique of Postcolonial Reason: Toward a History of the Vanishing Present*. Cambridge: Harvard University Press, 1999. Print.

———. "Three Women's Texts and a Critique of Imperialism." *Critical Inquiry* 12, no. 1 (1985): 243–61. Print.

Sprinker, Michael. "Marxism and Nationalism: Ideology and Class Struggle in Premchand's *Godaan*." *Social Text* 23 (1989): 59–82. Print.

Srinivas, M. N. *Caste in Modern India and Other Essays*. London: Asia Publishing House, 1970. Print.

———. *Social Change in Modern India*. Berkeley: University of California Press, 1971. Print.

Subaltern Studies Group. *Dalits, Muslims, and the Fabrications of History*, edited by Shail Mayaram, M. S. S. Pandian, and Ajay Skaria. Subaltern Studies 12. Ranikhet: Permanent Black, 2005. Print.

Subrahmanyam, Sanjay. "Diary." *London Review of Books* 30, no. 21 (2008): 42–43. Print.

Sunder Rajan, Rajeswari. *Real and Imagined Women: Gender, Culture and Postcolonialism*. New York: Routledge, 1993. Print.

———. "Society Must Be Led: Dilemmas of the Vanguard in Some Post-Independence Novels in India." In *The Postcolonial Gramsci*, edited by Bhattacharya, Baidik and Neelam Srivastava, 165–91. London: Routledge, 2010. Print.

Sumanakshar, Sohanpal. "Rangbhumi ko jangbhumi banane ke liye jimmedar kaun?" *Apeksha* 10 (2005): 16–18. Print.

Taakbhore, S. "Siliya." In *Dusari duniya ka yatharth*, edited by Gupta. Print.

Tendulkar, Vijay. *Kanyadaan*. Delhi: Oxford University Press, 2002. Print.

Tharu, Susie. "The Impossible Subject: Caste and Desire in the Scene of the Family." In *Signposts: Gender Issues in Post-Independence India*, edited by Rajeswari Sunder Rajan, 188–204. New Delhi: Kali for Women, 1999. Print.

Trivedi, Harish. "The Progress of Hindi, Part 2: Hindi and the Nation." In *Literary Cultures in History: Reconstructions from South Asia*, edited by Sheldon Pollock, 958–1022. Berkeley: University of California Press, 2003. Print.

Umrigar, Thrity. *The Space between Us*. New York: Harper Perennial, 2007. Print.

Valmiki, Omprakash. *Dalita sahitya ka saundaryashastra*. New Delhi: Radhakrishna, 2001. Print.

———. *Ghusapaithiye*. Nayi Dilli: Radhakrishna, 2003. Print.

———. *Joothan: An Untouchable's Life*. Translated by Arun Prabha Mukherjee. New York: Columbia University Press, 2003. Print.

———. *Juthan*. Nayi Dilli: Radhakrishna, 1997. Print.

———. *Salaam*. Nayi Dilli: Radhakrishna, 2000. Print.

Venkataramani, K. S. *Murugan the Tiller*. London: Simpkin, Marshall, Hamilton, Kent & Co., 1927. Print.

Viyogi, Kusum. *Dalit mahilaon ki carcita kahaniyam*. Dilli: Sahitya Nidhi, 1997. Print.

Viswanathan, Gauri. *Outside the Fold: Conversion, Modernity, and Belief*. Princeton: Princeton University Press, 1998. Print.

Woloch, Alex. *The One versus the Many: Minor Characters and the Space of the Protagonist in the Novel*. Princeton: Princeton University Press, 2003. Print.

Zelliot, Eleanor. "Dalit Literature, Language and Identity." In *Language in South Asia*, edited by Braj B. Kachru, Yamuna Kachru, and S. N. Sridhar, 450–66. New York: Cambridge University Press, 2008. Print.

———. "Dalit—New Cultural Context of an Old Marathi Word." In *Language and Civilization Change in South Asia*, edited by Clarence Maloney, 77–97. Contributions to Asian Studies 11. Leiden, Netherlands: E. J. Brill, 1978. Print.

———. *From Untouchable to Dalit: Essays on Ambedkar Movement*. New Delhi: Manohar, 1992. Print.

Zelliot, Eleanor, and Mulk Raj Anand, eds. *An Anthology of Dalit Literature: Poems*. New Delhi: Gyan, 1992. Print.

Zeno. "Professor Ahmed Ali and the Progressive Writers' Movement." *Annual of Urdu Studies* 9 (1994): 39–43. Print.

INDEX

abolition of caste in colonial census, 72
Acchutanand, Swami, 10, 26–27, 28, 33, 130, 132, 215
Ad-Dharmi, 26, 209
Adiga, Aravind, 131, 143, 145, 149, 151, 153, 158–59, 165–66, 226; *The White Tiger*, 131, 138–40, 141, 144, 148–51, 154, 158, 164–65, 227
Adi Hindu, 26, 33; movement, 130, 132
Adorno, Theodor, 1, 20, 23, 79, 197
aesthetics, 1, 3, 13, 17, 21, 22, 23, 30, 34, 36, 38, 40, 45, 54, 66, 71, 79, 97, 147, 150, 159, 171, 197, 201, 204, 212, 215, 216, 226, 228
Agyeya, 13, 71, 181
Ahmad, Aijaz, 80, 137, 138, 152, 157, 210; critical realism, 152; *In Theory*, 80, 152; "Reading Arundhati Roy," 137–38
alienation, 75, 78, 185, 189; and aestheticization of labor, 73–75; and consciousness, 80; and metaphor, 73–75
allegory, 141, 149–50, 210
Ambedkar, B. R., 1, 2, 5, 6, 7, 9–12, 16, 24, 25, 37, 97, 102, 129, 130, 132–33, 143, 168, 186–87, 199, 204, 208, 209, 223; *Essential Writings*, 9–12, 133, 222; and Gandhi, 172; on intercaste marriage, 136; public conversion, 187; Republican Party of India, 187; on village life, 97
Ambedkarism, 12, 97, 143, 182
Ambedkarite, 69, 88, 115, 118, 142, 199, 200
Amritsar, 186; massacre, 188, 231
Anand, Mulk Raj, 3, 69, 70–81, 87, 89, 129, 135, 145, 166, 181, 215, 225, 231; *Untouchable*, 69, 70, 72–81, 89, 129, 135, 166, 181, 215, 216, 218, 231
Ananthamurthy, A. R., 124
anchalik, 101, 109, 103, 110, 122, 219
anchalik sahitya, 4, 13, 99–103, 115, 119, 123, 218, 221; and description, 104; and ethnography, 104
anchalikta, 99, 101, 104, 107, 111–14, 117, 123, 124, 125, 219; and culture, 112, 114
anchalik upanyas (regional novel), 101, 107, 110. *See also* novel, regional; realism, rural
Anderson, Benedict, 10, 43, 212
Anglophilia, 66, 76, 77, 82
Anglophone, 4, 23, 69, 71, 72, 95, 129–31, 134, 152, 157, 159, 170, 201, 218, 224. *See also* novel, Anglophone
Anglophone fiction, 130, 133, 135, 139, 140, 142, 153–54, 164, 218, 224, 227; modernist, 135; nonrealist, 135; postindependence, 153; South Asian, 152; traditional realist, 135
anti-brahmanism, 97
anticapitalism, 97
anticolonialism, 68, 71, 110, 154
antigenealogy, 4, 23, 30, 100, 111, 171
antihero, 149
Appadurai, Arjun, 78
artlessness, 2, 82, 86, 94, 95, 193, 195, 204
atmacharitra, 177
atmavad, 146
atmavrat, 177
authenticity, 30, 140, 149, 169, 191, 220; of the autobiographical, 177
autobiography, 1, 2, 17, 25, 61, 64, 65, 67, 129, 130, 162, 170, 177–78, 182, 183, 192
Avadhi, 27

Awasthi, Rajendra, 101, 102, 104, 220; *Jangal ke phool* (Flowers of the Jungle), 104, 110, 111, 220

Bagul, Baburao, 163–64; "Mother," 163–64
Bal, Mieke, 74, 223; *Narratology*, 74; on metaphor, 74
Baldwin, Shauna Singh, 153
Balzac, Honoré D., 16, 43
Bechain, Sheoraj Singh, 177, 222
belatedness, 166
Bengali, 32
Bhakti, 25–26
Bharatiya Dalit Sahitya Akademi, 5, 33, 34
Bhattacharya, Bhabani, 71; *He Who Rides a Tiger*, 71, 216
bildungsroman, 60, 159, 188, 189
biography, 134
Bloomsbury Group, the, 71
Brahminism, 4, 5, 225
Brahminness, 52, 53, 136
Brajbhasa, 27
Brecht, Bertolt, 79
Brueck, Laura, x, 2, 207, 210, 230, 235
Buddhism, 12, 24, 187, 198

canon, 8, 25, 34, 53, 63, 83, 133, 166; countercanonicity, 68; revisionist critique, 195
capital, 151
capitalism, 74–75, 143
caste, 28–30, 38, 41, 42, 43, 44, 61, 67, 71, 96, 129–30, 132, 133, 134–35, 136, 138, 141, 142, 143–44, 147, 148, 149–50, 151, 152, 153, 154, 155, 156, 157, 158, 160, 162, 164, 165, 166, 168, 170, 171, 180, 181, 182, 184, 195, 200, 201, 212, 216, 227; abandonment, 148; abolition of, in colonial census, 72; and alienation and, 75; analysis, 143, 150, 154, 157, 159, 195; -as-family, 165, 203; assertion, 67; and class, 80, 96, 218, 224, 228; and economy, 78; as endogamy, 73, 89; and gender, 66, 147; as gendered atrocity, 89, 228; identity, 33, 60, 75, 137, 181; and international modernism, 72; and knowledge, 65; and labor, 73, 75, 82; literary, 43, 224, 226; and literary form/genre/type, 41, 53, 67; as literary object, 71; and marriage, 73, 136, 137; and Marxist analytics, 72; materialist critique of, 121; and mimicry, 76–77; and narrative, 72, 74, 211; politics, 66, 199; postcaste consciousness, 156; and Premchand, 37; and purity, pollution, 95; radicalism, 67, 208; as rape, 89; as relationality, 202–3; reproduction, 166; romance, 138; and social relations, 54, 60; as social reproduction, 89; superstructure, 142; and sympathy, 48–53, 64, 66–67; system, 37; and untouchability, 72, 82
casteism, 6, 57, 61, 161, 190
casteless, 129, 133, 137, 156; Anglophone sphere, 139; fiction, 133, 164
castelessness, 129, 139, 145, 154
census, 72, 104
Chakrabarty, Dipesh, 46, 47, 48, 52, 215
chamar, 7–8, 34, 37, 44, 53, 181–82, 186, 198, 202, 208, 210, 212, 213, 218, 231
character/characterization 7–8, 12, 13, 14, 18, 34, 37, 38, 39, 40–43, 44, 47, 49, 51, 53, 62, 63, 84, 89–93, 95, 99, 101, 105, 108, 114, 127, 135, 137, 140, 147, 148, 155–58, 175, 176, 177, 180, 181, 188–89, 190, 194, 195, 201, 210, 213, 214, 218, 220, 226, 230, 231
Charan, Ram, 26
Chatman, Seymour, 84
Chatterjee, Partha, 75, 231; on caste and wage labor, 75
Chauhan, Surajpal, 4, 86, 177, 217, 218; "Sajish" ("Plot" or "Conspiracy"), 86
Chavdar Tank movement, 187
Chhayavaad, 186, 220
chetna, 2, 68, 87, 89, 94, 97, 200, 229, 230, 235
Cixous, Hélène, 90
class, 80, 96, 131, 132, 133, 139, 144, 150–51, 153; agrarian class relations, 143; and caste, 80, 96, 99; positionality, 180; reproduction, 166; *ressentiment*, 144; struggle, 132, 147
cleanliness, 139
colonialism, 75, 135, 137, 192
commodity, 75, 77, 78
commodity fetishism, 78
communalism, 153, 154, 160, 180, 190
Communist International, 197

Index

Communist Party of India, 100; CPI-ML, 138
community, 145–46, 147, 151, 175, 177, 178, 181, 182, 183
composite protagonist, 92
Congress Socialist Party, 131–32
Conrad, Joseph, 95
consciousness, 24, 68, 70, 72, 87, 89, 93, 97, 229, 231; evocation of, 68, 69; false, 89; and literary revolt, 69; spatialized, 185; of the untouchable, 72. *See also* Dalit; Dalit *chetna*
conversion, 159
cosmopolitanism, 155, 197
Culler, Jonathan, 74, 93, 217; *Literary Theory*, 74; on metaphor, 74; *The Pursuit of Signs*, 74, 93

Dalit Panthers, 24, 199
Dalit Voice, 132
Dalmia, Vasudha, 98, 209
Dangle, Arjun, 24, 25
Darwinian meritocracy, 150
Deb, Siddhartha, 131
defamiliarization, 29
Depressed Classes Welfare Organization, 9
Desai, Anita, 139
description, 29, 84, 85, 93, 126, 127; and *anchalik sahitya*, 104; authenticity, 104; detail, 104; ethnographic, 110; and narrative, 84; "thick," 84, 197
Devi, Mahasweta, 182, 191, 230
Devnagari, 27
Dharamvir, Dr., 37, 132, 175–76
Dhareshwar, Vivek, 130, 134, 142, 151, 153–54, 157, 167, 224, 228
Dhasal, Namdeo, 24, 214
dialect, 99, 100; and vernacular, 104
Dickens, Charles, 75, 217; *Hard Times*, 75
Dom, Hira, 33
Dumont, Louis, 95
Dutt, Pandit Gauri, 32

Eco, Umberto, 94
economy, 95; casteized, 78; market, 103; peasant, 109; symbolic, 86; village, 98; village narrative, 124
epiphany, 89
ethnographic particularism, 127
ethnography, 18, 23, 30, 104, 144, 169, 170, 182, 192, 194, 169; and *anchalik sahitya*, 104; auto-ethnography, 126; genres of, 125; and native informant, 126; and Nehruvian developmentalism, 104; and transcription, 111
everyday life, 179, 190
existentialism, 80

false consciousness, 89, 142
Fanon, Frantz, 89, 111–13, 115, 117, 121, 126, 143, 149, 150, 221; *The Wretched of the Earth*, 112–13, 115, 227
feudalism, 140, 144, 148, 149, 172
folk, 22, 28, 199, 200, 204, 220; culture, 104, 114; genres, 107, 113; lyrics of Bihar, 100; song, 124
formal intertextuality, 115
form(s) (literary), 3, 15, 16, 22, 31, 33, 34, 35, 36, 39–43, 54, 55, 71, 79, 80, 89, 91, 122, 126, 170, 192, 198, 200; and caste, 41, 53, 67; and content, 80, 91; and ideology, 80, 200; and intertextuality, 115; and nationhood, 93; lowercaste cultural, 110
Foucault, Michel, 29
free indirect discourse, 44, 212

Gandhi, Mohandas Karamchand, 9–10, 12, 34, 35, 36, 37, 45, 71, 72, 77, 79, 96, 97, 102, 129–30, 136, 160, 172, 173, 181, 185–86, 199, 207, 208, 211, 216; and Ambedkar, 172; *Hind Swaraj*, 102; Satyagraha, 9, 24, 33; on village life, 97, 102–4
Ganesh, Mogalli, 151
Ganguly, Debjani, 178
Geertz, Clifford, 84, 222
gender, 46–48, 55, 56, 64, 66, 89, 147; and caste, 147; and Dalit *chetna*, 89; and Dalit exodus, 117; and perverse tradition in Dalit fiction, 117
genre, 3, 15, 16, 22, 31, 33, 34, 35, 36, 39–43, 54, 55, 71, 79, 80, 89, 91, 122, 126, 131, 193, 204, 209, 220; and caste, 41, 53, 67, 199
Ghosh, Amitav, 131, 139, 229
Gikandi, Simon, 69, 79, 95; "Modernism in the World," 69; *Writing in Limbo*, 79, 95
globalization, 140, 151, 197
Gonds, 104; *ghot*, 104, 110; *ghotul*, 110
Gooptu, Nandini, 131, 137; *The Politics of the Urban Poor*, 131
Gopal, Priyavada, 152, 191
Gorky, Maxim, 12, 160, 163; *Mother*, 160, 163
Greene, Graham, 95

Guha, Ramachandra, 104, 133
Gupta, Ramanika, 158, 174, 175, 191, 214
Guru, Gopal, 25, 29, 30, 169, 171, 190, 203, 209, 232; "Dalit Vision," 169; time and space, 171

Habib, Irfan, 95
Hansen, Katherine, 106, 220
Hariharan, Gita, 163; "The Remains of the Feast," 163
Harijan Sevak Sangh, 158
Harischandra, Bharatendu, 32
Hazari, Itwari, 82, 129, 130, 132, 137, 170, 183, 184, 185, 186, 187, 189, 190, 217, 222; *Autobiography of an Outcaste*, 82, 170, 181, 184; *I Was an Outcaste*, 129, 183
Hegel, G.F.W., 145, 150, 172
Heidegger, Martin, 165
high modernism, 95
Hindi, 1, 2, 3, 4, 5, 6, 8, 10, 12, 13, 18, 25, 26, 27-28, 29, 32-33, 35, 40, 54, 55, 56, 57, 58, 61, 62, 64, 66, 70, 71, 83, 93, 96, 97, 98, 99, 100, 101, 104, 116, 132, 131, 133, 135, 138, 147, 151, 155, 156, 159, 162, 163, 164, 168, 172, 174, 175, 177, 181, 182, 183, 193, 198, 203, 207, 208, 209, 210, 211, 214, 218, 219, 220, 222, 223, 224, 226, 229, 230, 232, 234, 235, 236, 237, 240, 241, 243, 244, 245, 248
Hindi Sahitya Sammelan, 101
Hinduism, 11, 28, 45, 136, 143, 199, 210
historical consciousness, 169, 183
historical materialism, 143
historicism, 16, 39, 170, 172, 173
historicity, 162, 169, 170,171, 172, 201; *savarna*, 176; Westernized, 176
history, 134, 169, 170, 201; historiography, 179, 183; revisionist, 168, 170; westernized conceptions of, 169
humanism, 8, 12, 40, 41, 142, 169, 170, 186, 191, 192
hybridity, 170

identarianism, 204
identity, 2, 3, 4, 8, 23, 33, 38, 43, 46, 53, 75, 81, 124, 129, 130, 132, 134, 137, 156, 169, 170, 173, 181, 182, 189, 197, 200, 202, 221, 222, 229, 237, 239, 243, 244, 249
ideology, 71, 93, 95, 98, 122, 126; and form, 80; of realist particularism, 93; of regional literature, 101

Illaiah, Kancha, 170, 172, 173, 222; labor-based knowledge, 172; "productive castes," 172; productive labor of the Dalit, 173
Indian Independence, 152, 154, 168, 178
Indian National Congress, 131, 181
Indian nationalism, 81
indigenous other, 151
individualism, 16, 21, 35, 38, 81, 90, 120, 165, 199, 203, 211
industrialization, 75
interiority, 42, 60
intertextuality, 23; formal intertextuality, 115

Jacobson, Roman, 75, 81, 93
Jallianwalla Bagh massacre, 185
Jameson, Fredric, 17, 18, 20-21, 119, 164, 178, 193, 195, 220, 224, 231
Jha, Raj Kamal, 131
Joseph, Manu, 150; *Serious Men*, 150

Kabirpanthis, 25
Kardam, Jai Prakash, 120, 123, 222; *Chappar* (Roof), 120, 125
Kesavan, Mukul, 153
Khakhar, Bhupen, 19
Khari Boli, 27
knowledge: by transcription, 111, 113, 122; untranslatable, of Dalit subject, 125
Kumar, Raj, 177; *Dalit Personal Narratives*, 177
Kumar, Udaya, 82, 217

labor, 70, 82, 85-86, 132, 143; aestheticization of, 73; and alienation, 75, 80; and caste, 73; and casteized singularity, 69; and consciousness, 80; forced, 132; and metaphor, 73; and reification, 73; relations, 75; and untouchability, 73, 82
Lallujilal, 32
land reform, 131, 143
language, 129; -as-form, 193; Bengali, 153; English, 144, 145, 152, 153, 155, 164; Kannada, 151; Maithili, 99, 220; Malayalam, 151; Marathi, 1, 6, 24, 25, 32, 151, 153, 164, 224; Urdu, 16, 27, 32, 93, 183, 208, 209, 210
Lazarus, Neil, 79, 200
Limbale, Sharankumar, 43, 64, 98, 143, 207, 229; *The Outcaste*, 177
literary countercanonicity, 68
Lodge, David, 93
Ludden, David, 102, 124

Index

Lukács, György, 16–17, 39–41, 53, 54, 60, 84, 108, 147–48, 161, 165, 195, 208, 211, 212, 217, 220; *The Meaning of Contemporary Realism*, 148, 165; on description, 83

Macaulay, Thomas Babington, 78, 82, 216
Mahabharata, 55, 62–63
Mandal Commission, 6, 57, 164, 207, 214
Manto, Saadat Hasan, 48, 218
Manusmriti, 5, 8–11, 25, 187, 208
Maoist guerilla movement, 146, 226, 227
marriage, 73, 158, 159; and caste, 73; fictional world of, 73
Marx, Karl, 79, 143
Marxism, 7, 70, 132, 211, 212; and aesthetics, 40; critique, 17, 20, 23, 24, 203, 224, 232; Indian, 143; and modernism, 81, 83
Mazdoor Sangh, 158
Meghawal, Kusum, 138, 227
Menon, Dilip, 129, 134, 151, 153, 190, 208, 211, 224, 228; "An Inner Violence," 129, 151, 190
metanarrative, 1, 19, 46, 55, 56, 141, 143, 153, 185, 198
metaphor, 1, 30, 54, 57, 61, 70, 73, 74, 81, 83, 85–6, 94–5, 204; and aestheticization of labor, 73; as epistemological mode, 74; and labor, 70; and localization, 83; and Marxist analytics, 75; and narrative distance, 85; and precision, 83; and reification, 73; and socialist realism, 74; and specificity, 83; metonymic, 94
metaphorization, 75, 95
metonymy, 25, 53, 70, 71, 72, 75, 82, 85–6, 94, 96, 201, 217; realist, 94
mimesis, 4, 16, 38, 191
mimicry, 76; and caste, 76–7; and Sanskritization, 77
Mishra, Shivakumar, 108
Mistry, Rohinton, 135, 229; *A Fine Balance*, 135, 216
modernism, 69, 70, 79, 80, 81, 95, 131, 135, 149, 165, 166, 199, 201, 215, 220; aesthetics of, 79; and caste, 69; Dalit, 21, 199; and decolonization, 69; epistemological and aesthetic debates inaugurated by, 69; high, 95; ideologies of, 69; Western, 22
modernist, 69, 70, 71, 76, 79, 80, 83, 90, 91, 92, 95, 96, 123, 135; aesthetic, 69; epiphany, 89; ethic, 69; fiction, 80; genealogical roots of contemporary Dalit text, 69; and Marxist, 83; narrative, 76; novel, 79, 80, 81, 85, 89; subject, 92; subjectivity, 72, 80
modernity, 77, 79, 89, 102, 106, 109, 113, 115, 118, 124, 129, 130, 135, 145, 153, 154, 156, 169, 197; and civilization, 102; and Gandhi, 102–4; loss and Dalit, 124; Western, 133
modernization, 75, 77, 78, 79, 103, 104; and modernist writing in the colonies, 79
Mohanty, Satya, 152; *Literary Theory and the Claims of History*, 152
Moretti, Franco, 22, 42, 84, 127, 188, 212, 229; on description, 84; *Signs Taken for Wonders*, 84, 127
Mufti, Aamir, 79
Mukherjee, Meenakshi, 35, 43, 44, 153, 208, 209, 210; *Realism and Reality*, 153

Nagarjun, 28, 99, 104, 218; *Balcanma*, 104
Nagaraj, D.R., ix, 28, 110, 114, 115–16, 168, 172, 190, 192, 196, 198, 199, 200, 217, 222; "Against the Poetics of Segregation and Self-banishment," 168; bonsaization, 168, 192; "The Disappearance of the Village," 116; intentionality, 173; lower caste cosmologies, 193, 199; "the moment of metaphorical birth" 172; origins, 172
Naimashraya, Mohandas, 28, 56, 116, 117, 123, 156, 169, 177, 180, 184–87, 190, 222; "Apna gav" ("Our village"), 116, 118, 119, 127, 178, 190, 222; *Apne-apne pinjare (Cages of Our Own)*, 169, 177–78, 180–84, 187, 214
Naipaul, V.S., 131, 136–37, 139, 141, 145, 149, 225, 226; *Guerillas*, 141; *Half a Life*, 136, 141, 226; *A House for Mr. Biswas*, 136
Nandy, Ashis, 135
Narayan, Jai Prakash, 101
Narayan, R.K., 139
narrative, 8, 23, 24, 34, 36, 42, 53, 54, 55–59, 60, 61, 63, 67, 71, 128, 135, 203; and caste, 72, 74, 204; and cultural difference, 111; and description, 84; and solidarity, 60–61; and space, 55; and time, 19, 201; Dalit, 22, 24, 26, 29, 54, 58, 65, 173, 203; forms, 90; indigenous forms of, 71; modernist, 76; realist, 17, 19, 34, 38, 53, 199, 200

narrator/narration, 26, 42, 57, 58, 62, 64, 147, 212
nation, 72, 77, 79, 96, 101, 104, 145, 170, 177; and region, 96, 104, 125; and rural realism, 101
national culture, 112, 115, 117; and Dalit particularism, 115
nationalism, 26, 35, 36, 38, 66, 81, 82, 106, 129, 132, 136, 139, 169, 188; anticolonial, 154; Gandhian, 71, 72; Indian, 74; regional, 71
National Sample Survey, 104
nationhood, 93, 110; and Urdu short story, 93
native informant(s), 111, 125, 212
naturalism, 36, 84, 108, 109, 123, 220; and rural regionalism, 109
Navariya, Ajay, 155–57, 159, 162, 165, 202, 203, 228; "Patkatha," 159, 162–64, 166, 202; "Usar mein kasht ki" ("To plow a Barren Land"), 156
Naxalites, 132, 146–47, 151, 198, 228
nayi kahani (new short story), 13, 101, 123, 219
nayi katha (new fiction), 101, 219
nayi kavita (new poetry), 107
negativity, 23, 24, 197
Nehruvian developmentalism, 103; five-year plan, 104, 105
Nehruvian socialism, 100
New Man, 145
novel, 15, 37, 41, 42, 44, 47, 54, 198, 211, 226; Anglophone, 4, 23, 69–71, 95, 129–31, 134–39, 140, 142, 145, 147, 150–54, 164, 182, 197, 218, 226, 227, 229; bourgeois, 85, 121; Christian, 35; Dalit, 55; Hindi, 27, 220, 223; modernist, 85, 89; and nostalgia, 116; progressive, 45; realist, 16–17, 20–21, 35, 42, 45, 211; and recovery of tradition, 108, 116, 117; regionalist *(anchalik upanyas)*, 101, 110; social reform, 23, 36, 46, 53, 60; vernacular, 35; Western, 16, 22

omniscience, 26
orality, 99, 115
Orsini, Francesca, 14, 209, 210

Panchayat election, 160
Panchayati Raj, 133
Pandian, M.S.S, 130, 134, 139, 150, 212, 213; transcoding, 150, 157
Paranjape, Makarand, 134, 135, 224, 225, 226; "The Caste of the Indian English Novel," 134

particularism(s), 92, 93, 110, 112, 113, 118, 165, 201; ethnographic, 127; and form and content, 92
Partition of India, 48, 103, 119, 153, 169, 170, 178–80, 181, 182, 188, 190
Patel, Nirav, 198
peasant (as literary type), 6, 33, 35, 38–41, 44, 46, 64, 65, 133, 152, 166, 175, 180, 210, 212
personhood, 75, 90
Phule, Jyotirao, 187
poetry, 27
polyglossia, 194
Poona Pact 178, 187, 188
popular cultural forms: ballads of Lorik and Bijaybhan, 109; Holi songs, 107; Maithili legend and song, 107; Vidhyapat dance-drama, 107
postcolonial literary analysis, 171; literary studies, 170, 191
postmodernism, 166, 178
Prasad, Chandra Bhan, 82, 231
Pratap, Rana, 158, 159; "Antata," 158
Premchand, Munshi, 3, 4, 5, 6, 7, 8, 13, 22, 27, 32–53, 54, 55, 64, 71, 72, 98, 103, 202, 207, 209, 210, 211, 214, 223, 225, 229; and caste, 37; *Gaban*, 37, 47, 212; *Godaan*, 36, 38, 40–42, 43–45, 54, 60, 65, 72, 98, 108, 120, 157, 211, 212, 220; "Kafan" ("The Shroud"), 174, 212; *Karmabhumi*, 36, 37, 40, 43; *Nirmala*, 36, 47, 60, 211, 212, 213, 215; *Rangbhumi*, 4–8, 16, 33–34, 43, 208, 212, 220; *Sevasadan*, 37, 212; and realism, 33–38; "Thakur ka kuan," 18, 211, 212
Progressive Writers Association (PWA), 15, 21, 36, 39, 71, 95, 100, 197, 208, 210
progressivism, 21, 23, 30, 34, 48, 66, 67, 176, 197, 198, 203, 204, 230
prose, 27, 32, 37
protest literature, 152, 155, 170, 177, 189, 192, 194

Quit India Movement, 160

Rai, Alok, 18, 40, 42, 44, 46, 48, 108, 209, 211, 212, 213
Raidasis, 25
Rakesh, Mohan, 123
Ramayana, 55
Ranga, N.G., 133
Rao, Raja, 71, 136, 145, 218; *Kanthapura*, 71, 136, 225

Index

realism, 1, 2, 3, 4, 5, 8, 12, 14, 16, 21, 29, 31, 35, 41, 46, 48, 54, 55, 59, 60, 64, 67, 70, 83, 127, 128, 131, 135, 140, 151, 152, 157, 162, 164, 167, 169, 170–72, 173, 190, 191, 195, 198, 200, 201, 213, 220, 227, 229; bourgeois, 22; contemporary particularist, 70; critical, 20, 29, 101; Dalit, 16–23, 27, 54, 88, 90, 122, 152, 161, 187, 189, 190, 191, 195, 202, 203, 204; and Dalit critique, 42, 43, 66–67; democratic, 19, 35, 38; Hindi, 32; historicity of, 84, 220, 229; and idealism, 3, 12, 17, 18, 34, 36; and individualism, 38, 39–40; melodramatic, 45, 65, 212; naturalist, 83; Premchand, 15–16, 33–41, 211; progressive, 35; and rationalism, 11, 17–18, 27, 59, 199; regional, 115, 123; rural, 101, 102, 109, 111, 115, 120, 124, 125, 126; social, 13, 15, 36, 65, 66, 68, 72, 80, 93, 166, 170, 175; socialist, 17, 67, 68, 71, 72, 74, 84; state, 19; subalternist, 70, 83, 204; *yatharthvad*, 109

realist, 70, 71, 84, 86, 90, 122, 127, 134, 135, 142, 146, 147, 149, 152, 154, 159, 161, 162, 164, 165, 175, 191, 192, 194, 196, 200, 208; metonymy, 94; particularism, 93

reality effect, 86, 163

referent, 38, 211

referentiality, 8, 18, 19, 69, 90, 122, 200; and character, 90–91; and Dalit realism, 122

region, 96, 97, 99, 100, 104, 106, 113, 123; and nation, 96, 125

regionalism, 3, 25

regionalists, 105, 106, 109

reification, 73, 110, 118; and aestheticization of labor, 73; and metaphor, 73

Renu, Phanishwarnath, 98, 99, 101,104, 107, 109, 157, 219, 220; colonialist anthropology in *Maila anchal*, 113; *Maila anchal (The Soiled Border)*, 98, 99–100, 105, 106–7, 110, 111, 113, 114, 116, 118, 119, 124, 157, 219, 220, 222, 223; *Parati parikatha* (The Story of a Barren Land), 105; "Rasapriya," 108, 120; "*Tisri Kasam*" ("The Third Vow"), 107

representation, 3, 7, 10, 12, 15, 29, 32, 34, 39, 41, 42, 57, 62, 63, 66, 67, 70, 72, 75, 98, 99, 101, 111, 112, 116, 120, 161, 167, 170, 175, 177, 191, 196, 201, 202, 213

Republican Party of India, 24

reservations, 6, 141, 207, 226

Risley, H.R., 104

Roy, Arundhati, 132, 137–38, 142, 156, 157; environmental criticism, 138; *The God of Small Things*, 132, 137–38, 142, 156–57, 164, 166, 226

Rushdie, Salman, 131, 139, 152, 153, 229, 231; *The Vintage Book Indian Writing*, 151

Sadana, Rashmi, 155, 225, 228, 231
Sahni, Bhisham, 180; *Tamas*, 180
Said, Edward, 20
Sankaran, Lavanya, 150; "The Red Carpet," 150
Sanskritization, 77, 213
Saraswati, 28, 209, 210
Sarkar, Sumit, 179
satire, 135
Satyagraha, 9, 24, 33
savarna, 98, 133, 169, 173, 174, 176, 186
Scheduled Caste Federation, 187
Schwarz, Roberto, 22, 47, 154, 166, 192, 193, 208, 211, 217
secularism, 129, 130, 133, 134, 142, 152, 153, 157, 167, 195
Seth, Vikram, 135; *A Suitable Boy*, 135, 198
Shirshir, Kurmendu, 83; "Daangar" ("Carcass"), 83–86, 93
Shivaprakash, H.S., 177
short story, 68, 93; Urdu, 93
shuddhi, 51, 213, 237
Shukla, Ramachandra, 96, 209, 210
Sidhwa, Bapsi, 153, 180; *Cracking India*, 180
Singh, Khushwant, 153, 180; *Train to Pakistan*, 180
Singh, Namvar, 125, 224, 232
Singh, Tej, 68; *Aaj ka dalita sahitya (Contemporary Dalit Literature)*, 68
social mobility, 82
social realism, 13, 15, 36, 65, 66, 68, 72, 80, 94, 131, 134–35, 152, 166, 170, 175; social realist, 69, 93. *See also* realism
socialist realism, 17, 67, 68, 71, 72, 74, 84. *See also* realism
Spivak, Gayatri, 20, 123, 126, 182, 191, 212, 223; *A Critique of Postcolonial Reason*, 123

subaltern, 12, 109, 110, 133, 147, 173, 199; critique, 20, 23, 28, 203; feminist critique, 89
subalternist, 70, 83, 121
Subaltern Studies Group, 187, 230, 231
Subrahmanyam, Sanjay, 140
sympathy, 6, 7, 23, 33–34, 37, 38, 42, 45–55, 58–67, 212, 213; and empathy, 64; and gender, 47–48, 64
synecdoche, 41, 75, 162

Taakhbhore, Sushila, 56, 138, 218
Tamil Nadu, 138
Tharu, Susie, 134, 163, 224
thick emotionalism, 203
Third World literature, 169
time, 174; and space, 186; vernacular conception of, 174; Western conception of, 174
Tolstoy, Leo, 16, 160; *War and Peace*, 160
totality, 16–17, 37, 41, 42, 65, 212
Tractor Art, 152
transcoding, 134
transcription, 2, 105, 111, 113, 115, 122, 127; and cultural difference, 111; of the folk song, 115; and the other, 111; and readability, 115; and representation, 111; "untranscription," 111; and utopia, 111
translation, 95, 150, 214; translatable, 115; untranslatable knowledge of Dalit subject, 125
type (literary), 34, 39–43; and caste, 41, 53, 67. *See also* form(s); genre

Umrigar, Thrity, 150; *The Space Between Us*, 150
universal humanism, 81
universalism, 96
unreading, 170, 175, 176, 186, 189, 191
untouchability, 72, 130, 140, 184, 191; and caste 72; and international modernism, 72; and labor, 73; and Marxist analytics, 72; and narrative, 72
urbanization, 82, 135
utopia, 19, 20, 23, 36, 152, 162, 169, 191, 197; and Dalit exodus, 117, 118, 119, 127
utopianism, 19, 20, 23, 36, 90, 95, 118, 119, 123, 204

Valmiki, Omprakash, 35, 43, 54, 56–66, 96, 97, 116, 125, 132–33, 156, 166, 168, 177, 184, 215, 218, 229; *Dalit sahitya ka saundaryashastra (The Aesthetics of Dalit Literature)*, 97, 132, 207, 224; *Joothan*, 168, 171, 177, 184, 208, 214, 215, 230, 231, 232
Varma, Pardeshiram, 193; "Phaansi" ("Noose"), 193
varna, 10, 208, 226
varnavyavastha, 87
Venkataramani, K.S., 70, 72; *Murugan the Tiller*, 70, 72
vernacular, 13, 69, 71, 98, 115, 131, 151, 152, 153, 154, 155, 166, 167, 199, 216; Bengali, 32; Brajbhasa, 27; dialects, 104; Hindi, 1, 2, 27–28, 32–33, 54, 57, 58, 61; literary production, 71; Maithili, 99; Marathi, 1, 6, 24, 25, 32; Urdu, 16, 27, 32. *See also* Language
vernacularization, 197
village, 4, 65, 97, 98, 101, 102, 104, 106, 107, 110, 113–15, 117–20, 123, 124, 127, 132–33, 136, 139, 141, 145–46, 156, 159, 160–61, 162, 166, 183–84, 186, 194; Ambedkar on, 97; as character, 114; content, 124; and Dalit theory of culture, 116; economy, 98; exodus, 117–19, 123, 148, 203; Gandhi on, 97, 102–4; India, 102; and intellectual, 120; life, 97, 132, 144; literary, 106; narrative economy, 124; representation of, 98; and *savarna* society, 98; as a space of culture, 102; as translatable object, 115; and untouchable society, 98
Viswanathan, Gauri, 130

water, 75; casteized valence of, 75; as commodity, 75
Westernization, 77
Westernized narrative forms, 90
Western modernity, 133
Woloch, Alex, 90
World *politik* model, 138

Yadav, Laloo Prasad, 144
Yashpal, 71, 171, 180, 229; *Jhoot sach*, 180
yatharthavad (realism), 109

zamindari, abolition of, 114
Zelliot, Eleanor, 2, 24, 207, 229

www.ingramcontent.com/pod-product-compliance
Lightning Source LLC
Chambersburg PA
CBHW031239290426
44109CB00012B/359